The Death of
Classical Cinema

THE SUNY SERIES

HORIZONS OF CINEMA

MURRAY POMERANCE | EDITOR

Also in the series

William Rothman, *Cavell on Film*

J. David Slocum, *Rebel Without a Cause*

The Death of Classical Cinema

Hitchcock, Lang, Minnelli

Joe McElhaney

STATE UNIVERSITY OF NEW YORK PRESS

Published by
State University of New York Press, Albany

© 2006 State University of New York

Printed in the United States of America

For information, address State University of New York Press,
194 Washington Avenue, Suite 305, Albany, NY 12210-2384

Production by Marilyn P. Semerad
Marketing by Michael Campochiaro

Library of Congress Cataloging-in-Publication Data

McElhaney, Joe, 1957–
    The death of classical cinema : Hitchcock, Lang, Minnelli / Joe
McElhaney.
        p. cm. — (SUNY series, horizons of cinema)
    Includes bibiographical references and index.
    ISBN-13: 978-0-7914-6887-6 (hardcover : alk. paper)
    ISBN-10: 0-7914-6887-9 (hardcover : alk. paper)
    ISBN-13: 978-0-7914-6888-3 (pbk. : alk. paper)
    ISBN-10: 0-7914-6888-7 (pbk. : alk. paper)
    1. Hitchcock, Alfred, 1899—Criticism and interpretation. 2. Lang, Fritz,
1890–1976—Criticism and interpretation. 3. Minelli, Vincente—Criticism
and interpretation. I. Title. II. Series.

PN1998.3.H58M37 2006
791.4302'33092273—dc22   2005036236

10 9 8 7 6 5 4 3 2 1

For Emilene

It would be untrue to say that in those days the palaces of Gabriel struck me as being of greater beauty than, or even of another period from, the neighboring houses. I found more style and should have supposed more antiquity if not in the Palais de l'Industrie at any rate in the Trocadero. Plunged in a restless sleep, my adolescence embraced in one uniform vision the whole of the quarter through which it guided it, and I had never dreamed that there could be an eighteenth-century building in the Rue Royale, just as I should have been astonished to learn that the Porte Saint-Martin and the Porte Saint-Denis, those glories of the age of Louis XIV, were not contemporary with the most recently built tenements in the sordid districts which bore their names.

— Marcel Proust, *In Search of Lost Time*

Unlike literature, a more evolved art, for example, where the writer can remain faithful to his style and technique throughout his life, the filmmaker does not enjoy the same freedom. . . . Genius in the realm of films must always strive toward the new. However beautiful it might be, any film that does not further the cinema is not wholly worthy of its name. It must mesh with the sensibilities in its era.

— André Bazin, *The Cinema of Cruelty*

Contents

Illustrations

Acknowledgments

First, an expression of enormous gratitude to my brilliant and inexhaustible series editor, Murray Pomerance, for his dedication to this project. Without his intervention, this book might have suffered a dire fate indeed.

Scott Bukatman and Thomas Elsaesser offered helpful criticisms of the original manuscript. I am deeply indebted to both of them.

For their comments on a much earlier draft of this manuscript thanks are also in order for Richard Allen, Gilberto Perez, Catherine Russell, Bill Simon, and Robert Sklar. Richard Allen and Sam Ishii-Gonzalès originally invited me to participate in their *Alfred Hitchcock: Centenary Essays* volume in which some of my material on *Marnie* first appeared, albeit in very different form, as "Touching the Surface: *Marnie*, Melodrama, Modernism." My thanks to both of them but especially to Sam for his superb skills as an editor.

At SUNY Press, the professionalism of James Peltz and Marilyn Semerad made the production on this book a very smooth one. Thanks to Howard and Ron Mandelbaum of Photofest for their generosity in terms of the stills and for their patience.

The process of writing and rewriting this book was made much less painful due to the loyalty of various friends. Special thanks here to David Gerstner, Frances Guerin, Sam Ishii-Gonzalès (yet again), Julie Kaplan, Noa Steimatsky, and Jay Weissberg. Most of all here I thank Ivone Margulies. Her friendship and her personal and professional dedication to me have been so enormous that I often question whether I am even worthy of them.

In my early years in New York City, the friendship of three people, now all deceased, was central in shaping my understanding of the cinema and I acknowledge their importance to me here: Tom Hopkins, Roger McNiven, George Morris. The more recent death of another dearly loved friend, Melodie Wertelet, has created another kind of profound loss and one totally personal.

Finally, thanks to those I cannot even begin to thank but I must. For nearly two decades, Steve Barnes has offered the kind of supportive environment that is far beyond anything I probably deserve. Without him, I would not have been able to return to film studies after an absence of several years, finally able to pursue the career path which he knew I wanted. What I owe him I cannot begin to repay, financially or emotionally. Not long before she died, our friend Melodie privately said to me, "Joe, I hope you appreciate what you have in Steve." I do. Every day.

My parents, Joseph and Louise McElhaney, and my sister, Diann Fish, have consistently given me their love and unwavering support for many, many years. They remain today what they have always been: the center of my life. As for the two youngest cinephiles in the family, Rachel and Lydia Fish, keep up with the obsessive viewing of films, girls. You've inherited it from your uncle.

Introduction

Writing the History of Classical Cinema

IN JEAN-LUC GODARD'S *CONTEMPT* (1963), the seventy-three-year-old director Fritz Lang plays a version of himself in an otherwise fictional scenario concerned with the production of a film version of Homer's *The Odyssey* being directed by Lang at Cinecittà studios in Rome. Lang and his producer, Jeremy Prokosch (Jack Palance), attempt to interest the writer Paul Javal (Michel Piccoli) in helping them create a workable screenplay for this project. At one point in the film, Lang tells Javal that he believes the particular power of *The Odyssey* resides in Homer's harmonious relationship with the world in which he creates. "The world of Homer," Lang says, "is a real world. The poet belonged to his own civilization, one that developed in harmony with nature, not in opposition to it. That is precisely the beauty of *The Odyssey*, its faith in reality as it exists . . . in a form that could not be tampered with." These lines were written not by Lang but by Godard and may be taken as Godard's attempt to define the nature of the moment in which his own film is being made—that of the early 1960s, at the height of the influence and creative power of the French New Wave.

An international coproduction packaged by Carlo Ponti and Joseph E. Levine, featuring a major star, Brigitte Bardot, and adapted from a novel by Alberto Moravia, *Contempt* was Godard's single major attempt to enjoy widespread international success and to create a film on a scale that would evoke, however distantly, the world of epic narrative. Within the context of film history up to this point, what such a citation of the epic inevitably suggested was classical cinema, a form which also, one could

1

argue, developed "in harmony" with civilization for approximately the first fifty years of existence.[1] And although written by Godard, these words are spoken by a filmmaker who, in Germany in the 1920s and early 1930s, forged not simply a style but, in the words of Noël Burch, "a series of achievements that match the history of the cinema's crestline of discovery stage by stage."[2] Unlike the improvisational Godard, Lang's cinema depends on a rigorous and inflexible preconception, working within a "form that could not be tampered with." In the grandiose and overdetermined world of Lang, little is left to chance.

Both Homer and Lang function for *Contempt* as the sites of far-removed and mythical realms, creating epic narratives designed for a wide audience and in worlds markedly different from the one in which Godard himself is now working—or at least that is the implication here. As many commentators on the film have noted, *Contempt* self-consciously draws on the language of this type of filmmaking to the point where the film becomes, as Jacques Aumont has phrased it, "a sort of compendium of classical cinema."[3] This relationship to classical cinema includes a narrative with an almost classical three-act structure; a fluid, long-take style; romantic musical underscoring; and a use of color and anamorphic widescreen that evokes the world of big-budget spectacle. But *Contempt* reproduces these elements in a very idiosyncratic manner so that the film seems to be, at once, an example of classical cinema and a commentary on it.[4]

As an extension of the element of commentary, *Contempt* cites numerous films and filmmakers whose origins are largely from what has been defined as cinema's classical period. Javal explains to Prokosch that his conception for *The Odyssey* is one that would revert to the style of D. W. Griffith and Charles Chaplin. In the film, a wall on the back lot of Cinecittà is covered with film posters from Alfred Hitchcock's *Psycho* (1960), Roberto Rossellini's *Vanina Vanini* (1961), and Howard Hawks's *Hatari!* (1962). Javal unsuccessfully attempts to convince his wife Camille (Bardot) to go to the cinema with him to see Hawks's *Rio Bravo* (1959) or Nicholas Ray's *Bigger Than Life* (1956); and while Camille sits in the bathtub reading Luc Moullet's study of Lang, Javal insists that he keep his hat on indoors in emulation of Dean Martin in Vincente Minnelli's *Some Came Running* (1958). These citations are not examples of Godard genuflecting to Great Directors of the Past. Instead they function as acts of mourning, an acknowledgement that a way of filming and looking at the world is passing out of existence. The posters on the wall at Cinecittà are not simply displayed but are peeling, fading away.

A year after *Contempt* was made (and most likely taking its cue from the film) Andrew Sarris wrote an essay on Godard in which he argued that the cinema:

Figure I.1. Jean-Luc Godard's *Contempt* (1963): Michel Piccoli as Paul Javal (left) with Fritz Lang. The backlot at Cinecittà.

may finally be passing out of its classical period, little more than half a century old, after all, and into a period of commentary and abstraction. The classicists from cinema's more instinctive past are either dead—Ophuls, Mizoguchi, Murnau, Griffith, Lubitsch, et al.—or aging—Renoir, Dreyer, Ford, Chaplin, Sternberg, Lang, et al. Even Rossellini and Welles, the great innovators (or conservators?) of the forties, seem to belong to traditions which have largely spent their force."[5]

Within *Contempt*, the films of Hawks and Hitchcock, of Lang, Minnelli, and Rossellini mark the end of an attitude toward cinema traceable back at least as far as the filmmaking of Chaplin and Griffith. Godard even includes a poster from one of his own films, *Vivre sa vie* (1962), on that wall of decay and reading these citations in allegorical terms is unavoidable. The Godard of 1963 was arguably the most historically self-conscious filmmaker of the French New Wave, and in *Contempt* he is already imagining the decline and irrelevance of his own work in the midst of the decline of his predecessors. Writing on the historical importance of *Contempt* seven years after its release, Serge Daney argues that the film raises the issue of whether "failure is not more profound than any success. That is, is it not the demiurges who fail?" Godard's film marks "a turning from which the cinema has scarcely begun to come back."[6]

During this period, the dominance of classical narrative cinema as an aesthetic force (as opposed to its dominance of a strictly economic nature) gives way to other methods that challenge this hegemony. Sharply defined alternatives to classical cinema are gaining widespread recognition, principally within the realm of European art cinema—especially that of the French New Wave but also certain developments within Italian cinema (particularly the work of Antonioni and Fellini) and a bit later still, New German Cinema. "For the first time since the silent period," Geoffrey Nowell-Smith writes, "the cinema, or part of it, found itself aligned fair and square with the artistic culture of modernism."[7] The methods of classical cinema up to this point are closely bound up with a filmmaking that became solidified in the 1920s and that emerged out of a highly developed industrial mode of production exemplified by the frequently imitated studio system of Hollywood. The decline of this cinema begins in the early to mid-1960s, when these industries are either suffering from economic problems or reorganizing their modes of production. In the past, Hollywood and classical cinema in general had often been able to absorb the lessons of modernist developments in film form easily. To varying degrees, they would continue to do so throughout the 1960s and 1970s although in a much more uneven and idiosyncratic manner. All of this creates a climate that seems to throw the earlier classical cinema into a state of uncertainty.

Three years prior to acting in *Contempt*, Lang directed what would turn out to be his final film, *The Thousand Eyes of Dr. Mabuse* (1960), made in Germany. Disastrously received by the press in Lang's native country, it did not open in the United States until 1966, as part of a double bill in a theater in Times Square, dubbed into English and released without benefit of press screenings. It did, however, make Godard's Ten Best list in *Cahiers du Cinéma* for 1961 (the year it was released in France) and finished sixteenth in the magazine's annual critics poll, just after Jean Rouch's *La Pyramide humaine* (1961) and John Cassavetes's *Shadows* (1959), two very different films that more obviously represented the changing direction of the cinema of the 1960s. Although indisputably one of the most innovative film directors in the history of the form, the Fritz Lang of 1960, returning to the country in which his reputation was established, no longer belongs "to his own civilization" or creates "in harmony with nature." The cultural environment and the technical resources that produced *Metropolis* (1927) and the earlier Mabuse films have ceased to exist. To many critics and spectators of the period, *The Thousand Eyes of Dr. Mabuse* is a film that seems to have been (to borrow a phrase from Manny Farber) "dropped into the present from a past which has become useless."[8]

Between 1960 and 1963, then, we have Lang's most recent film, largely regarded as a failure. Among the most vocal defenders of this work are the critics of *Cahiers du Cinéma*, many of whom (as filmmakers) are engaged in a significant rewriting and rethinking of the nature of cinematic form. Lang's work remains alive for these critics and filmmakers in a way that it is not elsewhere. But Lang makes no other films after *The Thousand Eyes* and later expresses regret at ever having made it. Although he was often publicly supportive of the work of the New Wave, it is a support marked by such ambivalence that one wonders if Lang even fully understands its most basic impulses: He is mystified by its concern with realism and improvisation, for instance, and considers this "the death of art."[9] In spite of their great admiration for Lang, the New Wave directors clearly, if they do not surpass him, move elsewhere and implicitly critique many of the assumptions of Lang's cinema. Unwittingly perhaps, their films and writings also magnify the general perception of Lang's decline. For the New Wave, the classical film auteur was first to be constituted as a model. But this process also entailed the necessity of foregrounding historical distance, of mapping out a distinct space within which new and distinctive forms of production could emerge. With this came major differences in the approach to film form between the Great Masters and the Young Turks of the New Wave. Whereas many of the Great Masters continue to make films during the 1960s, the nature of the investigations of the New Wave and other art cinema practices are such that this recent work by the canonical "first generation" of filmmakers was felt to suffer from historical dislocation by comparison. For the Great Masters who are still working and aware of this situation, the problem now is how to adapt and to continue creating a cinema that has not lost its historical relevance.

It is this *idea* of the death of classical cinema, its circumstances and implications, which are the primary concern of this book. The type of death I am situating here is not, by any means, a fact. Rather, it is a descriptive and historical attempt to give a name to a way of filming that, within several critical discourses of the period (and, to a certain extent, today as well), is regarded as being anachronistic. Numerous films and filmmakers from the period, stretching roughly from the late 1950s to the early 1970s, are relevant to the arguments I make here: the Jean Renoir of *The Testament of Dr. Cordelier* (1959), *Picnic on the Grass* (1961), or *The Elusive Corporal* (1962), the Michael Powell of *Peeping Tom* (1960), the George Cukor of *The Chapman Report* (1962) or *Justine* (1969), the Howard Hawks of *Red Line 7000* (1965), the Elia Kazan stretching from *Splendor in the Grass* (1961) up through *The Visitors* (1972), the John Ford of *The Man Who Shot Liberty Valance* (1962) or *Seven Women* (1966), the Robert Rossen of *Lilith* (1964), the Allan Dwan of *The Most Dangerous Man Alive* (1961). My primary concern, however, will be with three films: Lang's *The Thousand Eyes of Dr. Mabuse*, Hitchcock's *Marnie* (1964), and Minnelli's *Two Weeks in Another Town* (1962). My reasons for choosing these three films and filmmakers over the others is something that will become clearer over the course of this introduction. I cannot deny, however, that my choices are also the result of a personal preference or, to be more precise, a *passion* that is stronger than the admiration I have for the other films listed here. As we shall see, such apparent indulgences are not antithetical to the nature of my project.

As with many of the films listed previously, *The Thousand Eyes of Dr. Mabuse*, *Marnie*, and *Two Weeks in Another Town* were largely perceived as being not only failures but, in certain quarters, as catastrophes for these directors, clear indications that they were losing their relevance as filmmakers as well as being symptomatic of the declining power of classical cinema. But the word catastrophe also has another meaning for this book. Donald Kuspit has drawn attention to the recurring rhetoric of death, crisis, and catastrophe that invariably emerges when art is perceived to be in state of advance. "The birth of a new art is informed by a sense of catastrophe, displaced onto an old art by describing it as decadent, which it may or may not be," he argues. But the death of an old art is likewise informed by this sense of catastrophe. "The old art defends itself by regarding the new art as far-fetched and arbitrary," he writes, "or else the old art quietly assimilates the new art's advances, to stay in favor with the society that admires them."[10] What is taking place with the cinema during this period, however, does not precisely conform to any of these tendencies Kuspit outlines, although elements of all of them are at work here. In *Contempt*, for example, Godard may well view classical cinema as being in a decadent or ruined state. But this is far from being a simple negative evaluation, especially because Godard views his own work as engaged in a similar process of decay. And in spite of Lang's publicly expressed skepticism about the value of the French New Wave, Lang's own cinema, as well as that of Hitchcock's and Minnelli's, was clearly serving as a crucial model for a new type of modern cinema. Moreover, the admiration that both Hitchcock and Minnelli had for this new cinema emerging during the 1960s appeared to be quite strong—stronger than Lang's. A reversal of sorts begins to take place in which this new cinema itself became a type of model for these older figures and in ways that cannot be simply categorized as one of quiet assimilation.

To say that classical cinema has become a thing of the past is a statement fraught with historical problems. As an economic force within popular culture, classical cinema (particularly that of Hollywood) is as strong now as it ever was and it is still sometimes capable of producing works of interest. But my concern here is not with classical cinema as a monolithic cultural form practiced across twentieth-century history. Rather, I want to focus on the beginning of a specific historical moment when classicism is perceived to be in a state of decline. What are the implications of such a supposed decline in terms of how we understand, define, and historically locate this form so often identified as classical cinema? Or is this decline illusory, the subject of a melancholic fantasy about the cinema?

If we say that classical cinema is in a state of decline during the 1960s, and if we are to discuss this decline in relation to certain auteurs, how then do we account for the work of, for example, Hollywood filmmakers of the same approximate generation as Minnelli who do not appear to face the same problems that he did during this decade, directors such as Otto Preminger, Robert Aldrich, Don Siegel or, working completely out of Europe by this period, Joseph Losey? Any attempt to assess the development of classical cinema fully during the 1960s and after would need to address the ways in which these filmmakers, rather than going into decline, not only easily adapted to current trends but also arguably produced some of their best work during this decade and beyond it. Furthermore, how do we account for filmmakers of the same approximate generation as Lang or Hitchcock who continue to work during the 1960s but without feeling the need to adjust their filmmaking styles significantly in relation to changing fashions: Billy Wilder or especially Chaplin who, in *A Countess from Hong Kong* (1966), creates a film that seems to be willfully archaic? I raise such questions not to answer them here, but rather to pose them as historical problems. Although the concept of decline should not be entirely disregarded as a myth, arguing that classical cinema during the 1960s and early 1970s undergoes several important changes and transformations of which the films being discussed in this book are but three examples is more precise.

What Is Classical Cinema?

Before proceeding further, explaining how the terms *classical cinema* and *modernist cinema* will be used here is necessary. Defining them, like defining any historical and group style, is a complex, ongoing process. As Charles Rosen argues in his study of classical music, "the concept of a style does not correspond to an historical fact but answers a need: it creates a mode of understanding."[11] Consequently, I offer not one concise, textbook-like definition of either classical or modernist cinema, but instead negotiate my way among several major attempts to create a mode of understanding these cinemas.

David Bordwell and Kristin Thompson in *Film Art: An Introduction* and *The Classical Hollywood Cinema: Film Style and Mode of Production to 1960* (the latter cowritten with Janet Staiger) offer the most cogent definition of classical cinema. Although they were not the first to use the term *classical cinema*, the influence of their work has virtually enshrined classical Hollywood as a full-fledged academic category. Putting forth a cognitive approach to film form, strongly influenced by Russian Formalism and the work of the art critic and historian E. H. Gombrich, the authors define classical Hollywood cinema as one marked by a sense of "decorum, proportion, formal harmony, respect for tradition, mimesis, self-effacing craftsmanship, and cool control of the perceiver's response."[12] These qualities are achieved through the application of certain formal devices and storytelling techniques: the use of cause-and-effect narrative structures with strong goal-oriented protagonists; a reliance on the continuity editing system in which the action seems to unfold in a fluid and continuous manner; and a discreet use of lighting, camera movement, shot composition and sound that, while sometimes achieving expressive ends, are generally placed at the service of the narrative.

Bordwell's and Thompson's approach has its considerable appeal and usefulness, in particular an ability to offer a clear and sharply defined formalist system, a "group style" by which this cinema operates. Of the three directors who are the subject of this book, Minnelli belongs most firmly to this type of classical cinema. While often making use of expressive camera movements and of shot durations that were slightly above the norm for his period, Minnelli essentially creates within this group style. And in spite of his substantial contribution to the development of the musical genre (as well as to postwar melodrama and the domestic comedy), Minnelli's handlings of genre "only confirm the genre's fertility."[13] Hitchcock and Lang offer more complicated cases in that their work represents how an "intermittent and fluctuating" style may assert itself in a film, allowing these directors to "intrude more often than is usual." In Hitchcock this occurs through the emphasis on "optical subjectivity" and "blatant narrational intrusions," the latter occurring through the use of such devices as "unexpected" camera angles, symbolic inserts, and sound overlaps.[14] In the case of Lang, we have a filmmaker who creates a "paranoid" spectator through a strategy that initially appears to operate within classical narrative's investment in transparency, but that often "brutally and abruptly manipulates point-of-view to conceal gaps and force the viewer to false conclusions."[15]

However, neither Lang nor Hitchcock fully qualifies as modernist filmmakers according to the system that *The Classical Hollywood Cinema* constructs for itself. "Most often," Bordwell writes, "an idiosyncratic exploration of causality, time, or space works to reaffirm the norm by revealing the suppleness and range of the paradigm."[16] Bordwell, Staiger, and Thompson create three categories as alternatives to classical cinema: the art film, the modernist film, and the avant-garde film. Only the first two of these need concern us here. The art film, like classical Hollywood, largely conforms to a group style consisting of a greater attention to realism, a less tightly causal method of organizing narrative, and characters that are often ambivalent, less able to drive a narrative strongly forward as they are in classical cinema. A true modernist cinema is one in which "spatial and temporal systems come forward and share with narrative the role of structuring the film" in which "a dynamic of unity and fragmentation is set up within the text."[17] Examples are given: Yasujiro Ozu, Jacques Tati, Kenji Mizougchi, Dreyer, Rivette, Bresson, and Godard. Although mindful of ambiguities and exceptions, and while also arguing that "no absolute, pure alternative to Hollywood exists,"[18] *The Classical Hollywood Cinema* tends to position modernist cinema as a more formally complex and idiosyncratic practice than classical cinema. Film modernism here, as in most modernisms, retains its standard function as an aesthetic practice that challenges mainstream norms of perception and formal structure.[19]

However influential, Bordwell and Thompson's version of classical cinema has encountered a good deal of resistance. Miriam Bratu Hansen, for example, has questioned the validity of the very word *classical* (with its links to seventeenth- and eighteenth-century neoclassical ideals) as a way of describing a practice of filmmaking that may be more aptly defined as a type of "vernacular modernism."[20] Instead of a cinema devoted to principles of decorum, proportion, formal harmony, and a cool control of the viewer's responses, Hansen (influenced by Walter Benjamin and Siegfried Kracauer in their approaches to the culture of modernity) posits a cinema "anchored in sensory experience and sensational effect—in processes of mimetic identification that are more often than not partial and excessive in relation to narrative comprehension."[21] Where *The Classical Hollywood Cinema* erects a system to understand classical cinema, Hansen sees something closer to "a scaffold, matrix, or web that allows for a wide range of aesthetics effects and experiences. . . ."[22] Although less precisely defined than in Bordwell, Staiger, and Thompson's work, classical cinema in Hansen's essay also becomes something more disruptive and unstable, its films less strictly conforming to a precise system. Hansen argues (and she is not the first to have done so) that the "totalizing account " *The Classical Hollywood Cinema* offers also serves a potentially repressive function in its need to subsume genre completely into its paradigm.[23] Hansen does not, however, recommend dispensing entirely with the term *classical*, largely because she is unable to offer a more appropriate term and because the term itself still at least "names a regime of productivity and intelligibility that is both historically and culturally specific. . . ."[24] Eric Rohmer's prediction in 1949 that "classical cinema is not behind us, but ahead"[25] has yet to come to pass and most likely never will because from the moment that the cinema came into existence in the late nineteenth-century modernism was already substantially under way in the other arts. The cinema had to, in a sense, learn to be classical and modernist at once, resulting in its various modernisms very quickly perceived to be as out-of-date as its classicisms.

Although she does not specifically discuss any of their films, Hansen's insistence on connecting classical Hollywood to vernacular modernism opens up the work of Lang, Hitchcock, and Minnelli in some productive directions *The Classical Hollywood Cinema* does not offer. Modernism here is much more strongly tied to modernity in general and is not strictly related to modernism as an aesthetic practice that challenges traditional forms and modes of understanding. Within Hansen's matrix, Minnelli's work would not so much obey the dictates of a group style but instead be part of this history of vernacular modernism. As James Naremore has written, Minnelli's entire career (taking into account his early years as a window decorator and fashion photographer as well as designer and director of sophisticated Broadway musical revues) is "symptomatic of an aesthete's progress through the modern economy, [offering] a condensed history of the 'visions' offered by industrialized capitalism."[26] In terms of Lang and Hitchcock, the "intermittent and fluctuating" ways in which they negotiate between classical and modernist strategies within their respective filmmaking practices we may now see as being tied to how they also negotiate their way through the forces of modernity and popular culture. In particular, all three of these filmmakers rely on aspects of story construction, characterization, performance style, and stylistic details and iconography, which have some relationship to the world of melodrama: in *The Thousand Eyes* it is the serial pulp thriller; in *Marnie*, gothic melodrama and the woman's film; in *Two Weeks*, the Hollywood postwar domestic and psychological melodrama. Much contemporary writing on melodrama stresses this mode's relationship to the emergence of the modern but a modernity strongly connected to popular culture and to the supposedly shifting nature of visual and aural perception brought about by changes in modern life—of which the cinema's emergence in the late nineteenth century serves as a culminating moment. Melodrama is involved in a continuous search for plenitude and meaning in environments of social confusion and unrest. As Peter Brooks writes, "Melodrama starts from and expresses the anxiety brought by a frightening new world in which the traditional patterns of moral order no longer provide the necessary social glue."[27] Its investment in vision, in the act of looking and perception, is an attempt (often failed or frustrated) to regain for vision its lost classical primacy.

What is being offered in this book is not primarily a study of melodrama. But all three films in this book are, in different ways, concerned with this question of vision that haunts melodrama, of the attempt to project onto and control an image while at the same time being repeatedly marked by a sense of failure and frustration. In *The Thousand Eyes of Dr. Mabuse* this is articulated primarily through technologies of surveillance; in *Marnie* it is handled through the concept of both the male and female gaze, in which vision and perception are caught up in a system that is at once violent and erotic; whereas *Two Weeks in Another Town* directly concerns itself with the production of cinema and with a battle among multiple and conflicting visions of a film-within-a-film. But in all three instances these concerns are often done in an unusually intense and hysterical manner, as though the mode of melodrama itself has likewise reached a state of catastrophe, exhausting its potential to signify for these directors in the ways that it once had.

Furthermore, the very nature of the films that Lang, Hitchcock, and Minnelli are producing during this period, and the historical implications that these films raise, are in many ways consistent with how modernism is defined—specifically, the notion of a crisis of form or language that the artist acknowledges and then absorbs into the work itself. Daney's argument about the historical importance of Godard's direct acknowledgment of failure in *Contempt* is in itself a basic method of understanding modernism in which, as Irving Howe states, *"modernism must always struggle but never quite triumph, and then, after a time, must struggle in order not to triumph."*[28] Even if *The Thousand Eyes of Dr. Mabuse*, *Marnie*, and *Two Weeks in Another Town* do not, in many respects, conform to the Bordwell, Staiger, and Thompson's model of the modernist film, they nevertheless remain strongly modernist in impulse if not entirely in form as they struggle to give birth to a new type of cinema.[29]

Another major contemporary attempt to understand the relationship between classical cinema and modernist cinema comes from Gilles Deleuze's two-volume study, *Cinema 1: The Movement-Image* and *Cinema 2: The Time-Image*. For Deleuze, classical cinema has its origins in filmmaking prior to World War II. This cinema is not defined in conventional formalist terms but (working out of Henri Bergson and Charles Saunders Peirce) by its conception of movement, time and space, and signs. Classical cinema of the prewar period, while encompassing such seemingly irreconcilable conceptions of cinema as the Soviet school, Weimar art cinema, French impressionist filmmaking, and Hollywood, is linked by its impulse toward achieving unity between space and movement, a classical "movement-image" whose essence "lies in extracting from vehicles or moving bodies the movement which is their common substance, or extracting from movements the mobility which is their essence."[30] However different Soviet montage and classical Hollywood editing may be in their concerns, for instance, they are also linked in their concern with the subordination and conquering of the problem of time through movement. The modern cinema (rather than *modernist*, a term Deleuze does not use directly) that emerges in the wake of Italian neorealism is "not something more beautiful, more profound, or more true, but something different."[31] Here the "sensory-motor schema" that defined the classical movement-image collapses leading to the modern "time-image." Unity between movement and action slows down or stops, leading to "a new race of characters" that "saw rather than acted." Deleuze writes, "Time ceases to be derived from the movement, it appears in itself and itself gives rise to *false movements*."[32] At the same time, classical cinema and modern cinema do not necessarily stand opposed to one another but are engaged in a complex relationship in which the time-image "has always been breaking through, holding back or encompassing the movement-image."[33] Within Deleuze's system, all three filmmakers who are the subject of this book are placed somewhere between classical cinema and modern cinema. Lang (particularly in his American films) "becomes the greatest filmmaker of appearances, of false images";[34] Minnelli's "very great position in cinema" resides in his discovery of "the plurality of worlds" within a "dream-image" in which "every world and every dream is shut in on itself";[35] whereas Hitchcock becomes a filmmaker who is "pushing the movement-image to its limit" in his exploration of a "mental-image."[36]

Deleuze's writings on the cinema have inspired a wealth of academic material, from commentaries on and explications of his work to numerous Deleuzian readings of the cinema. Inevitably, reservations about his methods and historical arguments have been expressed, one of the most vociferous made by Bordwell who sees Deleuze practicing little more than an "orthodox historiography of style" largely derived from figures such as André Bazin, Burch, Marie-Claire Ropars-Wuilleumier, and the critics of *Cahiers du Cinéma*. For Bordwell, Deleuze demonstrates "how uncritical adherence to historiographic tradition can disable contemporary work."[37] When measured against the kind of formalist and art historical approach Bordwell himself practices, Deleuze's history of cinema must indeed seem somewhat trite. I question, however, whether Deleuze is even attempting to write a conventional history of cinema and at the very least I hope that the example of this book suggests that Deleuze's work is available to be used in ways more productive than Bordwell's reading allows for.

The Death of Classical Cinema follows in the footsteps of numerous contemporary texts on cinema that cite Deleuze although it is neither an attempt to further explicate his work in philosophical terms (a mammoth project outside the ambitions of this book) nor an attempt (in spite of the occasional use of certain terms taken from the texts) at yet another full-scale Deleuzian reading of films (if the latter is what emerges it is unintentional). The citations of his work that recur throughout this book serve a simpler purpose in that they will be used primarily for the manner in which they synthesize a wide range of film criticism, primarily French and primarily from the postwar period. Many of Deleuze's general observations on filmmakers are taken from various critical studies of these directors, something that Deleuze directly acknowledges, both in footnotes and interviews.[38] As Ropars-Wuilleumier has noted, this repeated use of secondhand references is an impulse "attributable to the cinema itself, whose singularity derives only from what it accomplishes by transforming itself into words." This strategy also allows Deleuze to break with "the empire of the sign" in which the original or established meaning of these texts is reinscribed into Deleuze's own system of thought.[39] I am aware that a limitation may consequently arise in my casual use of Deleuze in that simply drawing on his insights taken from the auteurist monographs may only serve to return those texts back to their original meanings. But as I have already noted, my attempt here is not to offer a Deleuzian text but to, at most, use Deleuze as one of several guiding spirits.

As a guiding spirit, one element that I am extracting from the two volumes is a sensibility informed by cinephilia, that fundamental, obsessive need and attraction for motion picture images as well as the attraction toward a culture more or less united in sensibility, which emerges out of this need. As Annette Michelson has noted, no single version of cinephilia exists, but rather different manifestations of it are seen across film history.[40] The version of it which informs this book is one in which cinephilia joined forces with auteurism, particularly as it took root in France after World War II. Although a backlash against this form of cinephilia over the last four decades resulted in its marginalization from film studies, it is gradually showing signs of a return (from essays to academic conferences and panels) of which this book is but one example.[41] *The Death of Classical Cinema* is an academic text written by someone who teaches film history within this academic world. I frequently draw on certain formalist approaches (as well as other methodologies) fully acceptable within academia. But it is also, for better or worse, influenced by an attitude toward the cinema that largely took root outside of the academy.

The Death and Resurrection of the Author

Today director-oriented studies commonly make defensive claims for themselves as avoiding traditional auteurism. I will not make such a claim, partly because I feel that auteurism as it was practiced in the 1950s and early 1960s was more varied and nuanced than it has often been given credit for and partly because the influence of auteurism on this book is too strong to deny. It was during the 1950s and early 1960s when the attempt to define classical cinema received one of its earliest and most sustained applications, from Bazin's "The Evolution of the Language of Cinema" to Rohmer's "The Classical Age of Film" to Godard's "Defence and Illustration of Classical Construction." Although much of what follows is strongly shaped by this period in film criticism, it is not shaped by it alone.

Paul Willemen has noted that a primary motivation behind cinephilia is the desire to bear witness, "the need to proclaim what has been experienced, to draw attention to what has been seen by 'the elect' but which may not have been noticed by 'routine' viewers. There is always something proselytising about cinephiliac writing, a barely contained impatience with those who have eyes but do not see."[42] Willemen creates a neologism of cinephiliac to refer to the attitude of necrophilia, which presides over cinephilia itself, the need to revive a past that is dead (or at least dead within certain dominant discourses), but that is alive in the memory and the consciousness of the cinephile.[43] In 1977 Daney wrote, "There is a dimension to cinephilia which psychoanalysis knows well under the name of 'mourning work': something is dead, something of which traces, shadows remain. . . ."[44] While the cinephilia that informs this book has always been fixated on narrative cinema above all others, the category of the "old man's film" has always been a central aspect to it: works dismissed at the time of their initial release because they were thought to be indications that greatness was now eluding the once-great, works that the cinephile transforms through the process of reading. *The Thousand Eyes of Dr. Mabuse*, *Marnie*, and *Two Weeks in Another Town* are all primary examples of this kind of cinema. Willemen and Daney (writing almost twenty years apart) were originally auteurist cinephiles who then moved "beyond" this position—even though Willemen declares, "I am still a cinephile."[45] But they both express a certain nostalgia for that earlier position and for what became lost when cinephilia gave way to other methodologies which contested its attitudes. Daney, for example, claims that the cinephilia of his generation was fixated on U.S. cinema above all else, but "often the most despised" type of American cinema produced within a thriving industry and a culture in which there is "a real consensus." This type of auteurist writing was central in the reevaluation of the American work of both Lang and Hitchcock and took Minnelli's work in melodrama as seriously as his work in the musical. Because both the nature of that industry and the surrounding culture has shifted, Daney feels that it is no longer possible to revive that particular practice of cinephilia.[46] Raymond Bellour has more recently contrasted the French cinephilia of his (and Daney's) generation with its fixation on Hollywood with a later cinephilia that emerges through the French New Wave and that reads Hollywood essentially through New Wave discourses and sensibilities while absorbing the cinema of the New Wave into its cinephilia.[47]

Lang, Hitchcock, and Minnelli all enjoyed extensive careers within the Hollywood studio system that was so fundamental to that earlier group of cinephiles and auteurists. Nevertheless, a primary reason I have chosen Lang and Hitchcock as directors for this book is that the formation of their filmmaking styles took place elsewhere (Germany and England, respectively) and consequently their relationship to the classical filmmaking practices of Hollywood is a complex one, allowing me to explore the possibilities of a less orthodox (and less distinctly American) version of classical cinema. Minnelli, on the other hand, is often considered a typical Hollywood filmmaker, the studio contract director who obediently and efficiently turned out film after film on assignment from MGM for more than twenty years. In this regard, he is a "minor" artist in comparison with Lang and Hitchcock and my inclusion of him here undoubtedly will seem like a provocation—which is partly my intention. But as I hope that the book demonstrates, and however different Minnelli may be in some ways from Lang and Hitchcock, his work is equally central to an understanding of the relationship between classical and modernist cinema. In this regard, I am undoubtedly attempting to elevate him to the status of a major figure, the proselytizing impulse of cinephilia manifesting itself once again.

Willemen states that the primarily French origins of cinephilia were strongly bound up with Roman Catholic–influenced concepts of revelation and with "the privileged, pleasure-giving, fascinating moment of a relationship to what's happening on a screen."[48] Many of the discourses and methodologies that supplanted cinephilia after the political upheavals of 1968 (semiotics and structuralism, psychoanalysis, feminism, cultural studies) were skeptical, if not hostile, to such moments of revelation. The marginalization or denial of the author as a stable center was a vital tool in these new debates. When Thomas Elsaesser's essay on Minnelli was reprinted in a 1979 anthology on the musical more than a decade after auteurism's decline, Elsaesser attached a new preface to the piece, establishing a distance from the approach taken in it and in a language symptomatic of structuralist discourses of the period. The victories of auteurist critics are, claims Elsaesser, "snatched from the jaws of common-sense."[49] But he also predicted that the need for such methods of experiencing cinema would continue: "The auteur is the fiction, the necessary fiction one might add, become flesh and historical in the director, for the name of a pleasure that seems to have no substitute in the sobered-up deconstructions of the authorless voice of ideology."[50] Furthermore, and as Hansen has noted, much of this post–1968 discourse was not startlingly new but indebted to earlier modernist practices and attitudes (sometimes self-consciously so, as in Godard's Dziga Vertov Group) in which a strong polarization between classical transparency and modernist materiality was often put forth, a manner of thinking of which traces can still be detected in *The Classical Hollywood Cinema*.[51]

Ironically, during this period of "the death of the author," film directors increasingly became celebrity figures in their own right, particularly in U.S. cinema when the so-called Film School Generation (Steven Spielberg, George Lucas, Brian De Palma, John Carpenter, Francis Coppola, Martin Scorsese) began to emerge in the aftermath of the decline of the traditional studio system. Many of these young directors were formed by the cinephilia and auteurism of the previous two decades, their work (like that of the French New Wave earlier) filled with citations from the work of favored films and filmmakers of the past: Scorsese's *Mean Streets* (1973), for example, lifts footage directly from Lang's *The Big Heat* (1953) as part of its final sequence, and Peter Bogdanovich includes an excerpt from Minnelli's *Father of the Bride* (1950) in what is arguably the ultimate "mourning work" of classical cinema from this later generation of filmmakers, *The Last Picture Show* (1971).[52] In interviews it was often de rigueur for these directors to proclaim their admiration for most of the same figures that the New Wave had already "discovered," whereas (particularly in the case of Scorsese), the New Wave and European art cinema began to be part of this history, available to be cited and absorbed into film practice: Scorsese's *Taxi Driver* (1976) simultaneously draws on Bresson and Godard as well as John Ford, Hitchcock, and Lang. Film studies increasingly became an academic discipline during this period. Many of the writings that appeared in *Cahiers du Cinéma* or in such English journals as *Sight and Sound* and the auteurist *Movie* were being read in classrooms (much of it, no doubt, by the film school generation) even though this writing was originally done outside the space of academia and largely by individuals who were not teachers or traditional scholars.

My own particular cinephilia is partly of Bellour's second category described previously, what may best be described as a French reading of U.S. cinema, although saying that for me French (as well as certain U.S. and British) film criticism merely confirmed and extended an already-held passion may be more accurate.[53] I did not discover classical Hollywood or the films and filmmakers who are the object of this study through the French New Wave. Rather, the New Wave refined and extended an interest created elsewhere. Moreover, this discovery of French film theory, criticism, and filmmaking took place for me more or less simultaneously with other discoveries, specifically New German Cinema and certain directors of the Film School Generation. My formation within film studies began during the late 1970s at a time when various discourses and methodologies were actively competing with one another. Within a single department, one class was often dominated by an instructor strongly influenced by post–1968 methods of film theory and analysis while another class would still be under the sway of traditional auteurism. No doubt much of this book shows my own history in this regard. However, the pre– and post–1968 discourses are not always as incompatible as they might initially seem and, in fact, many of the individuals who began to concern themselves with "the politics of representation" during the 1970s (Daney, Pascal Bonitzer, Jean-Louis Comolli, Jean Narboni, Sylvie Pierre) were shaped by the concerns of the previous decade. As Daney later said of the post–1968 period, "We wanted to re-read Ford, not [John] Huston, to dissect [Robert] Bresson and not René Clair, to psychoanalyze Bazin and not Pauline Kael." From the beginning of the history of the *Cahiers* up through its various transformations, the one constant for Daney is "a CINEMA HAUNTED BY WRITING."[54] The issue of authorship, however differently articulated, remains a central one throughout the later period and this book probably draws even more strongly on this period than it does the earlier one. For example, Jean-Pierre Oudart's argument in 1970 that the classicism of Lang and Hitchcock derives its force not from "its transparence and its contiguity with the real, but rather its anchorage in the obsessional" is central to this book (and will be extended to Minnelli as well).[55]

That cinephilia can ever be thoroughly and seriously reborn without the concept of images being traced to some kind of agency or intervention is unlikely. This sense of agency need not necessarily be the film director and indeed the cult of the film star has been a central aspect to cinephilia since early in the cinema's history. In spite of claims that auteurists are fixated on directorial style to the exclusion of other elements, a concern with the actor has not been absent from much of the film criticism that will be central to this book.[56] In particular, the notion that the actor is the film embodied, so to speak, is one which will be arise in all three chapters here. In the words of Jean Douchet, "The body's presence . . . or absence . . . its refusal, rejection, and repulsion . . . drove the story and guided the mise-en-scène."[57] This issue of presence and absence, of refusal, rejection and repulsion likewise manifests itself in relation to the three films under consideration here, in which the actor's presence (extremely problematic and controversial in all three films) becomes a crucial site of the expressive struggle at work.

Mise-en-scène criticism was central to much of early auteurism in which the style if not the vision of the filmmaker was articulated through camera movement, lighting, decor, staging of action, and the direction of performances. In some readings, such an investment could work against or significantly complicate the explicit content of the scenario producing, among other things, what Mary Ann Doane has referred to as a sense of "contingency" crucial to cinephilia.[58] Montage theory and criticism, such a major component of the discourse surrounding cinema during the pre–World War II era, briefly declined during this period. Its complicated revival is addressed in the first chapter of this book, a revival that also saw a gradual skepticism about not only the value of mise-en-scène criticism but also, as chapter three shows, even the very term mise-en-scène itself. For this book, although I will not dispense with such a useful term as mise-en-scène, I prefer to make use of the more general term *cinematic space* because it implies a relationship to mise-en-scène as well as to montage—the spaces of the film being created through the process of editing as much as through the pro-filmic. In either case the actor, as an element of staging or of a body or face being cut into through montage, will be crucial.

In a 1989 interview, Godard complained of the degree to which auteurism became co-opted by the forces of industry, that everyone talks of auteurs now and that it is part of the dominant discourse on the cinema: "Francois [Truffaut] spoke of 'auteur politics.' Today, all that is left is the term 'auteur,' but what was interesting was the term 'politics.' "[59] But Godard's solution (a slightly stale one, in my opinion), that we shift our emphasis to the study of individual great works rather than great authors, is not without its own problems: What will be the criteria for evaluating this tiny group of masterpieces worthy of serious study? And who gets to decide these matters? Consequently, I insist on the importance of the auteur, regarding him not as a fiction (film directing is, after all, a concrete act of labor and not something that exists within the realm of the imaginary, however elusive authorship to a film may often be) but as an active force within the films. This force is not static but subject to a variety of other factors, not all of them under the auteur's control. But in each instance here, the position and intervention of the auteur in the production of *The Thousand Eyes of Dr. Mabuse*, *Marnie*, and *Two Weeks in Another Town* is the one most worthy of serious attention, even (or perhaps especially) when that intervention is struggling to assert itself. Furthermore, these three films implicitly demand that the spectator take into account each respective filmmaker's body of work to fully grasp the richness of what they are presenting. Each is a type of testament film, a summation of each director's body of work done during a period of great uncertainty and possible transition.

What I hope to avoid, however, is to take a cue from *Contempt* and succumb to the appeal of melancholia in writing about these films, to create the kind of mourning work to which Daney refers. My interest here is not so much concerned with lovingly tracing out what is being lost to film history as classicism gives way to modernism, although such an approach certainly has its seductive appeal. Rather, I want to emphasize the relevance of these ostensibly old-fashioned testament films to the moment in which they were made and, by extension, their ongoing and contemporary relevance. Throughout the three chapters, the work of filmmakers associated with modernist or art cinema will be repeatedly invoked (Godard, Resnais, Antonioni, Fellini, Fassbinder), not to systematically set them in opposition to Lang, Hitchcock, and Minnelli, but instead to draw connections as much as differences and to complicate the temptation to read these films in terms of the simple notion of classical cinema in decline.

One reading strategy that emerges here is an allegorical one, attempting to trace out the process of ecriture at work in these films while attempting to trace out these filmmakers' own allegorical impulses. Lang, Hitchcock, and Minnelli are each, in somewhat different ways, writing over their own particular bodies of work at this time. If, as Craig Owens writes, the most fundamental impulse behind allegory is to "rescue from historical oblivion that which threatens to disappear" then these three filmmakers are attempting to rescue their own work from the onslaught of history, redeeming it for the present day.[60] In particular with Hitchcock and Minnelli, we find the desire to read one's own work through the work of another, not so much to restore original meaning as to rewrite and reimagine that work in relation to the present, whereas with all three filmmakers the need to cite and implicitly overhaul and critique their own earlier work is strong.

For Owens, allegory is repeatedly drawn to "the fragmentary, the imperfect, the incomplete," epitomized by the ruin.[61] One might also note here that cinephilia itself, in its fetishistic impulses, is often likewise drawn to a fragmentary cinema or to reading strategies that break into films, either to put the films back together again in new ways (particularly within certain kinds of traditional auteurism, in which the auteur becomes the coherent organizing principle) or by foregrounding the expressive incompleteness of the films (as in Surrealist cinephilia). When Owens writes that allegory is a way of speaking as "an expenditure of surplus value," a form of "excess," whereas "the suppression of allegory is identical with the suppression of writing,"[62] he is remarkably close to Daney's emphasis among the *Cahiers* critics who stressed "the excess of writing over ideology."[63] My own approach to the films over the next three chapters is no doubt torn between the need to defend, to explicate, to proselytize, but also to draw attention to the inexpressive, the imperfect, and the incomplete, to the allegorical impulse within these ostensibly classical films, an impulse that is also "at the origin of modernism in the arts."[64]

Opening and Closing Doors

As noted previously, fundamental to the analysis of the three films in this book will be how they treat the problem of cinematic space and how this, in turn, affects the relationship of these films to the ways in which we may understand classical cinema and modernist cinema. Lang and Hitchcock have been extensively analyzed in the past in relation to their treatment of architecture and also for the ways in which they organize their films, metaphorically linking shots in an architectural fashion, while Minnelli's treatment of decor and interior space is central to any formalist account of his work. As Vivian Sobchack has noted, film theory has traditionally been dominated by three metaphors, all of them drawing on tropes of space and decor: the picture frame, the window, and the mirror. The frame and the window both represent "the opposing poles of classical film theory," the frame largely concerning itself with signification in the formalist sense whereas the window represents the realist attempts to do justice to the concept of cinema as a transparent window on the world. The mirror, on the other hand, has been fundamental to psychoanalytic film theory and "represents the synthetic conflation of perception and expression."[65] Rather than limit myself to these three metaphors, I would like to add a fourth one that has received less attention but that may be even more pertinent to this study: the door.

In attempting to grasp a fundamental principle behind classical cinema, Daney has referred to the metaphor of "the secret beyond the door." Classical cinema creates a world in which our primary desire is always to know more and see more, not simply as part of the inevitable process of a cause-and-effect narrative unfolding, but also in terms of the organization of the images themselves.[66] Behind every image in classical cinema is another image and another, each of them linked in what Deleuze (in writing on Daney) has described as a "powerful beautifying organic totality."[67] Hence the importance in classical cinema of continuity editing strategies that fluidly link spaces together. I would also add to this that the door becomes a significant tool for articulating a sense of the frame within the frame, one with implications in terms of not only mise-en-scène but also montage. As one shot "logically" follows another, this momentum often complicates the desire to frame and possess the image in the fixed manner of a painting or photograph. The door (along with the picture frame, the window, and the mirror) supplies this desire for controlling and containing the image, directing the eye back toward the power of the single shot even if the entire rhythmic structure of classical cinema (and the technical apparatus of projected motion picture images in general) compels the senses to move on.

One can see this struggle between the static and moving frame clearly in the early work of D. W. Griffith. Not only do we find his well-known reliance on scenarios out of nineteenth-century theatrical and literary melodrama and their fascination with persecuted innocence played out in sealed rooms and behind locked doors (the spaces often serving as extensions of female bodies under siege), but also we find a certain reluctance to let the films move on, as it were. His actors will often enter or exit a shot very slowly from the far right or left, seeming to hug the frame itself, as though they cannot bear to let it go. The cut from one shot to another in Griffith frequently takes place as a character passes from one room to another, with the door marking the end of one shot and the beginning of another, the telegraph office of *The Girl and Her Trust* (1913) a primary case in point. The most startling sequence in that film is when the protagonist, Grace, attempts to keep two robbers away from the box in the safe of her office. She not only locks the door to the office but, in an extraordinary close-up, pounds a bullet into the keyhole with a pair of scissors, causing the bullet to go off, a literally explosive passage from one shot and one space to another. The door in cinema, then, is both a metaphor and a concrete object, a barrier to be crossed as it marks the passage from one shot to another, from one space to another.[68]

"The principal question posed by this cinema," Oudart writes, "indeed the only question, is that of the barred subject."[69] It is as though classical cinema itself is marked by the impulse to ostentatiously reveal and conceal, open and close while simultaneously evoking the world of traditional theater (the curtain raised and then finally lowered) and literature (the book as a physical object opening and then closing). Hence the recurrence of films that open and close with images of doors, from George Cukor's *Dinner at Eight* (1933) to John Ford's *The Searchers* (1956). "Why do they keep calling for metaphysics in cinema," Luis Buñuel wrote in 1928, "and failing to recognize that in a well-made film, the act of opening a door or seeing a hand—an enormous monster—pick up an object can encompass an authentic and novel beauty?"[70]

But the cinema need not be classical nor even be narrative to partake of the basic fascination with the door. The door manifests itself across film history and through many forms of cinema, given various articulations in the avant-garde, in animation, and the documentary as well as various genres and national cinemas. We may recall here that the

Figure I.2. Louis and Auguste Lumière's *Workers Exiting the Factory* (1895): First version.

first projected motion picture, Louis and Auguste Lumière's *Workers Exiting the Factory* (1895), is in itself a type of door film. If the three versions of this film are viewed successively, the subtle reworking of this film is clearly shown to involve methods of timing, staging, and reframing, which more strongly foreground the presence of the two factory doors, the large one at the right center of the frame and the small one at the left, as the

Figure I.3. *Workers Exiting the Factory:* Second version.

workers pour out of both of them. By the third version of this film, the opening of the larger door becomes a much stronger punctuation point than it had been in the first two, grandly announcing the opening of the film, whereas in this version the closing of the large factory door is likewise more strongly emphasized. (Note how the man responsible for opening the factory door in the third version is peeking out from behind the slightly open door at the beginning of the film, as though waiting for his cue.) It is as though the Lumière brothers kept remaking this film until they found the proper metaphoric image with which to usher in the beginning of projected motion pictures: doors opening and closing.

Nevertheless, this book will largely concern itself with classical narrative filmmaking, specifically certain treatments of the door within the world of gothic melodrama, of the fantastic, and of urban crime thrillers, all of which, in their fascination with hidden spaces, have their roots in much earlier folkloric and mythic storytelling traditions. We will be entering, then, a world of secrets kept locked away, of private spaces, hidden treasures, and dark pasts waiting to be uncovered.[71] The title of one of Lang's films could not be more explicit in its relationship to this: *Secret Beyond the Door* (1947). Gaston Bachelard has referred to the door

Figure I.4

Figure I.5

Figure I.6

Figure I.7

Workers Exiting the Factory: Third version.

as one of the primal images of the daydream, representing "the temptation to open up the ultimate depths of being, and the desire to conquer all reticent beings."[72] If we think of the cinema as a primary space of the dreamlike, the hypnotic, the erotic, then the door becomes one of its privileged motifs and Lang, Hitchcock, and Minnelli all explore its implications in various ways. Christian Metz has written, "Cinema with directly erotic subject matter deliberately plays on the edges of the frame and the progressive, if need be incomplete revelations allowed by the camera as it moves, and this is no accident . . . the point is to gamble simultaneously on the excitation of desire and its non-fulfillment. . . ."[73] Although an explicit treatment of the erotic is not given equal intensity to all three films discussed in this book, what will be of some concern is this question of the edge, of the border and the concept of passage in which an erotics of not simply the body but also of filmmaking takes place. It is an object of intense desire (although not always of a sexual nature) that is most often on the other side of this literal and metaphoric door for these directors. What exactly these objects of desire are and how they will be articulated are central to the three chapters that follow because these objects of desire increasingly become the source of a new kind of search, a new kind of secret, a new kind of image.

In *Contempt* we see an extended sequence (taking up almost one-third of the film's entire running time) in which Paul and Camille walk about their rented apartment, a space not entirely furnished or ready to be inhabited. Camille is uncertain where to place a mirror, which sits on the floor, propped against the wall. A large window offers a view of Capri but the view itself looks surprisingly flat and two-dimensional, as though resisting the possibility that it could represent a "window on the world." Godard shoots large sections of this sequence in extended takes, evoking a theatrical long-take, mise-en-scène–based cinema of the classical period: At one point, the camera slightly raises itself above Paul to show a print hanging on the wall behind him of what appears to be a nineteenth-century theater, surrounded by a white cardboard frame and all of it contained within a larger brown frame. Frequently, Paul and Camille pass through doors in this apartment, doors that do not seem to have locks or that are able to be closed firmly. The central door of this space is one in which the door's center panel is missing, allowing both Paul and Camille to simply pass through it without having to open the door at all while propped against the wall we are shown a row of similar doors, all taken off of their hinges. Paul and Camille seem to be walking through the final remains of a cinema which could once find meaning in this type of mise-en-scène.

Figure I.8. *Contempt:* Passing through an "empty" door.

One key question that will be addressed here, then, is how modernist cinema deals with this issue of the secret beyond the door in comparison with classical cinema. To what extent is modernist cinema caught up in many of the same fascinations of space and movement as classical cinema and to what extent does it break with or overturn them? And in what ways are Lang, Hitchcock, and Minnelli part of a classical tradition and to what extent do they equally complicate it? The value of paying particular emphasis to the door in relation to these three films is that, within a cinema so concerned with states of transition, with marking passages from one type of cinema to another, the door, that "entire cosmos of the Half-open,"[74] is an especially rich and potent metaphor. Georg Simmel has written that the door shows us "how separating and connecting are only two sides of precisely the same act"[75] and that the door also shows "the possibility at any given moment of stepping out of this limitation into freedom."[76] Lang, Hitchcock, and Minnelli are filmmakers perpetually standing on this threshold, this edge, between separations and connections, between "limitation" and "freedom." What *The Thousand Eyes of Dr. Mabuse*, *Marnie*, and *Two Weeks in Another Town* suggest, however, is that the threshold itself can no longer restrain these directors, and they must now finally attempt to pass through the door to the other side.

Dr. Mabuse, The Cliché

The Thousand Eyes of Dr. Mabuse

We are precursors, running along outside of ourselves, out in front
of ourselves; when we arrive, our time is past already, and the course
of things interrupted.

—Maurice Blanchot, *The Writing of the Disaster*

I F THE MYTH OF FRITZ LANG IS one enmeshed in paradox,[1] then few
of his films have found themselves caught up in this situation as thoroughly as *The Thousand Eyes of Dr. Mabuse*. While a box-office success
in West Germany (and popular enough to spawn several sequels, none of
them directed by Lang but featuring a number of his original cast members),[2] the film achieved this popularity by being marketed primarily to
adolescent audiences, as were Lang's two previous German-produced films,
The Tiger of Eschnapur (1959) and *The Indian Tomb* (1959), both released
two years earlier. However effective such a marketing strategy was in
economic terms, it fueled the overwhelmingly negative critical response
to these three films in West Germany: The legend responsible for
Metropolis and *M* (1931) was now out of touch with contemporary cinema
and reduced to producing absurd and recycled parodies of his earlier

successes. Although championed by auteurists and many of Lang's admirers, *The Thousand Eyes* (unlike Lang's earlier Mabuse films) has largely remained an object of cult veneration, a neglected and minor work within the larger history of cinema. Released two years prior to the Oberhausen Manifesto, and poised historically between the German cinema of its Weimar heyday and the New German Cinema to come, it would appear to supply evidence of Lang's irrelevance in relation to contemporary German cinema. A Lang biographer, Patrick McGilligan, for example, has characterized *The Thousand Eyes* as a film that "said less about the Germany of 'our time' than it did about a director stuck somewhat ambivalently in his own time."[3] But two years after the film's release, Alexander Kluge (who had worked as an assistant director on the Indian films) and other members of the Oberhausen group unsuccessfully attempted to recruit Lang for West Germany's first film school, the Institut für Filmgestaltung Ulm.[4] And Jonathan Crary has characterized *The Thousand Eyes* as being "precocious" rather than old-fashioned, a culminating point in Lang's attempt over the span of almost forty years to "chart the mobile characteristics of various perceptual technologies and apparatuses of power."[5]

The film appears at the beginning of a decade in which Lang's work was to become central to such major figures as Jacques Rivette, Claude Chabrol, Jean-Luc Godard, and later Wim Wenders and Jean-Marie Straub and Danielle Huillet, some of whom would produce work outside of the forefront of the commercial film industry—something that Lang himself never did. But the issues that his work raised would become fundamental to certain nonclassical filmmaking practices beginning to emerge in the 1960s. In their admiration for Lang, these younger directors did not work by pastiche or direct emulation. Lang's work and the issues it raised was the site of an epochal moment in the cinema, but it was a moment that, within certain discourses of the 1960s, was fading. The richness and complexity of Lang's work now became the site of an absence that allowed these later filmmakers to rearticulate, fill in, revise—a position seemingly unavailable to Lang, the product of very different historical circumstances.[6]

Within the context of the commercial film industry during this period, Lang's important role in elevating the spy and espionage thriller to the status of a major film genre (of which the Mabuse films and his 1928 *Spies* had been such seminal works) was being superseded by the enormous success of the James Bond films, which began to appear two years after the release of *The Thousand Eyes*. These films, expensively produced and fueled by the star charisma of Sean Connery, partook of the same fascination with visual and aural apparatuses of power and surveillance as Lang's earlier spy thrillers. But the Bond films were situated within a contemporaneous Cold War framework absent from the more abstract historical and cultural realm of *The Thousand Eyes*. Furthermore, the Bond films were ironic in tone in which everything from eroticism to politics to violence was transformed into camp, the kind of sensibility far removed from Lang's. In comparison with *From Russia with Love* (1963) or *Goldfinger* (1964), *The Thousand Eyes* is a bit prim and proper, humorlessly exploring some of the same terrain but without a charismatic and sexual star at its center and without beautiful starlets in bikinis scampering about and peering through binoculars. The presence of the actor Gert Fröbe (who plays Commissar Kras in *The Thousand Eyes*) in the role of Goldfinger only reinforces this sense of both connections and fundamental differences between Lang's approach and that of the Bond productions. For the commercial espionage thriller, this is an era presided over by Dr. No and not Dr. Mabuse.[7]

The Thousand Eyes was produced by Artur Brauner, as part of a series of films Brauner put together during the 1950s and 1960s in an attempt to recreate the films of Weimar cinema's heyday. It was the second collaboration between Lang and Brauner after the Indian diptych. Lang's return to Germany and the nature of the projects he was involved in at this time were typical of the Adenauer period of West German filmmaking. During this time, its cinema was dominated by numerous recyclings of titles left over from the Nazi and pre-Nazi regime. According to Eric Rentschler, about 70 percent of films released at this time were produced by figures that were active during the Nazi era. (Fröbe, for example, had been a member of the Nazi Party.) The continued presence of such figures and the indifference of the government in attempting to establish any funding for an alternative production outlet (such as existed in France) led to a cinema dominated by historical myopia. "West German films of the 1950s," writes Rentschler, "offered few examples of critical will, of a desire to confront and comprehend the Third Reich. . . . At its best, West German film of the 1950s pursued a displaced dialogue with the past; at its most typical, it took an extended vacation from history."[8] This "extended vacation from history" in an industry still dominated by figures from the Nazi era created an unusually difficult working space for Lang. The larger cultural environment in which he was filming appeared resistant to investigations into the persistence of Nazi ideology in the way that Lang claims he had originally envisioned for *The Thousand Eyes*. In addition, he encountered repeated problems from a contemptuous cast and crew. The film bears these marks. It is not as technically polished, elegantly scripted, or well acted as his Weimar and Hollywood classics. And yet this awkwardness also gives the film much of its strange and, at times, hallucinatory power. The film may periodically stumble but it never falls, and in this process articulates a particular vision of the relationship of the cinema to the postwar era that few other films of the same period matched. As Roger Greenspun has written, "From its audience, *The Thousand Eyes* asks both greater innocence and infinitely greater sophistication than most of us bring to the movies nowadays."[9]

Few fictional characters from the cinema's first fifty years of existence carry such a potent metaphorical relation to the cinema as both a powerful lure and a sinister trap as Dr. Mabuse. However, this metaphoric relation that Mabuse has to the cinema is not one that has remained stable. Mabuse, hypnotic master of disguise, changes with every film, in each case bringing into play a different set of relations to the cinema, from the rapidly shifting identities of *Dr. Mabuse, the Gambler* (1922), to his role as an all-seeing voice that is effectively substituted for the body of the master criminal in *The Testament of Dr. Mabuse* (1933), to his reincarnation in *The Thousand Eyes*. With each film, the sense of Mabuse as a specific fictional character declines, increasingly replaced by Mabuse as a concept, a signifier insinuating itself into the fabric of vision in the films. Furthermore, each of these alterations in Mabuse corresponds to shifting notions about the relations between power and vision that are taking place across the history of narrative cinema.[10] But one thread has remained constant and that is the notion of Mabuse as metaphoric double for the film director, the metteur en scène presiding over the work, controlling and manipulating other human beings, creating and staging scenarios of his own devising while often working through cinematic and proto-cinematic devices. In this regard, Mabuse has also functioned as a highly seductive and sinister double for Lang himself, the notoriously controlling, hypnotic, and manipulative auteur.[11]

However, only with *Dr. Mabuse, the Gambler* did Lang achieve a perfect balance between capturing the historical moment in which the film was made, employing the character of Mabuse as a melodramatic villain and as a metaphor of vision for that moment. As a result, the film succeeded as a thriller for popular audiences in Germany while also serving as a formidable instance of Weimar cinema as a newly emerging art form. Phrases such as "a document of our time" and "an archive of its time" recur in contemporary accounts, probably fueled by publicity surrounding the film that insisted on this parallel, by statements issued by Lang and screenwriter Thea von Harbou, and by the film's own subtitle: "A Document of Our Times." According to one reviewer, "Not one important symptom of the post-war years is missing." These symptoms included drug addiction, homosexuality, occultism, prostitution, gambling, hypnosis, jazz, and violence, and all of this appearing within the context of a narrative product that, in spite of a running time of more than four hours, managed to "work at a breakneck speed."[12] The popular press took the film's pacing combined with its highly sophisticated editing as yet another sign of the film's modernity.

Lang once stated that his idea for Mabuse in the first film was that he would be omnipresent but unrecognizable, a threat that could never be located. While characters in the film experienced this invisible omnipresence, the spectator does not quite have the same kind of knowledge about Mabuse. However disguised Mabuse is, the spectator is usually alerted to the nature of the disguise before many of the fictional characters concerned with detecting Mabuse's control over the narrative events. Not until the second Mabuse film does the character's insidious omnipresence begin to manifest itself more strongly. Crary has stressed the importance of understanding *Testament* in relation to early sound cinema, a moment in history when communications technologies (radio, television, and sound cinema) were opening onto broader fields of social influence and control.[13] In this second Mabuse installment, power has shifted from its origins in the visible to incorporating sound, as the now-insane Mabuse communicates by an ambiguous process of hypnosis to Professor Baum, who does Mabuse's bidding for him. This continues even after Mabuse dies and what appears to be Mabuse's ghost continues to speak to Baum. Under hypnosis, Baum assumes Mabuse's identity through audio technology, dispatching orders for criminal activities via recording devices and hidden loudspeakers to assistants who never set eyes on him. By the time of *The Thousand Eyes*, Mabuse's literal ghost no longer holds power. But his example continues to exert enormous control as it becomes reconstituted in his would-be inheritor, who assumes two primary disguises: Dr. Cornelius, the psychic, and Professor Jordan, the psychoanalyst. In Lang's final version of the Mabuse myth, video surveillance insinuates itself into the fabric of modern life and becomes associated with the twin mainsprings of social fear that the character repeatedly instills within his narrative universe, control and chaos.

The central space of *The Thousand Eyes*, the film's architectural, technological, and metaphorical centerpiece, is the Hotel Luxor. The idea for the Luxor was based on the Hotel Adlon, which the Nazis had planned to put into use after the war. This hotel was to contain an extensive surveillance system throughout its various rooms to monitor the activities of foreign diplomats and businessmen staying there. The film derives its title from this pervasive system. Out of the basement of the hotel operates Mabuse's inheritor, surveying the rooms through a bank of video monitors. But a fundamental problem that Lang's last film faced was that it was making use of a metaphor of ideological and state power in relation to acts of viewing and filming that, however apt it might be for the postwar era, was largely defined and expressed in the film itself in ways that evoked not the present but the past. If Mabuse was already an anachronism in 1933, his reconfiguration in 1960 presented Lang with a major obstacle: His film must legitimately revive a figure that seemed to belong to another era and another way of seeing.[14] The problem was solved in 1933 by killing Mabuse as a flesh-and-blood villain of nineteenth-century melodrama and transforming him into an "invisible" system of domination.

But Lang does something close to the reverse in 1960: Mabuse returns in the flesh and reassumes his role as the master of disguise from *Dr. Mabuse, the Gambler*. This new Mabuse is a madman who is obsessed with repeating the original Mabuse's criminal acts in the present day. Lotte Eisner justifies such a strategy by noting that "Lang was concerned with sounding a warning on dependence upon technology, the benefits of science that can turn into a menace in an age when one maniac might press a button and set off a nuclear holocaust."[15] But this reliance on placing the source for these concerns about technology on one maniac threatens to give the film a rather quaint and naïve air, the feeling of an "old-fashioned" pulp thriller. Eisner seems to unwittingly reveal this when she writes that in the film Lang became "elated by his love of whirlwind adventure."[16]

The Thousand Eyes opened in Paris in 1961. In marked contrast to the German response, Lang's film was generally admired in France. Jean Douchet published an important essay on the film, following in the postwar trend for reading Mabuse as a metaphorical figure who embodies the role of the film director as an all-seeing, all-powerful metteur en scène, someone who does not fundamentally wish to understand the world but instead wants to control and dominate it.[17] Released the same year as Lang's film was Rivette's *Paris nous appartient* (1960), a meditation on political conspiracy and paranoia set within a labyrinthine environment of Paris in the late 1950s. Not only is the film obviously influenced by Lang, Rivette even reinforces the parallel by the use of an excerpt from the Tower of Babel sequence from *Metropolis*. But apart from its general mood of anxiety and its desire to capture (as Lang himself so often did) a vast and complex network of relationships in a nightmarish urban space, it has a tone and style markedly different from *The Thousand Eyes*. Rivette is obviously trying to extend and rewrite the cinema of appearances and paranoia that Lang was such a central figure in developing. As Jonathan Rosenbaum has noted, Rivette's film negotiates its way between two seemingly antithetical approaches, the phenomenological and the formalist, and in such a way that the film seems to capture uncannily the mood of its historical moment.[18] At the center of the paranoid conspiracy theories imagined by the protagonists of *Paris nous appartient* lies nothing, no Mabuse, nothing behind it all except the feeling of paranoia itself. Instead of a world of chaos set into motion by one sinister figure, we have a world that no one seems to be in charge of or to possess an ultimate power over everyone else.[19] For Jean-André Fieschi, Rivette's modernism is strongly bound up with his apparent passivity as an auteur in relation to these kinds of scenarios, his refusal to partake in the "power fantasies and hypnotic overtures of Mabuse (that caricature and definitive metaphor for the average film director). . . ."[20] Although average is hardly the word one might use to describe Lang, Fieschi's attitude toward Mabuse does suggest that this metaphor has reached an exhausted state by the time of *The Thousand Eyes*. As I maintain throughout this chapter, however, a strategy of pointing toward this exhaustion in Lang while simultaneously brandishing the audacity of the latest examples of modernist cinema is insufficient. A primary reason why this is so is because *The Thousand Eyes* implicitly contains within *itself* an awareness of its own limitations while simultaneously offering particular insights into the issue of political and technological power, which are both related to and different from the more fashionable works of modern cinema that surround it during the early 1960s.

In the literature on Lang, the standard approach for many years had been to place the director's Weimar classics (most of them produced on an ornate scale when he was at the height of his influence and importance on the international film scene) against his Hollywood work, where the circumstances of production gave him far less freedom and where he sometimes worked on assignment: Fritz Lang the Weimar art filmmaker versus Fritz Lang the Hollywood director-for-hire. Auteurist writings beginning in the 1950s attempted to correct this limited method of reading Lang, drawing important links between the German and U.S. films. But the mythology of Lang as a fallen god, exiled from the Valhalla of Ufa studios to the mortal environment of Hollywood, has been a powerful one.[21] The auteurist approach to Lang was, I believe, correct in stressing the thematic and moral continuity of Lang's work across more than forty years of cinema, even if its awareness of the essential formal and historical differences in the three important phases of Lang's career—Weimar Germany, Hollywood, and Adenaur Germany—was not always strong. These phases are most productively thought of not in terms of binary oppositions or master narratives of decline and fall. Rather, each of these phases needs to be understood in terms of their complicated relationship to one another, in which breaks, continuities, and returns continually manifest themselves. Coming at the end of his career, *The Thousand Eyes of Dr. Mabuse* is in a unique position for allowing us to understand this. As the final film from one of the great masters of the form, *The Thousand Eyes* acutely demonstrates the complicated and uneasy nature of the relationship of Lang's work to classical and modernist cinema and its resistance to simple divisions between these two filmmaking practices.

One of Lang's assistants during the brief period of his return to Germany in the late 1950s was Volker Schlöndorff, and he has spoken of his impressions of Lang's historical and cultural otherness in relation to German cinema at this time:

> Lang's Viennese accent, his monocle, his trench coat, his way of interacting socially—these belonged to a Germany that no longer existed. Lang was past recognition. Since he couldn't go out without feeling like a stranger, he confined himself to the international anonymity of a hotel room. His films were from a different world. . . . His only thoughts were of Germany, of what it had been, of what it had done, of what it had become. He had to return, to the émigrés in France and to the U.S., in order to get back the feeling for the country he had always loved. Lang came back to Berlin with all his natural vitality, full of the desire to connect once again with his youth; Lang left Berlin, older, but not an old man.[22]

What is useful about this anecdote is that it easily invites a modernist allegorical reading of *The Thousand Eyes* with Lang as the film's anguished enunciator: A film in which Lang's desire to connect with his past and with the culture that had once formed his filmmaking practice— while simultaneously updating and revising those strategies for the immediate historical moment—is strongly apparent throughout. At the same time, the impossibility of this desire is likewise apparent. Lang's age and his status as a Viennese-born Weimar director who fled Germany for the United States indelibly mark themselves on both Lang as a person and an artist. The man, like the film, belongs to "a different world." Both director and film withdraw into the "international anonymity" of the hotel, in the case of *The Thousand Eyes*, the Luxor, a hotel with many secrets.

Throughout this chapter, two closely related issues will be central, both concerned with the matter of space in *The Thousand Eyes*: space as it is related to architecture (in particular, that of the Luxor); and space as it is created through the film's editing strategies. In both instances, these spaces are profoundly historical, not only in terms of film style but in terms of the history that precedes and surrounds the film. In style and structure, in story and thematic material, *The Thousand Eyes* not only draws on but also implicitly measures Lang's entire body of work (particularly that of the Weimar period) against the immediate historical and cultural moment in which he is filming in Germany in the late 1950s and early 1960s. *The Thousand Eyes* is a film in which the past and the present, the classical and the modernist exist side by side, all of them engaged in a tense relationship with one another.

Skepticism and Renewal

The Thousand Eyes opens, as many of Lang's films do, with a death, one that nevertheless animates the film and sets its narrative into motion. In this case, the death is the assassination of a television news reporter, Peter Barter. The assassination takes place in the midst of heavy traffic in a commercial area of a major city, as Barter stops for a red light. In the back seat of an adjacent car, we see a mysterious man in dark glasses anxiously tapping his fingers on top of what appears to be a violin case as he nods in the direction of Barter to his driver. These activities are suddenly interrupted by a cut to the homicide bureau where Commissioner Kras takes a telephone call from the blind psychic Dr. Cornelius, who informs Kras of his premonition about the assassination of a man stopping at a traffic light. As Cornelius climaxes his description of this vision to the skeptical Kras, he utters the word "murder," which acts as a sound bridge to a shot that returns us to the back seat of the car (now stopped by a red light) of the mysterious man, who quickly removes not a violin from his case but a rifle and takes aim at Barter. He silently fires at the back of Barter's neck and Barter falls at the wheel. This death immediately sets

Figure 1.1   Figure 1.2

Figure 1.3

The Thousand Eyes of Dr. Mabuse (1960): Opening sequence, the assassination of Peter Barter.

off a chain reaction as we are shown the responses and investigations surrounding Barter's demise: an on-air announcement of Barter's death from his television station; a meeting between Cornelius and Kras; scientists analyzing the murder weapon used in Barter's death; images of a clubfooted man at a radio dispatch, identifying himself as Dr. Mabuse (his face concealed), who appears to have instigated Barter's murder and is now sending his assistants out to investigate an American millionaire arms dealer; a discussion among Interpol agents about the shooting and its possible relationship to a series of murders, all of them associated with the Hotel Luxor (where Travers is now staying); and a meeting at the Luxor with Travers and various businessmen about an arms sale. All of this culminates in an exterior shot of the Luxor showing a woman (soon to become the film's female protagonist, Marion Menil) perched on the ledge of a high window, threatening to commit suicide.

This listing of story events gives no indication of the actual feel and structure of the first minutes of the film, one of the most impressive openings in all of Lang's work. Each of these events is tightly organized and interwoven through Lang's editing methods, either through parallel editing, establishing a strong visual and aural associations from the final shot of one sequence to the first shot of another, or a combination of both of these devices. Moreover, the opening is fast paced and elliptical, establishing a general rhythm for the film that Lang will largely maintain throughout, leading Eisner to characterize *The Thousand Eyes* as a film that is "lively, spontaneous, thrilling" and has "nowhere the appearance of an old man's work."[23] I would certainly agree with Eisner that the film is, in its singular way, thrilling. But this does not quite explain the atmosphere of uncanniness that pervades these images and the ways in which they are linked. Contrary to Eisner, it seems to me that *The Thousand Eyes* is very much an "old man's work," provided we divest that term of its negative connotations.

For anyone familiar with Lang's cinema, what is perhaps most immediately striking about this opening is the degree to which it is haunted by sequences from other Lang films, particularly those from his first German period: Barter's assassination is very close in manner and execution to the murder of Kramm from *Testament of Dr. Mabuse*; the phone call from Cornelius has certain relations with the phone call from Hofmeister to Inspector Lohmann near the beginning of *Testament* (including a similar establishing shot of the sign of the Homicide Bureau); the surprise on-air announcement of Barter's death evokes the on-air announcement of the death of Walter Kyne from Lang's penultimate American film *While the City Sleeps* (1956); the smoke-filled meeting rooms evoke similar spaces in *M*; and the elaborate parallel editing structure

itself seems to be an attempt to duplicate the success of the opening
sequences of *Dr. Mabuse, the Gambler* and *Spies* as well as certain elements
of the parallel montage sequences detailing the investigation into the
murders in *M.*

Throughout the rest of the film, we see additional revivals of famous Lang sequences: the séance that Cornelius holds in his apartment
evokes the one from *Dr. Mabuse, the Gambler* (a setting Lang had already
returned to in his Hollywood film *Ministry of Fear* in 1943); when Cornelius

Figure 1.4. *The Testament of Dr. Mabuse* (1933): The shooting of Kramm.

Figure 1.5. *The Thousand Eyes of Dr. Mabuse*: The shooting of Peter Barter.

Figure 1.6. *The Testament of Dr. Mabuse*: The death of Kramm.

Figure 1.7. *The Thousand Eyes of Dr. Mabuse*: The death of Peter Barter.

Figure 1.8. *The Testament of Dr. Mabuse*: Signage for the Homicide Bureau.

Figure 1.9. *The Thousand Eyes of Dr. Mabuse*: Signage for the Homicide Bureau.

Figure 1.10. *The Testament of Dr. Mabuse*: Inspector Lohmann with assistant.

Figure 1.11. *The Thousand Eyes of Dr. Mabuse*: Commissar Kras with assistant.

"accidentally" collides with Peter Travers's car one is reminded of a similar false accident in *Gambler*; the staged rescue of Marion by Travers in the Hotel Luxor is a variation on the staged rescue of Sonya by Tremaine in the Hotel Olympia in *Spies*; the character of Commissioner Kras is a variation on the far more colorful Inspector Lohmann from *M* and *Testament*; the idea of Kras's desk containing a bomb hidden within it and that explodes is reminiscent of the explosion of Inspector Von Wenk's desk from *Gambler* (the explosions and the desks in both films even look very similar); the sequences of video surveillance through the "thousand eyes" are an extension and hyperbolization of the video monitor in *Metropolis*; and the film's most famous set piece, the two-way mirror sequence through which Peter Travers observes Marion in her bedroom, is an idea that can be traced as far back as *Spiders* in 1919.

Why this constant duplication of effects from prior work? Why is Lang becoming an imitation of himself here? Although Tom Gunning argues that Lang's return to Germany allows Lang to resurrect the elaborate montage structures found in his early German works that he "had been forced to tame in his Hollywood films,"[24] what emerges through this revival is not quite a triumphant return to form. The history that has taken place in between *Testament of Dr. Mabuse* and *The Thousand Eyes* creates enormous difficulties for Lang and a simple return to form is not possible. Instead, the intervening years insistently speak through and within these images. Of course, for Lang we find nothing terribly new here in this almost self-parodic strategy. One may even see it as the inevitable extension of his tendency toward what Thomas Elsaesser calls "the Langian uncanny, of a reality appearing as its own copy" and becoming (or threatening to become) kitsch.[25] Still, there is something very specific and significant about the way that Lang's final film faces this issue of the uncanny. *The Thousand Eyes of Dr. Mabuse* is an extreme instance of Lang's tendency not simply to repeat but constantly write over his earlier films, modifying and revising the implications of the issues with which his work had always concerned itself.

"Every film is a palimpsest,"[26] Serge Daney has written. The film that inspires this statement is *Contempt*, in which Godard realizes the impossibility of both using and being used by his pro-filmic material and instead exposes that impossibility rather than masking it. Lang sits squarely in the middle of *Contempt*, a physical reminder not simply of the golden age of classical cinema, but of its repeatedly dashed hopes, its failures, its aborted projects, and its inability to realize successfully all of its promise. Years before Godard, Lang had already begun the process of writing over one's work and acknowledging its own provisional nature. By 1960, however, Lang is not simply writing over his prior work but expressing a certain anxiety about it being no longer relevant. In this regard, *The Thousand Eyes* has a clear allegorical dimension: A desire to rescue outmoded forms and bring them into the light of the present but achieving this through reinterpretation of these earlier forms rather than simple recreation.

Although Lang does indeed revive some of his former strategies of formal organization here and repeats many of the basic narrative situations and character types from his earlier work, his attitude toward them is now marked by a strong degree of skepticism. Skepticism is not new to Lang's cinema. In many ways, it had always been a central element of his work. In the past, this skepticism had most often revolved around the issues of sight, knowledge, and belief, which are at the center of Lang's cinema and which continue to be central in *The Thousand Eyes*.[27] Such concerns are at the very heart of skepticism as a philosophical problem and it haunts much of modernism as well. As Jacques Derrida writes, "Before doubt ever becomes a system, skepsis has to do with the eyes. The word refers to a visual perception, to the observation, vigilance, and attention of the gaze . . . during an examination. One is on the lookout, one reflects upon what one sees, reflects what one sees by delaying the moment of conclusion."[28] Through this process of reflection in *The Thousand Eyes*, Lang questions the validity of his own cinema (particularly that of the Weimar period) and his own role as authorizer and organizer of these images, which are now threatened with the possibility of becoming clichés.

From the beginning of his career, Lang trafficked in standard genre material; his film recycled myths and drew on stereotyped characters and situations, often the more clichéd the better. It was a cinema that seemed to thrive on cliché because it was cliché that allowed Lang more fully to tap into what Freda Grafe calls "a visual idiom that bypassed the domination of language."[29] But by the time of *The Thousand Eyes* (as well as in the Indian diptych), this drawing on stereotyped situations has intensified in that these clichés are those of Lang's own cinema and that Lang himself is now recycling. The film clearly establishes in the first Interpol sequence that Mabuse is a largely forgotten figure: a cutaway zoom shot shows Mabuse's grave overgrown with weeds. The new Mabuse sets into motion a revival of the old Mabuse's acts that had previously been the stuff of (as one Interpol agent puts it) "old cock and bull stories." Like Lang, this new Mabuse does not attempt to create a completely new set of crimes and situations but instead repeats old ones, modifying and rewriting them when necessary in relation to changing times. If the old Mabuse was a metaphor for the kind of filmmaker Lang saw himself as in 1922, the new Mabuse suggests that if Lang sees himself in this figure at all anymore it is negatively or, at the very least, ambivalently, as a figure who can only repeat and who has run out of ideas.

In all of his later films, Lang's skepticism about the value of his work begins to manifest itself more clearly. *While the City Sleeps, Beyond a Reasonable Doubt* (1956), *The Tiger of Eschnapur, The Indian Tomb*, as well as *The Thousand Eyes*, contain certain deficiencies of execution in comparison with his earlier films, from the casting choices and performances to some makeshift scenario construction along with apparently restricted budgets and shooting schedules. These ostensible flaws have long been noted and traditional film criticism has often regarded these works as stillborn objects. Whereas Lang's work in general makes unusual demands on the spectator, these later films go even further in that their perceived hollowness provides the spectator with very little in the way of conventional genre entertainment or narrative thrills—although to what extent Lang's work ever fully provided this is debatable. At the same time, these films are also prized among Lang aficionados, central texts within a certain auteurist, cinephile discourse, particularly for the degree to which they distil the very essence of Lang's cinema.[30] If *The Thousand Eyes* seems to me the most interesting of the later films in this regard, it is because Lang is reviving one of the great metaphoric characters of silent cinema. But *The Thousand Eyes* supplies us with neither Mabuse's ghost nor anyone who could furnish some kind of direct connection to the original. Instead, we have a copy, an imitator. Lang, who did not eagerly welcome the chance to film the character again, never convincingly revives Mabuse. As Lang himself said of Mabuse at this time: "The bastard is dead and buried."[31]

Dr. Mabuse, the Gambler has a séance that Mabuse, the Countess Told, and Inspector Von Wenk attend. The Countess disrupts the order of the séance by laughing at the solemnity of the occasion, her behavior particularly irritating the medium and her powers of concentration. *The Thousand Eyes* also has a séance. However, the medium presiding over this one does not possess any genuine contact with the world of the dead. The medium is Mabuse in disguise as Dr. Cornelius, and Cornelius has set up the séance ostensibly to convince Kras and Travers of his psychic powers to overcome their inherently skeptical nature. In fact, everyone at the séance is there under some kind of pretense. In the first Mabuse film, a single skeptic disrupts the proceedings. In Lang's final Mabuse film, the entire room is filled with skeptics and charlatans and an act of physical violence—a bullet fired through a window—disrupts the proceedings.

The word *skeptic* itself is directly used several times to describe characters in the film, particularly Travers, the nominal American hero, and Kras, the German inspector investigating Mabuse's crimes. In a sequence shortly before the séance, Travers and his secretary have a brief conversation about psychic phenomena. The secretary does not believe in any of it, whereas Travers, although identifying himself as fundamentally skeptical, expresses his desire now to at least believe in someone. Is it Mabuse, then, who is a double for Lang in 1960, pretending (as Cornelius) to get in touch with the world of the dead? Or is it a combination of the film's two major skeptics: Henry Travers, the American caught up in a situation beyond his control in postwar Germany, but who retains a certain tentative fascination for these elements; and Kras, the inspector struggling to unravel a mystery set into motion by a criminal who takes his cue from the spirit of Weimar Germany, a mystery that stubbornly resists detection?

What Does the Name "Mabuse" Mean?

In order to define this new Mabuse, it is best to begin by doing so in relation to what he is not, by what is absent rather than present.

First, this Mabuse has no face that clearly identifies him and no bodily wholeness. In *Dr. Mabuse, the Gambler* we see the "real" Mabuse and the disguises that he gets himself in to as he portrays other characters that circulate through the film's narrative world. Although the film never fully explains what drives this character or what causes him to create the kind of chaos he does, he has (at least in comparison with *The Thousand Eyes*) a stronger physical presence to him. He has a face that seems to be the "real" one from which he then constructs his other disguises—as the famous opening moments of Mabuse before the mirror trying on disguises demonstrate. *Testament* kills Mabuse and then ambiguously brings him back from the dead, as either a ghost or as a figment of Dr. Baum's imagination. In *The Thousand Eyes*, Mabuse makes a physical reappearance but in a highly displaced manner in which he winds up being little more than the sum of his two disguises, Cornelius and Dr. Jordan. The elaborate montage structure of the opening seemingly conceals Mabuse's face from us, suggesting that its eventual uncovering will be at the center of the film's fascinations. But we have, in fact, been looking at the face of the master criminal all along, in disguise as Cornelius and, a bit later, Jordan, while the face withheld from view is that of a minor figure. The clubfooted man, it turns out, is not Mabuse at all, and when we do see the clubfooted man's face near the end of the film—as he passes himself off as Marion Menil's husband and bursts into her hotel room—the uncovering is completely anticlimactic. Mabuse passes into the body and mind of someone who is, within the logic of classical narrative, never given a clear psychological profile, a set of drives and personality traits that would provide his duplication of Mabuse's criminal activities with some coherence.[32]

Second, he no longer possesses any real telepathic skills, any forms of extrasensory perception. Because the film must conceal Mabuse from the center of the narrative action, his function in relation to hypnosis and the forces of magic is embodied in Cornelius who, from the moment of his entrance, is skeptically positioned as part charlatan, part genuine psychic in a way that the original Mabuse never was. The original Mabuse's power as an occultist was always very real. In *The Thousand Eyes*, Cornelius's power is initially rendered in an ambiguous manner, simultaneously dismissed by Kras as a fake but a fake who also accurately predicts the assassination of Barter.

Finally, this Mabuse is essentially nothing more than an empty vessel who desires to repeat the acts of a long-dead master criminal from Germany's pre-Hitler past. During the opening montage, the question a policeman poses to his colleagues is not whether they remember Mabuse as a specific individual but whether the name *Mabuse* signifies anything to them. It does not. Only one particular policeman remembers because he was assigned to a case involving Mabuse in 1932. That situation was hushed up, the policeman maintains, by the Nazis as soon as they took power. A question remains, however: Is the name *Mabuse* forgotten because it no longer holds any mythological sway over postwar Germany and Europe? Or is it forgotten because it has been repressed, literally (first by the Nazis) and symbolically (by postwar Germany, disavowing any relationship to such a mesmerizing and hypnotic figure)? In *The Thousand Eyes*, Mabuse becomes a way of naming something that ultimately resists being named. Indeed, the act of naming (having a name, assuming another's, remembering someone else's, uncovering an alias) is central to this film produced within an environment of the utmost uncertainty. As Carlo Ginzburg writes, "the more complicated a society, the more a name is inadequate to circumscribe an individual's identity unambiguously."[33]

Both of the great master criminals in Lang—the first Mabuse and Haghi—are more fascinating for the possibilities they offer for metaphoric readings than they do psychological ones, continually playing a game of presence and absence within the films. In this game (as in many crime and espionage melodramas), the face and the name are shifting and unstable markers of identity—always a new face to assume, a new name to adopt.[34] Strictly in terms of the master criminal scenarios, the positioning of Haghi in *Spies* had already begun the process that is strongest in *The Thousand Eyes*. While undergoing various disguises in the film, Haghi is also just another disguise with a false beard and even a false physical malady: he pretends to be wheelchair bound. In a related manner, both *Testament* and *The Thousand Eyes* rewrite this notion of the master criminal in relation to his unstable face and identity, building on the implications of Mabuse in the first film. Instead of a face behind the mask, *Testament* and *The Thousand Eyes* use the face of Mabuse as the site of a fundamental enigma. In both films, Mabuse no longer ventures out into the world around him but instead he has all of his criminal acts performed by assistants under direct orders. But these assistants do not see him physically nor do they have any immediate face-to-face contact. All they know of him is his voice, a partial knowledge that creates their frustrated desire to set their eyes on him. In *The Thousand Eyes*, the man behind this disguise, the would-be master criminal, is once again someone who is strongly tied to notions of vision-as-power, to control over modern technology as well as control over older, more "primitive" methods of power such as disguise, hypnosis, and the occult. Once again, the master criminal causes death to circulate. But this master criminal in *The Thousand Eyes* is, in a sense, already dead before his plans are put into action—a death that is not physical (as in *Testament*), but cultural and historical.

Who Is behind All This?

Lang's departure from Nazi Germany in the aftermath of *Testament of Dr. Mabuse* has for years been enshrouded in legend: his refusal of Goebbels's offer to direct Nazi films and his hasty departure by train for Paris that same day (an anecdote repeated as fact in *Contempt* but whose veracity in recent years has been legitimately questioned); the Nazis' subsequent banning of *Testament*; and Lang's later and debatable declaration of the film as a parable about the dangers of the rise of Hitler. But separating fact from fiction is of secondary importance here in comparison with the ways in which, within the mythology of film history, *Testament of Dr. Mabuse* (along with *M* from the year before, both sharing the same central character of Inspector Lohmann) has functioned as a culminating moment in Weimar cinema at the same moment when the future possibilities for the example the film sets were abruptly terminated. With the rise of Nazi cinema, modeling itself on Hollywood's "art of the masses," we find "not the masses become subject but the masses subjected."[35] Classical American cinema, which perpetually connects physical states of movement to harmonious totalities, is something that fascist cinema now calls on to serve totalitarian ends.[36] Although certain stray aspects of Weimar cinema remain during the Nazi era, this cinema now becomes, in Rentschler's words, "a vehicle to occupy psychic space, a medium of emotional remote control."[37] It is, of course, emotional remote control that Mabuse practices as well. But such forms of control and overt methods of dealing with the nature of cinema and technology now become "hidden" in Nazi cinema in their emulation of Hollywood spectacle. Reading teleologically, one could say that the passage from Weimar to Nazi cinema is not simply one from (as Siegfried Kracauer has phrased it) Caligari to Hitler, but from Mabuse to Munchausen, from the hypnotic and all-seeing eye to the seductive charlatan storyteller. Rentschler notes that the images of Hans Albers in the 1943 *Munchausen* winking into the camera or flying through the sky on a cannonball absolutely define the cinema of this period when "cynical sophistication leads to a troubled subjectivity and a decided self-blindness."[38]

For Kracauer, the basic drives and fascinations of Lang's films, as with much of the art cinema of the Weimar period, anticipate the national psyche under Nazism. Referring to Lang's claim that in *Testament of Dr. Mabuse* the words and phrases associated with Hitler and the Nazis were put into the mouths of Mabuse and his criminal gang, Kracauer argues that *Dr. Mabuse, the Gambler* is "revealed to be not so much a document [of its time] as one of those deep-seated premonitions which spread over the German postwar screen."[39] Lang's dislike for Kracauer's book is well known, and he would often strongly deny the validity of these arguments.[40] Kracauer or no Kracauer, Lang's reputation as a filmmaker of major standing up through the time of his return to Germany in the late 1950s largely rested on these films from the Weimar period. Even if the tide had begun to turn in terms of the evaluation of his Hollywood films (with the critics for *Cahiers du Cinéma* in particular arguing for the major virtues of Lang's American work), the battle was not one that was going to be fought easily and Lang himself was often skeptical about some of the claims these critics made about his American films. This attitude is perfectly captured in *Contempt* when Camille expresses to Lang her admiration for *Rancho Notorious* (1952), to which an unimpressed Lang responds by claiming his preference for *M*.

However, the influence of Kracauer's book on later criticisms of Lang's work was very strong (particularly in the United States) and Lang seemed to pick up on it.[41] He began to express ambivalence publicly about some of the films from his Weimar period, being especially critical of the two films that Kracauer was also most critical, *Die Nibelungen* (1924) and *Metropolis*. The original dedication for *Die Nibelungen* ("To the German People") explicitly connects that film's mythological scenario to a much-desired-for collective body politic in the aftermath of Germany's defeat in World War I. In later years, Lang was always careful to point out the importance of situating this kind of impulse in relation to the historical context surrounding the film as he simultaneously expressed his own (by now) ideological distance from such a grandiose, mythologizing approach.

Die Nibelungen was a film that Brauner had originally wanted Lang to remake but Lang argued against it. His primary objections to doing it were both the expense of the project and the fundamental incompatibility that he saw between the subject matter of the film and sound cinema. For

Lang, *Die Nibelungen* was utterly connected to a mythology of the past, not only Germany's but the cinema's as well, that of its silent era.[42] Beyond this, however, to even implicitly dedicate a film "to the German people" in 1958 would have been ideologically problematic, to say the least, suggesting a continuity between the ideology of the film (one that evoked the sentiments of pre-Hitler Germany) and a reigning consensus within the country in relation to the film's project. German cinema was not alone in its inability to confidently draw on a classical filmmaking tradition during this period. But the specifics of Germany's situation—a country now literally divided between East and West, between communist and widely expanding capitalist, a country both recovering from and repressing its relationship to its immediate Nazi past—meant that the project of creating a cinema that could openly speak to large collective needs was an especially difficult one.[43]

Kracauer saw Mabuse as belonging to a "procession of tyrants" in early Weimar cinema who achieved domination through their insidious omnipresence in a confused and chaotic culture, one vulnerable and easily seduced by the hypnotic will-to-power of tyrants and master criminals. *The Thousand Eyes* cannot directly reproduce Lang's most famous master criminal in this way because not only is the post–World War I culture that effectively gave birth to the likes of a Mabuse no longer in place, but Mabuse (like *Die Nibelungen*) evokes a kind of pre-Hitlerian impulse that cannot be unambiguously revived. In *The Thousand Eyes*, Lang reproduces the basic structure of the master criminal scenarios so closely bound up with nineteenth- and early-twentieth-century concerns about the modern but only to render them devoid of a conventional underlying urgency. He positions a master criminal at the center of the film but only to displace his powers of agency and not give him a full melodramatic logic.

The connection between fascism and a fascination for the occult is an issue which, in the immediate aftermath of World War II, concerned not only Kracauer but also another member of the Frankfurt School with whom Lang was on friendly terms, Theodor Adorno. In *Minima Moralia* (published in 1951), Adorno draws links between hypnosis (perhaps Mabuse's most insidious tool) and totalitarianism, arguing that in the present day the two have become merged. In the midst of a society that believes it is headed for catastrophe, refuge in the occult becomes "the metaphysics of dunces."[44] Lang's treatment of Mabuse in *The Thousand Eyes* suggests a desire (possibly influenced by Adorno) to treat Mabuse far more critically. The film effectively breaks the fascination with the occult so central to the first Mabuse film, even if for much of its running time it tentatively suggests the possibility of the occult's persistence. In *The Thousand Eyes*, the eyes of Mabuse himself, as incarnated through Dr.

Figure 1.12. *The Thousand Eyes of Dr. Mabuse:* The eyes of Dr. Cornelius.

Cornelius, are blank. The look he returns to the camera and to the spectator (during the séance, for example) is a blind one rather than one whose power is immediately manifested through his hypnotic eye.

Nevertheless, Cornelius claims to be prey to visions, to be able to see into the future, and to communicate with the dead. Through Cornelius, the act of looking is constituted as something that is at its most powerful when it is associated with a literal blindness, articulated as a form of supernatural vision rather than a look immediately associated with forms of ideological power and control. Cornelius is able to predict Barter's death before it happens and calls Kras to warn him; Cornelius is able to "see" from his home that Henry Travers has cut himself while shaving in his hotel room; he also predicts a disastrous business transaction for Travers, a prediction that comes true when an atomic works plant, which Travers had considered purchasing, explodes. Furthermore, Cornelius explicitly situates his visionary powers within an archaic system of thought, specifically his roots in the mystical peasant culture of Ireland. The desire to know and understand the chaos of postwar western culture, to be able to see into its future and understand, is embodied in a blind clairvoyant, seated in an office with walls covered by astrological designs, evoking ancient Greece and Egypt, and who associates his visions with premodern (and non-German) forces. More than once, Cornelius makes a Cartesian claim for the special powers of his own blindness by suggesting that the blind see more clearly than those who have sight.

But the position Cornelius adopts is ultimately a false one. He is not blind at all. His "visionary" powers are the result of a network of concrete material forces that he organizes and controls out of the Hotel Luxor. He is able to predict bombings and assassinations because he has planned them. He knows that Travers cut himself because he watched it from the video control room of the hotel. The only genuine occultlike power he seems to hold is hypnosis, itself a form of "rational" mind control of which modern psychoanalysis has made use. Mabuse has hypnotized Marion Menil into pretending to be suicidal: She is induced to standing on the ledge outside of her room at the Luxor to lure Travers into rescuing her, thereby binding them as a couple. Although this is the only major act of hypnosis performed in the narrative, we do not actually see Mabuse performing it on Marion, obviously because if it was shown this early in the film then the withholding structure of the narrative would dismantle. But its absence from the spectator's field of vision is symptomatic of the film's central strategy of deferring and displacing the act of looking while simultaneously expressing Lang's increased skepticism about the forces of magic and the irrational that had formed his German work.[45]

Once this skepticism is put into play it effaces the very structure on which Mabuse's original power and fascination was based. The film multiplies Mabuse's act of looking from the hypnotic eye of his previous incarnations to the thousand eyes of the Hotel Luxor. But this also masks the fact that Mabuse himself, as a viewing subject, is becoming irrelevant. Although the original Mabuse and the cinematic apparatus were tied together in a reciprocal chain of looking, this is a Mabuse whose looks are always occurring elsewhere, outside of the pro-filmic. We do not see the act of hypnosis; we do not really see Mabuse watching through the hotel monitors. These activities are either not shown at all or are shown without Mabuse being clearly represented in the space, as when the bank of video monitors is first shown and only an unidentified male body (presumably Mabuse's) is at the control. Mabuse's absence from vision at these crucial moments occurs because he is caught up in something which even he is not permitted to control by now: the nature of Lang's cinema at this historical end point. Lang no longer wants Mabuse, no longer sees his own reflection in this kind of metaphoric figure. So he now must point to Mabuse's essential emptiness and take control of vision away from him. When Mistelzweig eventually exposes Cornelius's fake blindness (the agent throws a cigarette lighter at Cornelius and, in a classic Langian slip, the fake mystic catches it), Mistelzweig draws explicit attention to the clichéd nature of Cornelius's contact lenses, referring to them as looking like something out of an old American horror film.

This absence or deflecting of the sense of single agency is also the strongest difference between Lang's approach to montage in the opening sequence of *The Thousand Eyes* and the opening sequences of *Dr. Mabuse, the Gambler* and *Spies*. The openings of the earlier films derive their impact from the sense of simultaneous ellipsis and linkage, of control and dispersal, with their respective master criminals always implicitly or explicitly connected to the actions being represented. In *Dr. Mabuse, the Gambler*, the actions originate from Mabuse, as we see him in his apartment, in the midst of disguising himself. He looks at his pocket watch as there is an iris out to a robbery and murder on a train masterminded by Mabuse but actually performed by several of his assistants, all of them strategically placed on and around the moving train, as an important document is stolen, its original possessor murdered, the document tossed out of the train window to a man in a waiting car. This event is then witnessed by another assistant, perched on top of a telephone pole, who phones Mabuse to inform him of the success of the robbery.[46] The opening of *Spies* operates along similar lines, but delays the appearance of the master criminal until the end. Here we witness another robbery of vital documents, the surrounding violence and bloodshed, and various hysterical responses that take place in relation to these events before a question is explicitly posed by a character: "Great God! Who is behind all this?" The answer arrives in an intertitle, "I am," followed by a close-up of Haghi looking directly into the camera.[47] However elliptical both of these sequences are, they still fold back on the master criminal who controls the events, that someone "is behind all this." In the *Mabuse* opening, for example, not only does Lang periodically return to Mabuse looking at his watch as a way of clarifying the control that Mabuse exerts over the primary action of the theft. Lang also links the various shots across the various locations by the repetition of insert shots of pocket watches and through the graphic linkage of the shape of the watches with the iris effects.

But in *The Thousand Eyes* the master criminal's positioning as the instigator and focal point of the series of violent acts is camouflaged because the "grand enunciator" is actually Cornelius, assuming the appearance of a blind psychic, whereas "Mabuse" is nothing more than a henchman, dispatching orders in Mabuse's name.[48] The cuts in the opening montage that point toward the clubfooted man as being the center of the action have lied to us. Unlike the openings of the earlier master criminal films, *The Thousand Eyes* almost immediately introduces its detective figure into the action. But as a detective, Kras is a failure, never solving the case itself. So although the film displaces the function of its master criminal, it also does the same thing with its detective. Mabuse's downfall arises neither out of Kras's detective work nor (as in the earlier master criminal films) his self-destruction but through the simultaneous defection of Marion and the truly productive detective work Mistelzweig performs, the Interpol detective posing as an insurance agent, a fact concealed from the spectator until the end of the film. Furthermore, Travers also assumes the role of detective in the film as he begins to have Marion followed, although this is something the film never dramatizes, but only refers to after the fact.

In the opening, Kras is positioned in such a way that his entrance does not progress the action forward but instead interrupts it, as Cornelius's phone call takes us away from the principle narrative interest of Barter and the assassin in the street. Kras is shown at his desk reading a book on criminal psychology and initially refuses the call from the psychic (a call that itself is an interruption for Kras). The sequence implicitly establishes tension between Kras as a man of more rational and modern forms of thought (psychoanalysis) and the paranormal world of Cornelius. Cornelius's visions are confirmed in the shots that immediately follow the sequence in the homicide bureau as we witness the death of Barter. Kras's skepticism about Cornelius is temporarily undercut as the film appears to align itself with the world of the visionary rather than that of the rational. What is even more significant here, however, is how action itself (the assassination) is wedged in between two physically stationary characters, both of them seated at desks and seemingly powerless to affect the outcome of the assassination. At the same time, the movements of those who are caught up in the principle drive of the narrative action (Barter, the assassin, his driver) seem to be responding to forces that neither they nor the spectator can confidently trace to anyone or anything. *The Thousand Eyes* establishes a narrative world in which the various connections drawn between spaces and events, between the world of crime and the attempt to detect and uncover it, do not ultimately form a tight causal chain but instead only appear to. In retrospect, these cuts that seem to connect to one another actually point toward gaps. As a result, even on repeat viewings of the film, the opening loses nothing of its fragmentary power and in fact gains in intensity in this regard.

Door after Door, Shot after Shot

That the trope of the "secret beyond the door" becomes the literal title of one of Lang's films suggests that there is a fundamental link between this principle and Lang's cinema. In the silent films of Lang's Weimar period, the door will often literally be of an enormous scale, infusing the movements of the protagonists from one space to another with a solemn grandiosity: Siegfried's entrance through the gates of the castle of the Burgundiansin in the first part of *Die Nibelungen*, for example. Not only the door but also the window and the mirror recur throughout Lang's body of work and are frequently situated within vast and seemingly infinite architectural spaces containing trap doors and secret passageways. In the American films, this scale in terms of the treatment of the space is significantly reduced and domesticated but no less pronounced. Mise-en-scène in Lang, whether in Germany or the United States, is actively and literally filled with meaning.[49] Even in the low-budget American film *The Blue Gardenia* (1953) Lang maintains this kind of intensity within the mise-en-scène in which the attention to decor-filled shots can overwhelm the spectator with visual information. Although the three female protagonists of *The Blue Gardenia* live in a small one-room house, the entire space of the house is punctuated by an exaggerated profusion of doors that open on to closets, the bathroom, and the kitchen. But all of these doors ironically connote not a space continually opening up but a space marked by claustrophobia and lack of privacy. Moreover, Lang turns this emphasis on the door (as well the mirror) into a structuring element of narrative meaning. The descent of Nora into a night of drunkenness that culminates (or so she believes) in her murdering her date is marked by the repeated use of doors and mirrors, from her entrance into the Chinese restaurant through a set of double swinging doors marking the official beginning of this date (an entrance as portentous as Siegfried's into the castle), to the serenade within the restaurant by Nat "King" Cole in which a rectangular mirror is placed at an angle behind Cole, to the rectangular mirror in her date's apartment that she smashes in her struggle with him, to the set of double doors of her date's apartment building that she runs out of after the "murder."

Nevertheless, the meanings that arise through mise-en-scène in Lang are often intimately bound up with their relationship to montage, space being created at once through and within the images. But the sense of classical linkage in Lang frequently has enormous difficulty in giving itself over to this classical world of secret doors as Daney defines it. In Lang the secret beyond the door opens out not to another image that logically follows it but to images that complicate, interrupt, and contradict this logical unfolding. In Lang, what we find most often is that the passage from one space to another is played out not in relation to the door opening on to a transparent space in which a secret is revealed and a true sense of passage achieved. Instead, the door opens on to a space that further complicates a sense of passage, a space that may even be another door, an intensification of this basic trope that often serves as an end in itself rather than necessarily as a source of revelation.[50] In *Testament of Dr. Mabuse*, for example, there is a room where Mabuse ostensibly locks himself away and from where he issues his orders to his assistants. To get inside of this room, it is necessary to unlock two thick doors, the lock to one of which has a safe combination. Once inside, we find only a curtain and a silhouette of Mabuse speaking from behind it. But in a sequence near the end of the film, when that curtain is finally opened, we find no Mabuse inside, only a cardboard cut-out. After passing through two doors and a mysterious curtain, our expected moment of unveiling and revelation does not take place—at least not there and not quite in the way we expect. The moment of explanation itself (that Baum has been manipulating all of this from his office under Mabuse's name) is delayed as long as possible, and when it does arrive it is so full of inconsistencies and improbabilities that it carries an insufficient weight. It is as though the primary fascination here is with the sheer spectacle of the doors themselves being opened. In Lang the sense of unfolding and passage from one space to another and from one shot to another carries a power greater than any narrative revelation.[51]

Lang directed his first film, *The Half Caste*, in 1919, one year after the end of World War I. At this time Hollywood was not only beginning to establish its international dominance economically, but also establishing a form of continuity editing and of storytelling that has come to be associated with the most widely accepted definition of classical cinema. Central to this form has been the notion that the basic narrative drives and physical states of movement must ultimately revolve around a fixed point, in particular that of the strong, goal-oriented protagonist. The films are subjected to a process of analytical editing or decoupage, working on the principle that the actions and spaces of the film preexist the act of editing itself but are then broken down through cutting, most often in an "invisible" and fluid manner. Within this style, methods such as the eyeline match, the match-on-action, and the observance of the 180-degree rule work to connect closely states of movement with the linkage of shots because the cuts give the appearance of emerging directly out of the actions themselves. The highly seductive nature of this method was vital to establishing dominance of the continuity style.[52] Whatever its other virtues and possibilities, this type of editing became ideal for creating a world that seemed to be both fluid and logical.

As several of Lang's early films demonstrate, he had no difficulty in quickly mastering this language while frequently employing its devices for his own particular ends.[53] The classical concept of fluid and logical shot organization, offering a homogeneous and coherent conception of space, is one that Lang's films will sometimes directly reproduce but just as often complicate in a subtle and sometimes insidious manner. Throughout the American films as well, although the editing is seldom as obviously flamboyant as in most of the Weimar films, the viewer must work to create spaces out of problematic and incomplete material rather than having the space fluidly presented piece by piece, even though Lang will sometimes give an initial impression that he is playing by the classical rules of scene breakdown.[54] This method of cutting solicits the spectator's attention in an unusual manner because it so often points toward the gap that always materially exists between shots rather than attempting to cover over the gap smoothly with a continuity cut.

Furthermore, Lang's work is also strongly shaped by a drive, modernist in its implications, toward parallelism and contrast. It is, time and again, a cinema intent on drawing links and relations, comparisons and contrasts between spaces and actions: The opening of *The Thousand Eyes* is again a clear illustration of the ongoing importance of this approach to Lang. Parallel editing was crucial to the development of cinema during the silent period and the specific manner in which it has been practiced has taken place essentially along two lines, both of them relevant to Lang's work. The most common method is to cut between two or more lines of narrative action, most often (although not exclusively) for suspense; the other method draws larger thematic and graphic parallels among actions, spaces, and events. In different ways, both of these approaches may be loosely categorized as *montage*, a term that, in itself, has more than one meaning including an all-purpose term for editing. But during the silent era, montage most often referred to the second category of parallel editing listed previously, involving the editing together of two or more shots in such a way that meanings or actions could arise that were not otherwise in the individual shots alone. This second category is far more ambitious and frequently leads to an overtly metaphoric and rhetorical conception of the image than that for which traditional crosscutting methods allow.[55]

The technique of parallel editing in general came to play a central role in the development of what Deleuze has defined as the *large form* within classical cinema. In this form, the narrative environments, actions, and protagonists are individuated and concrete. The actions that the protagonists perform are responses to a threat being exercised against that environment by either outside forces or by corrupt ones from within it. These actions often play themselves out in a duel or series of duels, confrontations, and chases between the forces from within and those that are outside of or threaten it. Hence the key role played by crosscutting between lines of action, between positive and negative, organic and inorganic forces in which the moral and ideological battles are articulated in relation to opposing spaces and states of movement. These battles result in the restoration (often with modifications and transformations) of the environment prior to the threat imposed on it. The crime drama frequently makes use of the large form in which all actions, regardless of their extremity and violence, emerge directly out of a highly individuated setting. The criminal's actions are perversions, but they are also inconceivable outside of that environment, inorganic outgrowths and responses to it. Superficially, *The Thousand Eyes* (as with Lang's other espionage and master criminal thrillers) belongs to this tradition. Mabuse and his collaborators represent the sinister force bringing a threat of chaos to the urban environment in which the film is set. Duels, confrontations, and chases dominate here as Mabuse and his gang battle the police and Interpol in a desire for worldwide domination until Mabuse is finally defeated.

The climax to *The Thousand Eyes* even makes use of a completely straightforward type of parallel editing for suspense and in relation to one of the most basic of all suspense action forms: the chase. This alone does not signify a withdrawal into convention at the end of Lang's career because the previous Mabuse films (as well as *Spies*) also contained sequences of this nature. What is especially striking about the sequence from *The Thousand Eyes*, however, is its general lack of suspense and any conventional atmosphere of excitement. The chase is purely academic, a set of actions to be clinically observed as we wait for the inevitable to happen. We find no apocalyptic fire here (as there was at the end of *Testament*) or a theatrical coup d'etat (as there was in *Spies*, when Haghi shoots himself in the head onstage as Nemo the Clown). This fake Mabuse does not go insane (as did the original Mabuse), but remains comparatively lucid through the end. The traditional chase depends on an external playing out of narrative conflicts, a clear demarcation of heroes and villains, of pursued and pursuers. In his final encounter with Mabuse, Lang reproduces the mechanics of these traditional forms of shot organization but minus any underlying urgency or fullness. The fundamentally dualistic conception of the world that animates the most successful suspense-based parallel editing sequences (particularly as it has been practiced in U.S. cinema) and its basic drive toward the resolution of conflicts is ultimately foreign to Lang's thinking. If, as Deleuze notes, "Expressionism tells us: . . . *the non-organic life of things* culminates in a fire, which burns us and which burns all of Nature, acting as the spirit of evil or of darkness," *The Thousand Eyes* reverses the process of destruction from the prior Mabuse films and more mundanely dispenses with its master criminal by drowning him as his car loses control and plunges into water: a (quite literally) soggy climax.[56]

Although many national cinemas (particularly Soviet) have practiced some aspect of the large form, the American cinema has created the most formally and ideologically clear-cut example of it, a school of organic representation that insists on "unity in diversity."[57] In spite of the central role the large form has played in American cinema, Deleuze discovers the term itself in *M* where he finds "perfection" in this form. Here we see not only standard crosscutting between lines of action, but also a much more ambitious form of parallel montage that insists on strong structural and thematic links between characters and situations. Although Deleuze argues that *M* "prepared Lang's departure for America,"[58] the specific practice of the large form we find in *M* is quite different from the American version of it. Within this form (even in the United States), the social environment need not necessarily be presented as healthy and regenerative as long as "a kind of consensus reigns."[59] But in comparison with the classical gangster film, *M* considerably complicates the terms of this reigning consensus. In the gangster film, the organic world may not be directly presented (or it will be marginalized), but there is often a strong sense that it is out there—somewhere—within U.S. society.

M, on the other hand, has virtually no possibility of any positive reorganization of this society in the aftermath of the capture of Beckert. The crosscutting between criminals and government and police officials insists on a constant interweaving of criminality within the forces of law and pious sentimentality within the criminal world in its response to the murders. The world of the family is barely shown after the opening and what we do see looks exhausted. The two sets of opposing forces working toward the capture of Beckert are only seemingly opposed to one another, a structure that greatly complicates the sense of the duel or sets of duels that lead to the capture of Beckert as an organic action. The perpetual insistence on relations being drawn between these two worlds threatens to freeze the film's classical unfolding and its physical actions into sets of rhetorical and thematic oppositions. If *M* achieves perfection within the large form, then, it does so by refusing many of its fundamental terms.[60] While noting the film's ambiguity in realizing its own organic environment, Deleuze reads this largely in relation to the film's resolution.[61] But *M* seems a curious choice as an ideal instance of the large form in that the film has established an ambivalence about its own environment long before the resolution. In Lang's subsequent work in the United States, the ambiguous presentation of an organic society threatened by an external element often raises questions as to whether what is being threatened is worth saving at all. This is particularly the case in Lang's postwar American films.

Although many of the basic editing techniques already established during the prewar period continued on or were "refined" in various ways after the war, we also find the emergence of filmmakers who begin both to absorb and to amplify certain basic montage strategies from the prewar period: Akira Kurosawa, Robert Bresson, and the Orson Welles of *Citizen Kane* (1941) and *The Magnificent Ambersons* (1942).[62] But the most influential position on editing at this time was the notion that montage, as conceived during the prewar period was essentially an exhausted force, closely tied to manipulation of the spectator and to a distortion of the reality of what is being filmed. The emergence of Italian neorealism (particularly through the version offered through the writings of André Bazin) becomes paradigmatic, in which the role of montage is minimized or is very strongly defined in relation to less seemingly overt techniques of manipulation, such as the long take and deep focus.[63]

Lang's work bore little relationship to this development and in many ways would seem to be the antithesis of the kind of cinema Bazin was positing as most central to the postwar era.[64] When Bazin writes of the role of ellipsis in Rossellini's *Paisà* (1947), for example, this type of ellipsis could not be more different from Lang's: "The technique of Rossellini undoubtedly maintains an intelligible succession of events, but these do not mesh like a chain with the sprockets of a wheel."[65] In Lang, the events must precisely mesh like a chain with the sprockets of a wheel and the ellipses are not the after-effect of the spontaneous, documentary-like nature of the production process (as in Rossellini) but related to the power of the auteur in maintaining a firm control over the interpretations of the spectator. Bazin's single reference to Lang's use of montage is a sequence from *Fury* (1936), in which Lang dissolves from gossiping women to images of chickens clucking, which Bazin identifies as "a relic of associative montage."[66] Bazin's historical reading of montage within the postwar period would initially have a major impact on the French New Wave, however much their individual tastes may have diverged from Bazin's (including an enthusiasm for Lang, which Bazin did not appear to strongly share).[67] Nevertheless, the admiration for Lang's work throughout the 1950s on the part of figures like Rivette does anticipate a certain pulling away from Bazin, a break that will soon be much stronger and sharper.[68]

In a roundtable discussion with a group of critics and filmmakers from *Cahiers du Cinéma* the year following Bazin's death, the Bazinian position on montage clearly is being seriously thrown into question, primarily due to the release of a new film, Alain Resnais's *Hiroshima mon amour* (1959). Godard claims that the film "is the very idea of montage, its definition even," whereas Rivette calls attention to the film's "splitting of primary unity—the world is broken up, fragmented into a series of tiny pieces, and it has to be put together again like a jigsaw."[69] Although Resnais's film does not stand utterly alone in its desire to return to the fundamental issues that montage raises in relation to film form, it is arguably the boldest of these new montage films. Its release will mark the beginning of a decade in which montage again begins to play an active role, doing so with a certain awareness of the weight of the historical implications of montage itself, reviving certain discredited approaches from the prewar period, but without necessarily rejecting wholesale the Bazinian position. The classical cinema once so highly regarded by many *Cahiers* critics now begins to undergo a serious interrogation, a cinema now often being rejected for its "illusionist" principles as we enter a self-conscious period of "political modernism."[70]

We are increasingly in a cinema governed by what Deleuze would later term the "irrational" cut in which images refuse to be linked in the manner of classical cinema: "Instead of one image after the other, there is one image *plus* another, and each shot is deframed in relation to the framing of the following shot."[71] At the beginning of Resnais's *Muriel* (1963) we see this approach clearly. In this highly fragmented opening, set in an apartment, a dialogue about interior decoration between two middle-aged female characters takes place (one of them is Hélène, an antiques dealer and the film's central female protagonist and the other woman is Hélène's customer), while a young male character (Hélène's stepson, Bernard) makes espresso in the background. The dialogue is seemingly banal and much of the content revolves around the client's anxiety about her decor being old-fashioned, this content making an especially pointed and ironic counterpoint to the extremely modernist approach to cutting here. The very first image is of an open door, a woman's gloved hand on the knob. This shot (held so briefly that fully registering its meaning on a first viewing is difficult) is followed by a series of equally brief shots, most of them close-ups or medium close-ups: Bernard's hands as he boils water, Hélène's hands and face as she smokes a cigarette, various pieces of decor in the room, the customer's hand on her purse, an overhead shot of her hat, and so forth. Resnais uses the shot of the gloved hand on the door five times here, more than any other image. But instead of this door serving as the metaphoric opening onto a world of classical narrative, a door that characters open, close, and pass through as they move from space to space, this door neither opens nor closes. When the woman finally does leave the apartment, she turns and in a false match-on-action she is shown exiting through another door, the actual door to the apartment itself. The door we initially glimpse in the opening shot, never shown in its entirety here but only in fragments, remains poised between opening and closing, the site of a potential abyss.[72] The shots here neither link fluidly according to the traditional rules of decoupage nor does a clear idea emerge out of the disjunction of shots as in earlier forms of montage.

Figure 1.13. The opening of Alain Resnais's *Muriel* (1963).

Even during his Weimar period, Lang never goes to the extremes that Resnais does here. Nevertheless, Lang's cinema will continue to be central during this period of political modernism. But the interest shifts from concerns with Lang as a moralist, as articulated through his approach to mise-en-scène and to the scenario, to Lang as a formalist and modernist, with particular emphasis given to his approach to montage.[73] A more immediate question for my own purposes here is, to what extent can a film such as *The Thousand Eyes* be understood in relation to these significant developments in cinema of the early 1960s? If cuts in the postwar modern cinema often refuse to link spaces and phenomena classically, if they lay bare a world that is fundamentally disconnected, the montage in the opening of *The Thousand Eyes* might not initially appear to adhere to this postwar trend completely, still maintaining as it does an earlier tradition of perpetually linking spaces and events. It is true that in the opening Lang does seem to be tightly holding onto the reins, refusing to allow even the briefest of sequences or shots to stand alone but always immediately insists on relations and parallels being drawn from one sequence to another.[74] However, one of the more striking aspects to the opening of *The Thousand Eyes* is how resistant the entire editing structure is to the convention of drawing classical parallels and linkages between actions and characters. Seeing these shots as significantly complicating the kinds of relations so central to classical cinema's conception of montage is important. This complication had always been present to varying degrees in Lang's work but given the larger film culture surrounding *The Thousand Eyes,* and the rethinking that is taking place in relation to montage, the historical importance of Lang's final film needs to be further contextualized.

Forgery and Death

On one level, what is clearly at work through much of *The Thousand Eyes* is a relationship between film and spectator that has strong roots in Weimar cinema in which the development of narrative filmmaking—however impressed the Germans might have been by the American version of it— was subjected to a fundamentally different practice: the fascination with embedded narratives or any type of storytelling in which the story functions more as a trap for the spectator, filled with detours, bizarre ellipses, and false leads; characters who do not seem to be in control of the action or serve as conventional fixed points; a cinema in which the filmmaker assumes a role of power over the spectator rather than "invisibly" setting into motion a transparent narrative world; and a cinema in which time often plays a fundamental and often anxiety-producing role, both within the diegetic worlds of the films, where characters attempt (but ultimately fail) to control and dominate time, and where the spectator likewise experiences the temporal unfolding of the action in a manner different from much of classical narrative. In spite of the contemporary German critic Eisner cites who remarked on *Dr. Mabuse, the Gambler's* speed, one of the most frequently remarked-on aspects of the original Mabuse film in the years after its release is its slowness and lack of conventional cause-and-effect narrative drive.[75] This is a quality that most of Lang's silent German films possess. They are not simply slow-moving but clearly aim to impart a hieratic and almost hypnotic sense of rhythm, as the films drag on for hour after hour.

By contrast, Lang's American films are far more economical in all senses of that term. Several of his most-admired American films (*Fury*; *You Only Live Once,* 1937; *The Big Heat*) are ninety minutes or less and only one runs longer than two hours, *Hangmen Also Die* (1943). However, the experience of time a spectator has when watching *The Thousand Eyes* is different from *Dr. Mabuse, the Gambler* or much of Lang's earlier German work. Not simply the opening but the entire film is marked by a propulsive narrative drive, one that only intermittently manifested itself in the earlier German thrillers, which tended to alternate between fast-paced and elliptical set pieces and far more deliberately paced sequences most often built on a structure of alternating montage. The general pacing in *The Thousand Eyes* suggests a perpetually nervous forward movement while at the same time Lang will frequently cross cut from one space or action to another as though they may be taking place simultaneously. The series of events we witness from the assassination through Marion standing on the ledge occur over several days. But the persistent linkage of images and sounds from sequence to sequence, in combination with the rapid pacing, creates a sense of frantic and impossible simultaneity. Events seem to be following one another and happening at the same time, as though the entire logic of traditional parallel editing is being pushed to the breaking point.

Lang's mise-en-scène here also reinforces this because most of the opening shots are clearly done in the studio. Although economic necessity may well have been the primary reason for shooting the opening in this way, Lang takes maximum advantage of this ostensible limitation. The cars move on platforms in front of a rear projection screen, creating a floating-like sensation rather than an effect of simple forward movement as we are immediately plunged into a world in which action and movement seem to be shaped by mysterious outside forces. At the same time, neither the editing itself nor the organization of the narrative are strictly linear or causal in nature, but instead are subjected to a process of frequent interruption and concealment.

Barter's dash to the television station is doubly interrupted, first by the formal strategies of the film through the cut to the dialogue between Cornelius and Kras; and then within the narrative world itself, through the assassin's bullet in the back of the neck. Whereas agency for this violence is quickly posited (via the shot of clubfooted Mabuse figure) the withholding of a shot of Mabuse's face immediately creates an atmosphere of obscurity rather than clarity in relation to this agency. Why bother to withhold this information? On one level, this withholding places the viewer's knowledge about Mabuse within an ambiguous realm, knowledge that is much higher than that of Kras or anyone else investigating the crimes and slightly higher than that of Mabuse's assistants. A primary effect that this creates is one of frustration for the viewer, in which knowledge is given but just as clearly is blatantly withheld by the film. The cuts will often signify enormous gaps, not simply in terms of time and space but more significantly in terms of knowledge.[76] Furthermore, knowledge is explicitly linked in the opening sequence with death itself. In the brief dialogue sequence immediately following the assassination, when the driver expresses his desire to see what Mabuse looks like, the assassin tells him that anyone who attempts to get close enough to Mabuse to see what he actually looks like is immediately killed. In this film, to see, to know, and to believe is to die.

In this regard, the cutting here assumes a role that has always circulated through Lang's work but that achieves a particular clarity in this film. The type of cut I am referring to is not simply a moment of transition, a passage from one image to another. Instead, it is an overt act of manipulation and control, a form of violence performed by and on the film. The first major cut from one space to another is from the backseat of the car of the assassin (as we see him tapping his fingers anxiously on his gun case) to the office of Kras. Lang does not cut directly to Kras but to a sign hanging in his office explicitly announcing the fact that this is a homicide bureau. We move, then, from an image of a potential murder abruptly interrupted—the action suspended—to an image that is a literal sign of death, marking death's absorption into the world of criminality and its detection. Likewise, at the end of this sequence as Cornelius attempts to tell Kras about his vision of an assassination in a crowded street, he utters the word "murder," which acts as a sound bridge across a shot that shows the assassin taking the rifle out of its holder and aiming at Barter. From Cornelius to the assassin, this word links the two shots and contaminates both of them as it spills over from one frame into the other, appearing to activate the actual firing of the rifle. Death, then, permeates not simply the actions being represented within the narrative world of the film but is also at work in the relations between shots.[77] The cut itself may also carry the mark of death on it, be a violent form of rupture rather than part of a process of unfolding or of drawing simple relations between images.

As many commentators on Lang's work have noted, death is at the center of his cinema and, paradoxically, seems to animate it. This central role for death exceeds that of the simple recurrence of murders, assassinations, and suicides that run throughout film after film of Lang's. After all, this piling up of dead bodies is the crime and detective film's stock-in-trade. Rather, the effect of death, its mortifying impulse, permeates Lang's cinema. In this claustrophobic world, actions and responses to those actions always seem off-kilter: the wrong person accused of a crime, a death undeserved, the relations between a crime and its punishment unfair and uneven. This is not the glamorous and ironic world of many crime and detective fictions. *You Only Live Twice* the title of a 1967 Bond films tells us. That film presents us (as so many Bond films do) with a world in which, no matter how many characters lose their lives, the finality of death never manifests itself but is always kept ironically at bay. Thirty years earlier, Lang tells us something different: *You Only Live Once*. That film presents us (as so many Lang films do) with a world in which death is everywhere and in which the basic drive of the narrative is an attempted escape from the reality of the social world that puts the mark of death on its protagonists.

No death in Lang ever stands alone. It always sets off a reaction, with the death of one person affecting the ability of those who were close to the dead to continue remaining fully alive themselves. Consequently, Lang's protagonists often become emotionally frozen, poised between life and death.[78] By extension, this battle marks itself on the film. All this trafficking in death, all this investment in tracing out and filming its various implications, often threatens to turn the film itself into a kind of death work.[79] So much of the mythology surrounding Lang is that of the Teutonic martinet, meticulously mapping every camera angle, every aspect of design and lighting, and browbeating his actors and crews into submission. What this points toward is Lang's desire not simply to create but also to aggressively control that creation, however much that kind of control runs counter to the industrialized and collaborative methods of film production. But the example of Lang's career equally and repeatedly points toward loss of control: the cutting and destruction of major films in both Germany and Hollywood, the humiliation of commercial assignments, interference from studios, contentious movie stars, and hostile producers. Beyond this is the curious tendency on Lang's part to sometimes walk away from a film in the final stages of postproduction to go on to another film, leaving the final cutting of that earlier work in the hands of others.[80] It is as though the initial intensity of Lang's investment in the need to dominate all aspects to his films exhausts itself, realizing it would never be able to achieve the sense of absolute control desired. Lang's role as auteur is often implicated within a reading of the modern world in which "authorship often slips into an identification with the impersonal system."[81]

This position Lang assumes for himself is a familiar one within certain late-twentieth-century debates about the nature of authorship in general. The modern artist must confront the ruination or erasure of his or her own work, the possibility that what is being created may not matter at all, that it reflects a basic emptiness; or once it is finished and circulates through the culture it will no longer belong completely to the artist but now also belong to the reader or spectator for whom it may acquire a meaning of a very different nature from what the artist intended. Whatever its other possible generic and historical functions, death in Lang may also be read as a symptom of this acute awareness of the loss of artistic control. If the characters in Lang must continually confront death, then so must the filmmaker who forcefully makes death felt in the formal strategies of the film, a death's hand that also grips the spectator.

In spite of the central role of death in most of Lang's films prior to the late 1950s, however, the relationship between organic and nonorganic forces was usually situated in such a way that a type of dialogue was at work between them. From the murder of Elsie Beckmann in *M* to the dynamite in the car that blows up Dave Bannion's wife in *The Big Heat*, death and violence in Lang are always associated with the emotional and physical scars they leave behind. We see an overwhelming sense of loss in the treatment of death, a brutal extinguishing of the physical and organic. But by the end of his Hollywood career, in *While the City Sleeps* and *Beyond a Reasonable Doubt*, Lang presents a world that often seems to be drained of organic life, so much so that the films have been read almost exclusively in relation to the supposed contempt Lang has for the characters, for the world being depicted and, finally, for the Hollywood environment out of which they were produced.[82]

The return to Germany, on the other hand, did initially suggest a possibility for renewal and the Indian diptych shows a degree of what Martin Scorsese has called "purely physical pleasure" lacking in the later American works.[83] Aside from its "rediscovery" of montage, *The Thousand Eyes* is colder and more abstract, withdrawing from "purely physical pleasure" and closer in tone to the last two American films. In *The Thousand Eyes*, the presentation of the film's environment is consistently dry and spare. The film is totally closed in on itself, scarcely going anywhere in terms of location, essentially alternating between the Hotel Luxor, the office of Commissioner Kras, and the home of Peter Cornelius. (When Travers suggests to Marion that they go out for a night on the town he ends up taking her to the nightclub on the first floor of the hotel.) Sequences set on the streets or anywhere outdoors are marked by second-rate process work, as though Lang has simply lost interest in this kind of technical meticulousness. He does not create a great social panorama here that exists under the watchful and hypnotic eyes of a master criminal threatening to dominate that world as he does in *Dr. Mabuse, the Gambler* or *Spies*. Instead, the events in *The Thousand Eyes* happen to a highly limited group of individuals who lack a strong cultural or psychological specificity and in which the culture outside of the Hotel Luxor appears to be in little danger.[84] The only major glimpse of a "real" world outside the Hotel Luxor is the crowd that gathers to watch the suicidal Marion on the ledge. They respond to the event strictly as an inhuman mob, fascinated by the spectacle of impending death. The world into which these acts are launched is not an organic one, threatened by this alien force, but a world represented as largely nonorganic and sterile.

In *The Thousand Eyes*, not only is this Mabuse a forger without a name, but he also sets off a chain of essentially false protagonists, of pretenders and impostors.[85] Except for Kras, every major character operates under at least one alias or assumed identity at some point. The closest to a character assuming an overtly physical function is Hieronymus Balthazar Mistelzweig, whose very name evokes bodily excess and who repeatedly draws attention to his protruding belly. But Mistelzweig is no less a part of this false network because he is working undercover for Interpol. Even Kras does not escape from the sense of forgery that exists everywhere in the film as he begins to pass off Barter's girlfriend as his wife, placing her photo on his desk at work and taking her to Cornelius's séance. But this lack of a center to the characters reaches an extreme degree with Marion Menil. The spectator is continually uncertain until the resolution of the film of the extent of her relationship to the various criminal activities of Mabuse's. All of Marion's behavior and activities (her hysteria and suicide attempt, her apparent depressions, the selling of her jewels and purchasing of airline tickets to get out of town in which she books four flights under four names) contain a double register of significance in which they may be read as indicating either her complicity with Mabuse or her attempts at disentangling herself from him.

Furthermore, the editing structure of the film continually reinforces her essential ambiguity. Not only does the opening montage sequence culminate with Marion on the window ledge at the Hotel Luxor (the very center, we have already been told, of a series of violent deaths), but also throughout the film is sometimes a cut from a grisly murder done in Mabuse's name to Marion as though linking her with these acts of violence (such as when we see a shot of the dead body of Kras's assistant dissolving into an image of a necklace she is trying to sell in a jewelry store, the dissolved image of the necklace around the assistant's head evoking strangulation). On one level, this ambiguity is not radically different from the manner in which the traditional femme fatale of the detective film is presented in which her ambiguity ultimately resolves into a coherent characterization once her motives are revealed. At the end of *The Thousand Eyes*, Marion's behavior is likewise given an explanation as her connection with Mabuse is confirmed. Her hysterical and sometimes emotionally distant responses may now be read as indices of her divided emotions as she is torn between Mabuse and her love for Travers. But the film never supplies us with any definitive information about her or even provides her with a coherent motivation for her involvement with Mabuse. (Unlike Cara Carozza in *Dr. Mabuse, the Gambler*, she does not appear to be in love with Mabuse, nor does she have deeply personal and political reasons for associating herself with the world of crime the way that Sonja does in *Spies*.) Like the new Mabuse, she exists as an abstraction. She has a narrative function (as the seductive bait for Travers) and a symbolic one (as the morally ambiguous female protagonist of the pulp thriller or, perhaps in a Proppian reading of the film, the princess is need of being rescued) but she has no organic function.

If the characters in *The Thousand Eyes* have this mark of forgery about them, the performances in the film likewise complete this aspect. Some of the casting choices seem quite peculiar, in particular Peter Van Eyck as the American Henry Travers. Van Eyck was, in fact, German. Although he became a U.S. citizen in 1943, his thoroughly Aryan features (magnified in *The Thousand Eyes* by hair that is bleached) inevitably led to his being cast in Hollywood films as a Nazi, most notably in Billy Wilder's *Five Graves to Cairo* (1943), Henry Hathaway's *The Desert Fox* (1951), and Robert Aldrich's *Attack!* (1956). Aside from his association with playing Nazi officers, his most notable roles prior to *The Thousand Eyes* were as "heavies" or at least morally ambiguous characters in films such as Henri-Georges Clouzot's *Wages of Fear* (1953) and Welles's *Mr. Arkadin* (1955). He speaks German throughout *The Thousand Eyes*, even to ostensibly English-speaking characters, and in all of his scenes with the English actress Dawn Addams[86] (who plays Marion) he continues to speak German while she appears to be mouthing her lines in English. (In the German-language prints, Addams is dubbed whereas in the English-language prints both Van Eyck and Addams are dubbed.) Although this is not atypical of postwar international coproductions, it is symptomatic of the film's essential dryness of tone that its two great lovers do not, if observed closely, even communicate in the same language with one another.[87] Van Eyck's features seem to be locked in a malevolent expression of coldness and barely concealed contempt, more appropriate for playing Mabuse than for playing the leading man here. Gunning is certainly correct in complaining about the "soporific" nature of Travers's romance with Marion in opposition to the "truly sensual love affair between Tremaine and Sonja in *Spies*."[88] But this kind of sensuality really has no place in *The Thousand Eyes*, a film in which the struggle to communicate and the threat of inexpressiveness manifests itself through the relationship between body and speech as much as through image.[89]

The brief final sequence of the film is particularly symptomatic in this regard. In a hospital bed, a seriously wounded Marion (to whom Travers attends) opens her mouth and attempts to speak. No sounds emerge and her head falls to the side. The camera pans down to Marion's hand resting against Travers's palm as his hand touches hers against the white hospital sheets. These images suggest not the unmistakable sign of Marion's recovery, but the even stronger possibility of her eminent demise, a simultaneous bonding of the romantic couple and the end of that romance through death. The austere beauty of this final shot, however, merits attention in that it speaks to a desire for communication, a desire for the tactile and the erotic within a cinematic environment that conspicuously resists it at every turn.

The Thousand Eyes fails, then, at the basic level of providing the spectator with a convincing romantic couple pitted against the arch villainy of a master criminal. But this "failing" also allows the film more fully to join company with a major tendency of postwar modernism as it attempts to deal with the notion of conspiracy. If the presence of Gert Fröbe as Kras anticipates the ironic approach toward international espionage the Bond films took, the presence of Howard Vernon as the assassin looks forward to another very different classic film of the period, Godard's Alphaville (1965). In Godard's film, Vernon plays Professor Leonard Von Braun, designer of Alpha 60, the computer that serves as the central brain for Alphaville itself. Von Braun, Mabuse-like, rules Alphaville primarily through his computer, which exerts a totalitarian drive to eliminate all nonconformists. Although both Alphaville and The Thousand Eyes give their master criminals a name, the very instability of those names (Von Braun, for example, was originally called Leonard Nosferatu, a name clearly intended to evoke the legendary vampire of Weimar cinema) is but one indication of the movement away from a sense of single agency so central to traditional notions of conspiracy. Instead, power now gains its control through its sheer insidious persuasiveness, simultaneously visible and invisible.[90]

In Testament of Dr. Mabuse, Dr. Baum has a feverish monologue in which he describes, in a combination of extreme fascination and horror, the hideous and diseased brain of Mabuse, something both rotten and brilliant. Even though Baum is describing the internal operation of Mabuse's mind, his language and manner of delivery impart an almost physical dimension to this brain, as though it were an object in its own right, apart from the body of Mabuse. The notion of the brain as something that continues to live after it has been removed from the body of the person in whom it originally lived is a staple of the horror genre. But such a brain/body split still presupposes a biological relation, albeit of a perverse nature, for example, The Brain That Wouldn't Die (1963). By divesting its Mabuse of biological specificity, The Thousand Eyes refuses this more conventional relation between body and brain. The brain possessed by this Mabuse is closer to the artificial one of Alpha 60 than it is to his namesake thirty years earlier.[91] In Godard's film, the erasure of collective memory under Von Braun is essential to the operation of Alphaville, a type of erasure utterly familiar, of course, in totalitarian regimes. Alphaville typically links this erasure to the repression of emotion and spontaneity, a world in which thought and emotion become criminal acts.

It is not an overtly totalitarian regime that Lang is presenting in *The Thousand Eyes*. But the failure of collective memory and responsibility in the aftermath of World War II in the world of Lang's film is no less essential: A film in which crime is rampant but cannot be traced to a single source; a film in which the act of criminal detection is equally off center; and a film in which the environment and all other characters are marked by falseness, stiffness, and a lack of physicality. In *The Thousand Eyes*, we have bodies that seem to be barely inhabited, voices that emerge from them that have little expressive function, inexpressive faces that approach the status of masks. It is as though the characters are responding to a mind that is not their own and that empties out their bodies, draining them of the possibilities of "normal" movement and action. If anything, Godard's film is more romantic, more utopian than Lang's: The struggle by detective Lemmy Caution (Eddie Constantine) to restore the memory of Natasha Von Braun (Anna Karina), a memory repressed under her father's regime, the escape from Alphaville by the couple as Natasha ("A name from the past," Lemmy says) haltingly utters the words, "I love you"—no real equivalents of these appear in *The Thousand Eyes*. Where Godard has charismatic actors who suggest the expressive potential of a return to the physical in a totalitarian world, Lang has mannequins who dryly and automatically go through the romantic motions. Where Lang has a polyglot international cast covered over with some bad dubbing, Godard has a cast of largely non–French speaking actors for whom the act of speaking itself forms part of this struggle to feel and to be understood. It is as though Godard's film picks up from the rubble of ambivalence and skepticism that Lang has left behind and constructs something both more despairing and more optimistic, a film that is not only more physical, more sensual than Lang's but also, at times, quite comic as it gives itself over to moments of pure physical slapstick. Vernon's presence, then, could not be more ideal for *The Thousand Eyes*: a tall, gaunt body encased in a black suit and tie, eyes permanently shaded by sunglasses, a man of no curiosity, whose brain functions automatically in relation to Mabuse's commands, he is as mortifying as the figure of Death in Lang's *Der müde Tod* (1921). But unlike that figure he has no remorse, no pity, no melancholia.[92] The fingers that anxiously tap on the surface of the gun case at the beginning of *The Thousand Eyes* are not the sign of the activity of a human brain, but of the brain of a machine programmed to go off in relation to certain stimuli. He is a man with no name at all, only a number: 12.

Figure 1.14. Howard Vernon as No. 12 in *The Thousand Eyes of Dr. Mabuse.*

Figure 1.15. Howard Vernon as Leonard von Braun in Jean-Luc Godard's *Alphaville* (1965).

Death Enters the Hotel

One of the major spaces of *Alphaville* is the hotel in which Lemmy Caution stays. In reality, the hotel Godard chose as the location site for the film had been one in which Nazi officials had resided during the occupation of Paris. In the film, the women who work in the hotel wear numbered tattoos on their backs, like survivors of a concentration camp. If some of the older European hotels that survive the postwar period sometimes carry with them the taint of association with fascism, the hotels built since the war sometimes represent not a symbol of renewal but a symbol of an attempted cover-up and denial of the past. Although works of narrative (classical or otherwise) containing their basic concerns within certain highly restricted architectural spaces is not unusual, the hotel presents a particularly privileged method through which these concerns may be addressed. In the cinema, the secret beyond the door is here multiplied in relation to the sheer size of the central architectural structure. The vast modern hotel suggests a perpetual regeneration of story after story, of many secrets behind many doors, but all within an atmosphere of anonymity and transience and with a realization that most of these secrets will remain just that.

A Hollywood film such as *Grand Hotel* (directed by Edmund Goulding and released in 1932), acknowledges the nonclassical effect that such spaces may create. As in *The Thousand Eyes*, we are in a large modern German hotel (here explicitly situated in Berlin), although not even indirectly does *Grand Hotel* refer to the political situation in Germany or anywhere else in Europe at the time. Underneath the credits, we see dizzying kaleidoscopic designs (as we also see in the credits for *The Thousand Eyes*) while a fast-paced waltz plays; during the opening sequence an extreme overhead shot, taken from a high position in the central circular staircase down to the hotel's lobby, points to the labyrinth-like nature of the space. The film's two most famous lines (Garbo's "I want to be alone," and Lewis Stone's "Grand Hotel: People coming, going, nothing ever happens") suggest the modern hotel's appeal as well as alienation as it provides not only the means of escape from a conflicted identity, but it also has the power to erase and create a world in which "nothing ever happens" because everyone within it has become emptied out and in which the revolving door (the penultimate shot of the film) becomes the ultimate emblem of a fundamental transience.

But the basic drive and structure of *Grand Hotel* is one that moves toward renewal and regeneration. For all the sickness and death and neurosis shown (including a dying protagonist, played by Lionel Barrymore), the film takes great pains to compensate for each of these

Figure 1.16. Edmund Goulding's *Grand Hotel* (1932): The central staircase.

with a presentation in the final sequence of healthy bodies and minds, such as the birth of a child and the appearance of the young aviator couple who check into the hotel. The construction of the scenario (with its extended dialogue sequences in a restricted number of settings and with a limited number of characters) is obviously derived from its conventional theatrical source material with its rising and falling dramatic arcs, with characters entering and exiting through doors, with its lessons learned and a sense of "life" continuing after the resolution of the narrative. But also what is magnetically beyond each door in this hotel is not only a secret but a movie star (Garbo, Joan Crawford, John and Lionel Barrymore, Wallace Beery, all at the height of their popularity) and not simply narrative but also spectacle (a film lavishly produced by MGM, the most self-consciously glamorous of all Hollywood studios, with "more stars than there are in Heaven"). These doors are all very beautiful, Art Deco in design, heavy and expensive-looking. This Grand Hotel was constructed as a monument to the power and appeal of the system that produced it, the system that has also been most responsible for institutionalizing classical cinema.[93]

Figure 1.17. Alain Resnais's *Last Year at Marienbad* (1961): Endless hallways and open doors.

The hotel in postwar modernist cinema continues to make use of this basic framework while also altering it in significant ways. In the postwar period, the passage from the closed door to the open door lacks the necessary metaphoric power, either in relation to the shot change or to the conception of space and the narrative enigmas contained within. The door (be it the door of a hotel or any other work of architecture) is more likely to be open than closed. This is not because the cinema now lays any great claims to having more direct access to the truth as it shakes off the power of the gothic mysteries and secrets kept hidden away that exerted such a strong appeal in classical narrative. On the contrary, the doors that have now been opened raise several complicated questions rather than supplying direct answers. In *Last Year at Marienbad* (1961), Resnais and Alain Robbe-Grillet present us with a hotel with seemingly endless hallways and perpetually open doors. The film's narrator refers to the hotel's false doors, false bottoms, and perspectives: "Everything was deserted in this immense hotel, empty parlors, corridors, doors, salons." We have a hotel that is haunted, populated by zombie-like figures who evoke the late 1920s, a hotel in which mysterious events have at one time taken place, although what precisely took place is something that is never clarified. The very openness of the hotel's space creates not a sense of transparency but one of obscurity and agoraphobia.

In many of Lang's films, for all of their spectacular parallel editing effects and for the manner in which the sense of a vast (and usually urban) environment is created, we see a tendency for this environment to collapse ultimately, either onto a single location that serves as a nucleus for the film's concerns (as in the Chuck-a-Luck ranch in *Rancho Notorious*) or for the seemingly infinite urban world of the film to tightly and implausibly connect, demonstrating relations and proximities of an unsettling nature: the New York of *While the City Sleeps*, for example, is used as though it were a small town in which virtually the entire cast of characters seems to live and work within a three-block radius of one another. In neither of these tendencies do we find a suggestion of a classical center to these worlds. Instead, they create an effect of both claustrophobia and infinity, of worlds carefully mapped out and diagrammed and yet finally beyond containment. This is precisely what takes place, and to an extreme degree, in *The Thousand Eyes*. Not only does the Hotel Luxor replace a master criminal as the film's fixed point, it is even equated by Mistelzweig with the human: "People aren't the only ones influenced by the constellations upon their birth. A building is, too."[94] While the ever-skeptical Kras denies that a building can be born in this way, Mistelzweig argues that the placement of a building's cornerstone is its birth hour and that the Hotel Luxor was built "under a bad star." Mistelzweig describes the hotel as having been constructed during a late period of the Nazi era (its cornerstone laid in May 1944) causing it to be haunted by this historical moment.[95] The new Mabuse's plans were adapted directly from those the Nazis were hoping to put into use in the hotel for surveillance. In this regard, the film is making clear links between the tactics of Mabuse and the Nazis, pointing to the persistence of this ideology even when appearances during the Adenauer era suggest otherwise.[96]

In a well-known essay on the hotel lobby, Kracauer argues that this lobby functions as "the inverted image of the house of God . . . a negative church."[97] In the church, the relinquishing of an individual's name and identity allows for a solidarity with the collective—a higher collective in which the congregation joins to face God. But in the modern hotel lobby, this loss of identity loses it positive relationship with a higher realm. Here the name "gets lost in space" because "anonymity no longer serves any purpose other than meaningless movement along the paths of convention." People become empty forms, mannequins as they "now file by as ungraspable flat ghosts."[98] The detective novel, with its "emptied-out individuals," is a particularly privileged form for exploring the kind of space the hotel lobby suggests. Kracauer quotes a passage from a 1921 Swedish detective novel, *Death Enters the Hotel*: "Once again it is confirmed that a large hotel is a world unto itself and that this world is like the rest of the large world. The guests here roam about in their light-hearted, careless summer existence without suspecting anything of the strange mysteries circulating among them."[99] Several aspects to both Kracauer's arguments and the passage he cites from this detective novel are of interest in relation to *The Thousand Eyes*: the issue of the disappearance of identity as names get lost and individuals become emptied out and become ghostlike; the relationship between the hotel and detective fiction in general, as though the space of the hotel is by its very nature a space lacking in transparency, a work of architecture that creates the need for detection and unmasking; and how all of this leads to an atmosphere of paranoia, surveillance, and anonymity. The hotel is a crucial location throughout Lang's work in both Germany and Hollywood.[100] Given the central role the hotel plays in many detective and espionage thrillers, and given Lang's frequent reliance on these genres, such a recurrence is hardly surprising. In this regard, the Hotel Luxor is simply the last in a long line of Lang's hotels. However, the Luxor's absolute centrality to *The Thousand Eyes*—the way in which it becomes the film's major location in terms of both the frequency with which it is used and in terms of how it contains the film's concerns within a precise architectural structure—makes the Hotel Luxor not simply the ultimate in Langian hotels, but the one in which Lang pushes the function of the hotel within classical cinema to its limit.

In comparison with its function in classical cinema, the hotel in modern cinema has an identity strongly bound up with its relationship to two of the central topics of modernism: time and memory, both personal and historical. The hotel is no longer a world of secrets carefully hidden away behind closed doors, but a space in which everyone is being watched while the possibility of ascribing that look to any individual is obscured. What connects these two approaches is the idea of paranoia and conspiracy, of the intense desire to engage in acts of detection whereas the difficulty (if not the impossibility) of fully uncovering the enigmas contained within the hotel are also frequently raised. The hotel contains "too much" in the way of history and memory; it permeates and often overflows the architectural confines.[101] In relation to the Luxor, the history that threatens to overflow its confines is the "bad star" of Nazism. The name of this fictional hotel is the same as that of another Luxor, the Egyptian city located on the southern half of what was once ancient Thebes. While a modern environment now, Egypt's Luxor was built on the magnificent ruins of a once-great empire. Some of these ruins (particularly the Luxor Temple) still exist and continue to exert their fascination within contemporary Luxor. Lang's hotel does not visually evoke the idea of ruin in an explicit way. The decor is dominated by an austerity, simplicity of form and a lack of apparent evocation of any past. In contrast to the mise-en-scène of many of Lang's films, the fascination with visual density and frames overflowing with information is largely absent here. Instead, the spaces (particularly that of the Hotel Luxor) look stripped to the bone and have a somewhat unsettling sense of scale: high ceilings but narrow

Figure 1.18. *The Thousand Eyes of Dr. Mabuse*: The space of the Hotel Luxor.

doors and decor that seems to be dwarfed by its surroundings. Even when the decor makes a clear visual impression, as in the Japanese motifs of Travers's room, its expressive value in relation to the film's thematic concerns is not always clear. But whereas this Luxor has the appearance of absolute newness, of a space without memory, it is in fact constructed on repressed history and memory.[102]

Two popular images dominate the urban space of postwar Germany. The first is that of the immediate postwar period, an urban landscape of ruin in the aftermath of the Allied assaults of 1944 and 1945, images repeated incessantly in newsreel footage, photographs and in narrative films such as Rossellini's *Germany, Year Zero* (1947), Jacques Tourneur's *Berlin Express* (1948), Billy Wilder's *A Foreign Affair* (1948), and Sam Fuller's *Verboten!* (1959), as well as the numerous "rubble" films of postwar German cinema. The second image is that of the urban landscape as it began to develop during the 1950s when the ruins were cleared away and a certain postwar strain of functional modern architecture replaced several of these ruins. The desire to eliminate the Nazi past was manifested in this embracing of an architectural modernism that had the appearance of something utterly new and untainted by history, but that often merely served as a covering over of history, more a work of repression than recovery.[103] There is a shot in the first of Fassbinder's trilogy of films dealing with the period of Germany's postwar recovery, *The Marriage of Maria Braun* (1978), which concisely articulates this notion. Maria and a friend tour the rubble of a school they attended as children. Embracing one another as they sing, Fassbinder cuts to a long shot of the two women overwhelmed by the ruined architecture. The camera slowly pans to the left and then begins to tilt up to an image of a ruined fragment of a wall on the floor above where the women are sitting. In the middle of this wall is a tightly closed door, one that, if suddenly opened from the other side, would cause a person to fall to his or her death. With the sounds of construction heard in the background (and which seem to be quite consciously designed to sound like gunfire as well), Fassbinder briefly holds on this image as the final shot of the sequence.

In *The Thousand Eyes*, the central space within the Hotel Luxor is the basement, a typical strategy of Lang's, who often stages crucial sequences in the lowest regions of a particular work of architecture. This fascination with the lower regions shows a strong debt to the world of the gothic and the fantastic in which the highest or lowest areas of a primary architectural space also become the space of both repression and power, where the secrets (and often the bodies) are buried and where the past must eventually come to light. It is significant, then, that Lang does not have his new Mabuse presiding, godlike, over his video monitors from a luxury suite (similar to Joh Fredersen in *Metropolis*), but from the space of repression, the basement. In this regard, the film still clings to a nineteenth-century conception of conspiracy, creating a vertical space in which the truth is carefully tucked away, just below or beyond what is immediately visible and that is simply waiting for the appropriate forces of detection to uncover. This happens here when Mistelzweig sees the Hotel Luxor's elevator doors descending to basement level while noting that the elevators actually contain no signs or buttons indicating the presence of a basement.

But as with so much of this film, the sense of cliché and exhaustion brings it closer to the concerns of the postwar period than one might originally believe. After all, what else can one expect from a walking cliché like this new Mabuse except for him to launch all of his fantasies from these exhausted spaces? What else is he capable of drawing on except the ruined plans of others—those of the first Mabuse for his criminal actions and of the Nazis for surveillance in the Hotel Luxor? In a case of life imitating cliché, we may recall that Berlin is a city in which approximately 15,000 unexploded bombs from the Nazi period are buried throughout its landscape, all with the potential to explode and that no work of architecture can possibly suppress.[104] Within the realm of poetics, the lower regions may be a tired metaphoric space for representing repression but within the concrete facts of history this notion is not entirely exhausted.

Beyond this, however, Lang's fascination with the lower regions of a space combined with the ambivalence with which he treats the notion of the secret beyond the door suggest that the basic drives of his cinema are less toward getting to the other side of something (a space, an image) as to get to the bottom of it, literally and metaphorically. Such a drive toward the bottom is bound up with the relationship between act of uncovering and forms of abasement and degradation—with dirt—and this is likewise extended to the treatment of the body in which the feet may assume a role as central as the face or the hands: The one specific shot from a Lang film that Paul cites in *Contempt* is in *Rancho Notorious* in which Mel Ferrer places his foot against a loose board in the floor of the gambling casino, allowing him to control the gambling wheel, an elegant and discreet gesture nevertheless tied to corruption. The clubfooted man in *The Thousand Eyes*, by contrast, is utterly lacking in this kind of elegant physicality. The foot is heavy, inexpressive, awkward, suggesting not so much the physical as the mechanical. Even a sense of the bottom in this film, then, is hollowed out. The basement of the Hotel Luxor suggests less a space of elemental lower regions as a space in the process of a rather mundane modernizing through a row of television monitors.

If certain aspects of postwar modernist European cinema may be seen as a response to fascism then we must also look to the altered function of space and architecture in this cinema and their relationship to history. In Resnais's *Night and Fog* (1955), Jean Cayrol's voice-over narration refers to the concentration camps being built along the lines of a stadium or a grand hotel, drawing a link between the large collective spaces of modern urban life and the architectural banality of the camps. We see a repeated emphasis in the film on closed and open doors, on the relationship between the unprepossessing exterior to a building and the horrors that took place behind it. Near the end of the film, we see the doors to the camps being opened as the camps are liberated, the nightmarish reversal of the doors to the factory opening at the end of the Lumière films. But this opening is also a form of closing down, as we see a brief montage of Nazi officials denying any accountability for the events that took place within the camps and Cayrol's voice-over directly asks the question of who precisely is to be held responsible if these people are not. In the final moments of the film, we see the ruins of the camps and are told that they provide the illusion that what took place there lies buried underneath the rubble and will never occur again. Throughout the present-day color footage of *Night and Fog*, Resnais's camera relentlessly tracks through what is left of the camps, the doors now open. But only traces of what took place there remain and as the camera tracks it assumes the role of a melancholy detective, searching for clues at a crime scene, one that contains both too much evidence and too little.[105]

Figure 1.19. Alain Resnais's *Night and Fog* (1955): The closed doors of the camps.

Figure 1.20. The open doors of the camps in *Night and Fog*.

The detective and thriller format is one to which modern cinema returns again and again (either directly through pastiche, as in *Alphaville*, or indirectly through narratives constructed in the form of an investigation or trial, as in Resnais's 1974 film *Stavisky*). The use of such a format may be read as the search for a fundamental truth in relation to historical trauma, but a truth that often refuses to be located. This is not what happens in *The Thousand Eyes*. The mystery is solved, the villain is unmasked and destroyed, the key space of conspiracy traced to the basement. But the hollowness with which the film approaches the basic drives of detective fiction suggests a link to more contemporaneous modernist approaches to the question of detection and uncovering.

For example, although the assassination of Barter is indeed essentially a copy of the assassination of Dr. Kramm from *Testament* one significant detail is changed: the nature of the object that kills its recipient. In *Testament*, it is an actual bullet that ends Kramm's life while he stops at a red light. In *The Thousand Eyes*, not a bullet but a steel needle enters the back of Barter's neck and then travels to his brain, killing him. Moreover, this needle enters its assailant silently. It is a "clean" murder, leaving no apparent trace, no visible point of entry—very different from Kramm's death. Unlike Lang's earlier crime films, this crime leaves no immediate traces. Only after an autopsy can this needle be discovered within the body of the assailant. This, then, is a crime without a firm indexical sign of death attached to it. Kras's fundamental source of frustration in the film as a traditional detective figure is that he must proceed "blindly," as Mabuse's crimes, which do not have any indexical signs left behind. Within the film's opening montage, we see a brief sequence of Kras visiting Barter's ransacked office. In *While the City Sleeps*, the serial killer leaves his mark behind in the space of one of his victims by writing "Ask Mother" in lipstick on the wall. This trace is, as a character in the film describes it, a deliberate "impertinence," a parody of a clue rather than a genuine one. The idea of the lipstick trace reappears in the sequence in Barter's office, where an imprint is found on the back of a photo from the reporter's girlfriend. Unfortunately for Kras, it's just a trace—she is not the criminal, and the imprint is a sign of her love for Peter and nothing more. What both Kras and Lieutenant Kaufman (Howard Duff) in *While the City Sleeps* state in slightly different ways is that criminals have now become so aware of the idea of the clue left behind at the scene of the crime (primarily through other forms of detective fiction) that they have been able to devise their own thorough methods for erasing all firm traces of their presence. What *While the City Sleeps* initiates and then *The Thousand Eyes* pursues even more fully is the notion that the index itself has become a cliché.

Although *The Thousand Eyes* suggests that a total investment in the indexical world of the detective film is becoming a thing of the past, the film also suggests that the notion of the secret beyond the door is equally threatened with extinction. This may already be seen in *While the City Sleeps*. The locked doors in that film (mainly those of real and potential female victims of the serial killer) are flimsy, easily available to be manipulated, the reflection of a conception of space in which public and private are collapsed. In the film, the walls of the offices in the Kyne headquarters are all of made of glass, allowing for all the employees to spy on everyone else. When the characters are in apartment settings, they express anxiety about the possibility of the walls having sliding panels with microphones behind every picture. By the time of *The Thousand Eyes*, the door itself has lost much of its earlier power to conceal and create enigmas. Kras has no trouble getting into Cornelius's apartment when Cornelius is not there; he simply lets himself in, as though opening a locked door is the most natural event in the world, a minor occurrence. This basic idea is repeated later in the film after Travers and Marion have returned from the séance. Travers, believing that he is alone, looks out of the window of his hotel room. Suddenly, Marion's voice speaks to him from off-camera, and as he turns, he is startled to see her standing in the archway to his sitting room. She explains that the door was unlocked and so she simply walked in. In spite of the fact that the film is set in a luxury hotel, this is a film in which a closed door or a locked door no longer carries any great significance. Indeed the scale of the set design often emphasizes small and narrow doorways and archways, often tucked away in the rear or to the side of a set, rarely commanding any significant attention. In a film in which all spaces are under the watchful thousand eyes, of what relevance finally is a closed door or a locked door?

The two central devices that take the place of the door in Lang's final film for assuming the crucial role in marking a sense of passage are the two-way mirror connecting an empty suite in the hotel with Marion's and the monitors through which Mabuse surveys the space of the hotel. This two-way mirror, in particular, is a culminating moment in Lang's conception of the frame-within-the-frame in that it brings together three of the major framing devices that occur throughout his work: the door, the window, and the mirror. The very conception of the frame-within-the-frame is one that often involves an intensification and doubling up of the basic desire to seize an image. Lang's origins in Weimar cinema create an especially fruitful environment for a decor, which not only establishes setting, but which also self-consciously frames, reframes, and reflects images.[106] In writing of the shifts at work during cinema's postwar period, Kerry Brougher notes that the cinema now becomes rather like a "hall of mirrors" in which "reality and illusion often co-mingle. This is also a dialogue that returns time and time again to the cinema's origins, holding the past up to the present, cinematic spectacle up to the mirror of contemporary culture, splintering it and re-arranging it into new, self-reflexive [*sic*] experiences that highlight and subvert screen practice." The crucial moment here is the funhouse sequence from the end of Welles's *The Lady from Shanghai* (1948) in which one "cannot distinguish between the real and the reflection."[107] But if the shattered mirror is an emblem of postwar cinema, it is equally evocative of more classical forms of narrating. The very gesture of shattering a mirror is a grandiose melodramatic one, a destruction of an element of decor that looks back at and negatively reflects on the individual. This is part of Lang's heritage and was fundamental to Weimar art cinema's revival of nineteenth-century gothic elements. In this regard, *The Lady from Shanghai*'s funhouse mirror sequence partakes not only of a postwar shattered mirror syndrome, but also a prewar syndrome, a gesture the film is self conscious about, as in the obviously Expressionist-influenced decor of the funhouse evoking Robert Wiene's *The Cabinet of Dr. Caligari* (1920). Nevertheless, one may also read Welles's strategy here as one that seeks, through its highly elliptical and fragmented editing strategies, to "shatter" this heritage as strongly as it draws on it.[108]

Although the basic idea of the two-way mirror in Lang's career goes back to *Spiders*, in *Spiders* it simply allowed Lio-Sha to spy on her colleagues from a privileged space that these other men could not see. In *The Thousand Eyes*, the two-way mirror gives Travers the illusion that he is spying on Marion, allowing him to voyeuristically survey a private space as he observes Marion getting dressed or weeping as she receives flowers from him. As such, the mirror serves as not only a window through which Travers is able to watch Marion but also a frame that catches and reflects Travers's own desires. On one level, this is simply a variation on an approach to the mirror that has its basis in Romanticism in which the reflection caught within the mirror also looks back at its subject, seizing and reflecting the subject's unconscious desires.

But, in fact, this mirror is designed as a trap by Mabuse: Marion knows that Travers is watching her so that Travers is, in effect, being indirectly watched in return. It is a performance that she gives in a private film designed specifically for Travers with Mabuse as its invisible metteur-en-scène. This sequence serves as the only moment of eroticism between the two characters, the only moment when Travers communicates a directly carnal desire for Marion. When she steps up close to the mirror and adjusts her lipstick, fully aware that Travers is on the other side of this looking glass, she seems to be offering herself directly to him in a

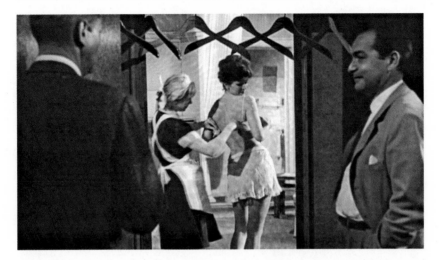

Figure 1.21. *The Thousand Eyes of Dr. Mabuse*: The closet, the door, and the two-way mirror.

way that we never see her doing at any other point in the film. But this rare moment of eroticism depends on the impossibility of touch taking place here because the barrier of the mirror prevents this from happening. In Lang's earlier films, when characters gazed into a window it was most often a shop window within which their material or physical desires were framed, as impossible objects of desire were just within reach but impossible to touch or possess. In *The Thousand Eyes*, however, the idea of the public space of the shop window has invaded the false private space of the hotel room. It is no longer a world in which public spaces create and reflect private desires but a world in which any distinction between these realms no longer exists.

Lang does not completely discard the idea of the secret door here in that the mirror is kept locked up, within a closet, so that Travers must still unlock and open a door. But the sense of passage is much more heavily blocked. The moment in which Travers breaks through the two-way mirror is a crucial one in this regard. Travers ostensibly breaks the mirror when he observes Marion's husband abusing her and he cannot bear to watch the physical abuse any longer—he shatters the glass and, under orders from Marion, shoots her husband. At last, we might think, we are on the road to truth, to the moment of revelation when Marion's full identity and her relationship to Mabuse is made clear. The film seems to be aiming for a moment of release in which the structure of appearances begins to shatter as the mirror itself shatters. Even on a first viewing, however, the possibility of reading the sequence in this way is complicated by the shots of a figure (in reality, Mabuse) observing all of this activity from monitors in another space (in reality, the basement of the Hotel Luxor). If these shots have an uncanniness to them it is because of the sense they are not only being watched, but are also controlled by someone else: a metteur en scène. Hence the importance of the monitors being switched off after the shooting rather than voyeuristically continuing to observe the response to the murder. The murder is a scenario that has played itself out according to plan. Not only is the resolution foregone by this point but the metteur en scène must also now assume his role as actor and play Dr. Jordan in the subsequent sequence. Travers has broken the mirror not to move from a position of spellbound passivity to action in which he controls a space and the narrative events. Instead, he merely passes into another space of appearances. Even the act of shattering the mirror will mean little: We are told that the pieces of the mirror will be very quickly cleaned up and the mirror restored.

In *The Thousand Eyes*, then, the mirror shatters only to be put back together again while the film itself still has another reel to go with a botched escape from the hotel by Marion and Travers (Marion gets shot), a trip to the basement for some plot explanations, and a car chase. Welles's film would appear to be more audacious, more modernist in its treatment of the mirror in relation to the formal structure of the film overall: shatter the pieces of the mirror, let the rubble fall where it may, and just walk away. Lang, on the other hand, glues the pieces back together because his film is not structured on a drive toward the idea of the shattered mirror. Instead, Lang restores the mirror as his film takes refuge in clichés rather than attempting to "highlight and subvert screen practice." But once this mirror has been restored, looking at it (or the film) in the same way again is difficult. The cracks will always be apparent no matter how strenuous the attempted cover-up. All of Lang's work is engaged in this perpetual dialogue between the shattered mirror and the restored one, between the closed door and the open, between the classical and the modernist. But no other Lang film is as strongly marked by its struggle to achieve a sense of passage from one space to another, no other Lang film has such small doors, such sterile characters, such a nonorganic environment. In *The Thousand Eyes* of Dr. Mabuse the shattered mirror ultimately cannot be restored.

Fascination and Rape

Marnie

The cinema is necessarily fascination and rape. That is how it acts
on people.

—Jacques Rivette, "Time Overflowing"

❦

OF ALL OF ALFRED HITCHCOCK'S major works, the critical reception of *Marnie* has undergone the most extensive reappraisal
since the film's release in 1964. Its reevaluation initially took place
through auteurist writings of the 1960s; feminist and psychoanalytic approaches in the 1970s and 1980s have been equally important in moving
Marnie into the Hitchcock canon. But in spite of this body of academic
writing, *Marnie* remains (like the title character herself) something of a
problem child. Unlike *Vertigo* (1958), another Hitchcock film that was initially a critical and financial failure, *Marnie* has repeatedly encountered
certain pockets of resistance in the Hitchcock literature. For example, in a
1992 anthology on Hitchcock, edited by Slavoj Žižek, Žižek breaks
Hitchcock's work into five periods, the final period being one of "disintegration." For Žižek, this period begins not with *Torn Curtain* in 1966 (the
site of the standard auteurist beginning of Hitchcock's decline) but with

Marnie. During this period, we see a "breaking apart of Hitchcock's universe into its particular ingredients" in which only "isolated touches of brilliance" remain.¹ Žizek feels no need to explain his decision to posit *Marnie* as initiating this period of disintegration, in spite of the fact that it runs counter to an important body of work on the film over the last thirty years.

François Truffaut has more productively categorized *Marnie* as belonging to the category of the "great flawed films." Truffaut defines the great flawed film as "a masterpiece that has aborted, an ambitious project weakened by some errors in the making: a fine screenplay that is 'unshootable,' an inadequate cast, a shooting contaminated by hatred or blinded by love, or an inordinate gap between the original intention and the final execution."² This type of film essentially belongs to the cinephile who is able to recognize the nature of the film's ambitions much more immediately than the general public or the average film critic. Certainly *Marnie*'s financial failure can be partly attributed to the kinds of expectations Hitchcock had built with general audiences in the preceding years. The huge financial success of *Psycho* as well as the less successful but still profitable *The Birds* (1963) had made Hitchcock's name virtually synonymous with the horror film, a genre he had never directly touched prior to this. But this is a genre to which *Marnie* does not belong. Nor could the audiences for *Spellbound* (1945), *Notorious* (1946), *Rear Window* (1954), *To Catch a Thief* (1955), or *North by Northwest* (1959) have been particularly taken with the idiosyncratic manner with which elements of the psychological and romance thriller function in *Marnie*.

But reading the film from an auteurist perspective, *Marnie* does emerge in a certain line of development out of *Psycho* and *The Birds*.³ Not the least of *Marnie*'s ties to *The Birds* is its self-conscious incorporation of certain formal aspects of 1960s European art cinema. Although such a strategy does push Hitchcock's cinema into some new directions, this was scarcely the first time in his career that Hitchcock used modernist or avant-garde developments in film and the other arts. His ability to incorporate various modernist strategies (Soviet montage, Expressionist lighting and decor, Surrealism, Symbolism) into mainstream commercial projects strongly shaped his initial fame as a director in Britain in the 1920s and 1930s.⁴ But the influence and importance of this European work in the early 1960s clearly represented for Hitchcock a force to be reckoned with and in a way that he had not experienced since the 1920s. Prior to shooting *The Birds*, Hitchcock screened films by Godard, Bergman, and Antonioni with the influence of the last of these filmmakers ultimately making the strongest mark on *The Birds* and *Marnie*. "Hitchcock," writes Robert Kapsis, "wanted to be taken seriously as an artist."⁵ The release of *Marnie* came in the aftermath of several events around which Hitchcock was indeed being taken seriously as an artist: the 1963 Museum of Modern Art retrospective, the choice of *The Birds* as the opening night feature of the Cannes Film Festival, and an accelerating body of auteurist writings placing Hitchcock at the forefront of the development of cinema. In a review of *Psycho*, Andrew Sarris went so far as to write that Hitchcock was "the most daring avant-garde filmmaker in America today."[6] Truffaut's lavish interview book with Hitchcock served as the culminating moment in the attempt to solidify Hitchcock as a filmmaker worthy of the utmost seriousness. Truffaut had begun the interviews shortly after *The Birds* was released although the first edition of the book would not be published until 1967, the same year in which Truffaut made his own Hitchcockian film, *The Bride Wore Black*, which contains a Bernard Herrmann score and numerous *Marnie*-like elements.

In spite of this, all three of Hitchcock's films from the early 1960s received largely negative reviews in the mainstream press (and *Marnie* was even dismissed by Sarris, although this unexpected auteurist swipe at the film appears to be an isolated one).[7] Hitchcock's desire to be viewed as a serious film artist of the caliber of Bergman or Antonioni was not taken seriously anywhere except where it had always been—on the pages of *Cahiers du Cinéma* and *Movie*—where the nature of Hitchcock's ambitions was duly noted. Despite *Cahiers du Cinéma*'s increased skepticism about Hollywood and classical cinema as it was being produced during the 1960s (a subject to be dealt with in more detail in the following chapter), a belief in the contemporary relevance of Hitchcock's work continued unabated. *Marnie* finished third in the magazine's annual year-end poll in 1964, preceded by Godard's *Band of Outsiders* and the final masterpiece of another great aging filmmaker with roots in the silent era, Carl Dreyer's *Gertrud*, a film perhaps even more despised on its initial release than Hitchcock's. A year prior to this in the magazine, Jean-André Fieschi linked *The Birds* with Resnais's *Muriel*. "*Muriel*," he stated, "is to me the equivalent of the first hour of *The Birds* expanded into a full-length film," while also noting the references to Hitchcock in both *Muriel* and *Last Year at Marienbad*.[8] It was, in fact, this connection to art cinema strategies in *The Birds* that was causing a great deal of confusion and anger among some of Hitchcock's nonauteurist followers. The public's anger with the film is traceable to the film's ambiguity on two points: its failure to supply a concrete explanation for the bird attacks and the ambiguous, Antonioni-style ending.[9] These responses are symptomatic of Hitchcock's increased distance from his mainstream audience at a moment when, in the aftermath of *Psycho*, factors would seem to point in the opposite direction. A certain expectation about a Hitchcock film is now being frustrated. It was within this context of mounting popular frustration and disappointment over Hitchcock's work that *Marnie* was released.

For Hitchcock, *Marnie* was to be a continuation of the expansion of his universe into the realm of European art cinema already begun with *The Birds*. As has often been noted, the film does have some suggestive parallels with Antonioni's *Red Desert*, released the same year (although Hitchcock was most likely not aware of this particular Antonioni film before making *Marnie*). Furthermore, *Marnie* was intended to be his response to critics who had dismissed his approach as being excessively concerned with form at the expense of psychology and characterization. Hitchcock saw the film as primarily a "character study"[10] and only secondarily a thriller, a claim that suggests that the film not only bears some relationship to European art cinema, but also to a postwar American cinema with a strong basis in psychological realism.

Unlike *The Birds*, however, *Marnie*'s critical and financial failure at the time of its release was not based on its supposedly modernist strategies or on its desired-for great psychological depth. Instead, the film was often attacked for its "old-fashioned" nature, burdened by a conventional melodramatic scenario with ties to gothic "woman's fiction."[11] Furthermore, critics felt the film possessed an archaic visual style, particularly apparent in its reliance on obvious matte work and rear projections.[12] Debates about the nature of the film's process work continue to this day.[13] All of this gave *Marnie* the aura of a slightly stale studio product at a time when the traditional Hollywood studio system itself was in its final days.

Compared to *The Thousand Eyes of Dr. Mabuse*, however, the production circumstances on *Marnie* were luxurious: A director at the height of his fame and power, given virtual carte blanche by his studio, Universal Pictures, to embark on a project quite unlike his recent successes. Whereas *The Thousand Eyes* lives in the shadow of the James Bond films that would follow it, Hitchcock was able to get James Bond himself, Sean Connery, for his male lead. (This film was made between *From Russia with Love* in 1963 and *Goldfinger* in 1964). Hitchcock began *Marnie* with the utmost enthusiasm and dedication, not only in terms of the material, but also in terms of the treatment of the film's star, Tippi Hedren, on whose performance he lavished an unprecedented amount of attention. But as is well known, by the end of the production their relationship had become extremely tense and, according to some sources, Hitchcock lost interest in the film as a result, becoming careless in the final stages of production and postproduction. Hitchcock had hoped to turn Hedren into a major star with *Marnie*. Instead, the film's failure virtually finished whatever chances she might have had for a major career.[14] After Hitchcock's death,

Truffaut maintained that the failure of *Marnie* was especially painful for Hitchcock and that he was "never the same afterwards." Truffaut ascribes this entirely to Hitchcock's falling out with Hedren.[15] The specific psychosexual details of his interest in Hedren (if they are true) are of no concern here. What is of interest is this desire to launch her as a film star and the film's enormous investment in this process. By 1964 the career Hitchcock must have envisioned for her was in many ways an anachronism, a throwback to the kind of star created in the Hollywood studios of the 1940s and 1950s. The glamour female stars beginning to emerge in the 1960s (Julie Christie, Catherine Deneuve, Monica Vitti, Jeanne Moreau, and Faye Dunaway) pointed toward a reconceived notion of glamour, one closer to "reality" in which the star's acting ability comes ready made and is not necessarily dependent on the smoke-and-mirrors manipulation of studio machinery. Hedren, a former fashion model, represented a more remote and idealized notion of femininity, a quality that specifically evoked the 1950s icon Grace Kelly, Hitchcock's original choice for the part. With the production and reception of *Marnie*, Hitchcock seemed to suffer both a private and public humiliation and one in which his integrity and relevance as a film artist were questioned.

However, Hitchcock's investment in Hedren may also be seen in relation to a postwar European art cinema that often thrived on a mythology (and one that certainly exists outside of the boundaries of this period) in which actresses served as muses to gods of inspiration behind the camera, particularly if any kind of romantic relationship existed between director and star: Antonioni and Monica Vitti, Godard and Anna Karina, Bergman and Bibi Andersson or Liv Ullmann, Fellini and Giulietta Masina. In all of these cases what we find is a director transforming an actress of previously minor standing into a major art house star. Hedren's almost total amateur standing as an actress prior to *The Birds* makes her an ideal candidate for assuming this kind of Pygmalion/Galatea fantasy role for Hitchcock.[16] But she does so within a cinema that is now attempting to give rise to a new kind of image and to join ranks with what it perceives to be a fully modern type of filmmaking. Hedren consequently finds herself much more uncomfortably poised between two kinds of cinemas—in looks, personality, and physical bearing evoking a certain kind of glamorous Hollywood star of the past while at the same time she is called on to embody a new direction in Hitchcock's work.

Seen in this light, the circumstances surrounding *Marnie* have a very seductive appeal for any Hitchcock fanatic in that the theme of "degradation for love" that recurs throughout his cinema now spills over into the mythology surrounding *Marnie*'s production.[17] The "slice of cake" that Hitchcock called his cinema suddenly becomes not so much a slice of life as a kind of unwitting form of self-exposure, one with bitter consequences. This is finally not a case of Trilby and Svengali in which the woman escapes from or destroys the powerful creator.[18] With *Marnie*, Hitchcock and Hedren go down together, destroying one another and leaving the beautiful ruin of the film behind them. Although I certainly wish to avoid a simplistic reading of *Marnie* in which Hitchcock's personal obsessions with an actress spill over into all of the film's formal excesses (especially because much of what makes the film idiosyncratic is the result of far more complex historical matters), this mythology (which is two decades old at this point and has no relationship to any of the early, groundbreaking analyses of the film) does have a certain degree of usefulness. It suggests that Hitchcock's authorial control of *Marnie* is "off," unsure of itself as it struggles within both the more traditional forms of his cinema and the new ones he is attempting to adopt. His position as authorizing agent seems unusually vulnerable here, more easily lending itself to a reading in terms of private obsessions.[19] While at the center of all of this is a woman (both the fictional character of Marnie and the real-life actress portraying her) who is the source of both a great problem and a great fascination.

In a 1968 interview, Jacques Rivette stated that near the end of shooting *L'amour fou* (1968) he and his cast and crew members went to see *Marnie* again. Rivette says, "not only did we have the feeling that Hitchcock had already filmed the whole subject of *L'amour fou* and beyond, but afterwards this vision of *Marnie* integrated itself into the film for us."[20] How is it possible that a plush studio film like *Marnie* could ever integrate itself into and implicitly move beyond Rivette's 252-minute film, part 16mm cinema verité, part 35mm psychodrama, dealing with a theatrical couple (a director and his actress wife) whose marriage breaks up in the midst of a production of *Andromeche*? Rivette does not elaborate and the two films would appear to be the product of such completely different approaches that Rivette's comment might seem mystifying. But if we turn to Rivette's review of Elia Kazan's *Splendor in the Grass*, written six years earlier, we may get a somewhat clearer idea of what he is responding to in *Marnie*. In his review of *Splendor in the Grass*, Rivette writes of this film's "stumbling, disruptive construction" through which he detects a "conflict between traditional dramatic elements and free structures." Rather than positing this as a negative, Rivette argues that Kazan's film is "a decisive step towards that fully atonal cinema adumbrated by the great films of today."[21] Fieschi sees in this review "a dream of a film" that would ultimately become *L'amour fou*, "the fruit of an impossible encounter between the two extremes of absolute control and absolute freedom."[22] What we find in *Marnie*, on the other hand, is another kind of dream and another "impossible encounter," certainly not unrelated to Rivette's but one in which the dynamic is played out differently. Here, as in almost all of Hitchcock, we find the sense of absolute control at work, the Hitchcock of the suspense film and psychological thriller in which the relations among all the formal elements of the film are rigorously thought through. But we also find here a desire for "freedom," a certain looseness of form, not one given direct expression but achieved periodically and in a somewhat cautious manner because a more direct confrontation with this kind of "freedom" might threaten to topple the very foundations on which Hitchcock's cinema are based.

Marnie is arguably the Hitchcock film that inspires the most feverishly intense cinephilic and cultlike devotion. Films such as *Rear Window* or *Psycho* are too popular and widely accepted as major Hitchcock works to achieve this status, whereas *Vertigo* has assumed such a canonical role within Hitchcock's corpus that it has long surpassed its original position as the director's major cult film. Much of the discourse surrounding *Marnie*, by contrast, is defensive in tone, alternately extolling the work's power and beauty while also feeling the need to construct a wall around the film, protecting it from any further hostile invasions. Robin Wood's proclamation on the making-of documentary on the DVD release of *Marnie* may serve as the ultimate statement in this regard: "If you don't like *Marnie* you don't really like Hitchcock. I would go further and say if you don't love *Marnie*, you don't love the cinema."

Several of Umberto Eco's notions of what constitutes cult cinema are of direct relevance to *Marnie* (as they are in different ways to all three films discussed in this book): the importance of the work's organic imperfections; the sense that the final result is beyond the conscious control of the author who has conceived it; a work so dominated by clichés and stereotypes that, rather than undercutting its effectiveness, allows the work to achieve "a glimpse of the Sublime";[23] a work that, because of its imperfect nature, is perpetually broken into, quoted, and fetishized by its admirers.[24] What is especially central here in relation to *Marnie* is this notion of the spectator breaking down the work, breaking into it, reading it in a variety of often contradictory ways. *Marnie* is a film that encourages the spectator to see it as a film of pieces so that at times it achieves a state of "glorious ricketiness"[25] far more compelling than the perfection of an accepted masterpiece. What is "in pieces" in *Marnie* is not simply this film alone but virtually all Hitchcock's cinema, which *Marnie* exhaustively calls on in its attempt to create a new kind of Hitchcock film.

An Empty Platform

Throughout the various stages of *Marnie's* preproduction phase (and long before Hedren's involvement), an image remains constant in the early treatments and screenplays (by three writers: Joseph Stefano, Evan Hunter, and Jay Presson Allen) and finds its way into the final product. This image is the one we see a variation of in the opening of the film, immediately after the credits: a woman alone, in a train station, seen only from behind, with shiny black hair, clutching a mysterious, bulging purse. This image would be gradually refined to what we have in the film now: an extremely close shot of a yellow purse, tightly held in a woman's arm, against a dark green tweed jacket. The camera tracks behind her, the two movements at one, until she picks up speed. The camera recedes and then stops until she is farther away, walking along what is now revealed to be a train station platform, suitcase in hand. She rigorously maintains a straight line down the completely empty platform, the only sound being that of her high heels clicking on the pavement. She eventually stops and we observe her in long shot in the middle of the platform. Her face is never shown. This opening has been the subject of several well-known analyses, including those of Ian Cameron and Richard Jeffrey, V. F. Perkins and, especially important for my concerns, Raymond Bellour. At the risk of redundancy and inevitable overlap, I review much of this same footage here, but in doing so I hope that some new issues will emerge.

Figure 2.1. The opening of *Marnie* (1964): Close-up.

Figure 2.2. The opening of *Marnie*: Long shot.

This shot of the purse has its obvious narrative function, immediately announcing to the spectator that what is contained within the yellow purse will be of vital concern to the narrative that follows and that the mysterious woman carrying the purse is possibly Marnie herself (a suspicion confirmed two sequences later). In some ways, this is a typical Hitchcock image, one that seems to speak directly to the spectator through the clarity of the framing, the precision in the details within the shot, and the handling of movement. Furthermore, and again typical of Hitchcock, viewer interest and curiosity are achieved through a process of contrast and relation: Between the yellow leather purse and the green tweed suit and black hair; between an apparently deserted train station and a lone figure within it; between movement and stasis; and between close-up and long shot The suddenness with which we are plunged into this first image is always startling, regardless of how many times we see the film. The camera is so close that we have no time to get our bearings. The impact is even stronger in relation to the credit sequence preceding it, which is visually barren (the credits appearing on ordinary-looking flip pages) but aurally rich and intense, alternating between Herrmann's love and madness themes, an alternation that prepares us for the close links in the film between desire and psychosis. We then move to the first postcredit shot, in which all sound abruptly drops out (except for the rhythm of the clicking heels), and we see an image of maximum intensity, one that is at the same time predicated on it being withdrawn from us as quickly as it is given. Still, something about the shot itself is a bit idiosyncratic as soon as we attempt to situate it more thoroughly within the broader context of Hitchcock's cinema.

Pascal Bonitzer has described the movement from far away to close up as Hitchcock's most characteristic device, a passage from the large picture to the small, from environment to object.[26] The opening to *Marnie* is one of the rare instances of a reversal of this process, the implications of which are especially significant here in that this image sets into motion a sustained form of reversal and displacement of many of the standard elements of Hitchcock's cinema. Bonitzer has drawn attention to the role of editing in Hitchcock and in suspense cinema in general, making distinctions between early cinema in which editing was absent or minimized, to the later development of cinema in which editing becomes increasingly pronounced. On the one hand exists an early cinema that is "innocent, joyful and dirty," and on the other exists a later cinema that is "obsessional, fetishistic and frozen." The "dirtiness" of early cinema becomes interiorized by the introduction of the gaze that in itself becomes increasingly central as the relative freedom of the gestural body in early cinema gives way to the power of the close-up and to performances that are as strongly shaped in the editing room as they are in front of the camera.[27] Although problems occur with this kind of historical argument (in particular, the way that it effectively sweeps aside an entire history of gestural cinema that takes place alongside of the cinema of the gaze), it is useful for understanding Hitchcock. Within this history, the gaze becomes strongly linked with crime and death, and Hitchcock has drawn the widest-ranging consequences of any filmmaker of his generation in this linkage between the gaze and its criminal component. Hitchcock's cinema indirectly responds to that of the Lumière brothers that, in its respect for the integrity of the pro-filmic event, "does not in fact see death" but instead "makes do with life."[28] The gaze's relationship to crime creates narrative, puts fiction into play, as opposed to the world of early cinema, where narrative has a largely sketchlike quality. A character in Hitchcock notices something off-kilter, a "stain on the landscape," within an otherwise natural (and sometimes quite storybook-like) setting. Occasionally (and particularly in the color films), this stain is literalized, as in *The Man Who Knew Too Much* (1956) when the dark makeup that covers the face of Louis Bernard (disguised as an Arab) is smeared onto Ben McKenna's hands as the murdered Bernard falls to the ground. But most often the stain is simply an object or prop whose natural use is "perverted" in some way, turned against its normal functioning.[29]

If Hitchcock's cinema indirectly responds to that of the Lumière brothers, the opening shot of *Marnie* may be seen as an indirect response to one of the Lumière brothers' most famous films, *Arrival of a Train at*

La Ciotat (1895).[30] Both Hitchcock and the Lumières take their cameras to train stations and film their respective actions in a single shot. The Lumières film from a static camera position and, in effect, let life take over as the train follows its normal schedule, stops at the station, and the passengers disembark. The very simplicity of this method of filming reinforces the sense of life captured spontaneously. In certain versions of this film (as in their factory film, more than one exists) some of the passengers notice the camera and briefly stop and return the camera's gaze before, in some cases, clearly being told to move on by an off-camera presence (most likely by one of the Lumière brothers). Here, the gaze upsets the reality effect, threatens to draw attention to the presence of the camera, thereby in effect preventing the sense of a spontaneous event being seized.[31]

What we find in *Marnie* is a form of double inversion in which not only the logic of the Lumière film is resisted but also the logic of much of Hitchcock's own cinema prior to this. Hitchcock begins his film in close-up before we can completely see the surrounding space. The camera aggressively forces our attention on an object that is attached to a body we are only permitted to see part of before the camera is willing to

Figure 2.3. Lumière's *Arrival of a Train at La Ciatot* (1895): A crowded train station.

let go of this body and the object it is holding. Even by the end of the shot, when we see Marnie's body in its entirety, we see only the back of her; the sense that the camera is withholding something from us in relation to her remains very strong. Where the Lumière film shows us a train station overflowing with bodies as they disembark, move about the platform, and eventually exit the frame, Hitchcock's train station is empty with the trains all at a standstill in an ominously quiet station. Marnie seems to be utterly alone in an environment as uncannily depopulated as the town Sandro and Claudia stumble on in *L'avventura* (1960). In an earlier sequence in that Antonioni film, Claudia, like Marnie, walks down a train platform. But in comparison with Hitchcock's film, Claudia is surrounded with a greater sense of activity than Marnie, and the shot itself belongs to a realm somewhere between the Lumière films and Hitchcock's. She moves much more freely than Hitchcock's heroine, and she walks toward the camera and not away from it.[32]

As with *The Thousand Eyes of Dr. Mabuse, Marnie* creates a world that often seems to be without a strong sense of organic life.[33] Unlike Lang's film, however, *Marnie* looks both plush and austere, a hothouse plant of a film. Set primarily in Philadelphia, Baltimore, and the surrounding areas, it often lacks a strong and consistent sense of verisimilitude. As has sometimes been noted, both visually and in terms of the social behavior of some of the characters and in some of the performances, the film often seems to be set in a displaced English world (partly traceable to the English setting of Winston Graham's source

Figure 2.4. Michelangelo Antonioni's *L'avventura* (1960): An empty train station.

novel) rather than an eastern Atlantic one with sequences revolving around afternoon tea rituals or ridings of the hounds and with a miscast (albeit charismatic and attractive) leading man, whose Scottish accent repeatedly interrupts his attempts at portraying an upper-class Philadelphian.[34] In this film of a woman in constant flight, inhabiting deserted train stations, going on loveless honeymoon cruises, and riding a horse as it gallops on a moving platform in the studio, movement itself becomes abstract and formalized.

In its brief running time, the Lumière film constantly suggests an organic world, not only the one directly in front of the camera, but also in the offscreen space to the left, right, and bottom of the frame as well as at the extreme rear of the shot (a landscape). In contrast, the opening shot of *Marnie* suggests a closed world, which alludes to nothing substantive or alive on any sides of the frame. It is not simply that Hitchcock's single shot employs camera movement and the Lumière film does not, especially because the movement in the Hitchcock film is not substantial. Rather, it is a question of placement and framing, of staging of action, of the strong sense of portions of the image being sectioned off, of attention being directed, and of the sense of the spectator being addressed by the image.

The notable Hitchcock camera movements prior to this one from *Marnie* that take us from environment to object all convey a similar kind of message: Within this vast, seemingly anonymous space with everyone going about their business oblivious to any kind of disorder, is an object or an element of some kind that threatens the illusory harmony of this environment. The yellow purse in *Marnie* does fit into this tradition in some ways. The tightness of the close-up on the purse immediately announces to the spectator that this purse is also something else, assuming a function much larger than what a normal handbag ever would, and the vivid yellowness of the bag against the green tweed jacket and the blackness and grayness of the entire space of the train station creates a staining-like effect, reinforcing the sense of its perverted role. But the fact that Hitchcock begins the film by showing us the object in close-up before pulling back to show the environment surrounding it also suggests that the notion of the stain on the landscape is itself undergoing a shift. Rather than showing us a natural world against which the perverse object emerges, in the opening of *Marnie* Hitchcock *begins* with the stain before pulling back to show us the world around it. What we finally see is not a natural world that is oblivious to the stain, but a world in which the stain does not hold the same intensity of contrast it once did for Hitchcock.[35] Is this why the film not only contains instances of literal staining within its diegetic world (black hair dye insinuating itself into the water of a bathroom sink, drops of red ink accidentally spilled onto Marnie's white blouse, the blood soaking the white t-shirt of the sailor the child Marnie kills) but also the subjective red suffusions that periodically fill the frame whenever Marnie sees that color? It is as though the stain is not simply within the diegesis, but has begun to spill over onto the very surface of the image itself.

This is a film, then, of intense surfaces of which its controversial use of "bad" rear projections and "faulty" matte work is especially symptomatic. Although finding a Hitchcock aficionado who is not fond of this obviously artificial production and postproduction work is increasingly difficult today, *Marnie* has occupied a particularly crucial position in relation to the rear projection and matte work controversy, and the film separates the Hitchcock diehards from the dilettantes. Purely in terms of technical execution, *Marnie* is no more obvious and (to my eyes, at least) no cruder in its use of similar devices found in *The Birds*, *North by Northwest*, or the 1956 version of *The Man Who Knew Too Much* and appreciably *better* from a technical and expressive standpoint than what can be found in *Notorious*, *Spellbound*, or the 1934 version of *The Man Who Knew Too Much*. Why would these devices be such a problem for many spectators (and most critics) on *Marnie* and not on these other, more popular films? The most obvious explanation would be that these devices were falling out of fashion by 1964 and that this, combined with *Marnie's* perceived old-fashioned scenario, reinforced the strong sense of anachronism. Hitchcock's inability to see that anything was wrong with these shots during the production of the film cannot simply be attributed to his indifference to the final result. More likely he did not see that anything was wrong with these shots because, within the logic of his own filmmaking system, there is nothing wrong with them. They convey the necessary information (she is very happy riding a horse, she is very upset when sees red) while maintaining a balance between fluidity and abstraction, surface and depth, realism and artifice, which is at the heart of his cinema.[36] Numerous films (Hollywood and otherwise) made throughout the 1960s relied on traditional rear projection and matte work, often in a perfunctory manner. (See, for example, Don Siegel's deadpan, almost pop-art use of rear projections in his remake of *The Killers*, also shot at Universal in 1964.) One major difference in the case of *Marnie* is that Hitchcock is asking these "archaic" devices to serve a strongly expressive function, hence the quality of historical dislocation, of an emotional excess bordering on kitsch.

But another reason may exist why this process work has caused problems. *Marnie* travels across several locations on the East Coast (and contains an extended sequence on an ocean liner), but its first unit footage is shot almost entirely in the studio. In comparison with most of Hitchcock's films of the 1950s and early 1960s it stands in contrast to either the more rigorous use of studio work in *Dial M for Murder* (1953) and *Rear Window* or the mix of location and studio work found in all of the other films up through *The Birds*. The few exterior shots used here are done rather hastily and the film does not exhibit the strong sense of place that much of Hitchcock's work of the 1950s and 1960s does. The blatant use of studio work and the film's apparent lack of interest in masking these technical devices to make them appear seamless within the film's continuity boldly announces that the natural world's relation to the artificial and the perverse, a tension so central in much of Hitchcock's work prior to *Marnie*, is being overtaken by a more insular world, a more fully stained environment that, as Truffaut told Hitchcock, is "stifling, a little like a nightmare."[37]

Coming through the Door How?

If Lang resists a capitulation to the conventions of the secret beyond the door by intensifying it to such an extreme degree that the possibility of ultimately uncovering secrets is frustrated, Hitchcock's simultaneous fascination with and resistance to this trope takes another route. Examples of Hitchcock's fascination with the closed door abound: the door to Rebecca's bedroom to which the nameless heroine is drawn, the locked door to the wine cellar in *Notorious*, the door to the cellar where the corpse of Norman's mother is kept in *Psycho*, or the door to Cathy's bedroom which Melanie, Pandora-like, cannot resist opening in *The Birds*. In spite of this apparent fascination with the closed door, however, it is equally central to Hitchcock's cinema that the doors (and windows) of his universe be perpetually poised between the open and the closed. As he said once, "I am from the Man Comes through a Door How? school of dramaturgy."[38] The primary interest in Hitchcock does not reside in whether the protagonist will ever gain access to the secret beyond the door. That is virtually a given. Instead, the question is how the protagonist will interpret what he sees once he has crossed that threshold because in Hitchcock the door which metaphorically presides so often over his cinema is that of the mind itself. In *Spellbound* we find this realized in an almost parodic form in which a continuous equation of the door exists as a metaphor for the mind with the film stressing the necessity for opening the "locked door" of the neurotic psyche as key to achieving a properly functioning mental state. The great love scene of the film is an image of John Ballantine kissing Constance Petersen for the first time, an extreme close-up of her eyes closing shut dissolves to a Surrealist-influenced image of a series of doors opening.[39] In Hitchcock, the world must be visible and seemingly transparent before the mind is called on to interpret what it is seeing.[40] Hitchcock's work has a repeated emphasis on a position (sometimes a voyeuristic one but not exclusively that) of seeing from just slightly outside of the essential situation—close enough to see almost everything, but far enough away to create the necessity for interpretation. Even in a gothic melodrama such as *Under Capricorn* (1949), with its mysterious mansion of Minyago Yugilla, we find not so much a world of locked doors as one in which the doors and windows to the mansion are open, fully allowing for Charles Adare to observe all the activities taking place from a view immediately outside of the house. We get a repetition of this in *Marnie* as Lil (Diane Baker) looks down at Marnie and Mark from her bedroom window, eavesdropping on their conversation. Even when a door is closed in the film Lil is able to stand outside of it and listen in on Marnie's telephone conversation with her mother. The knowledge of a character or of the spectator is almost invariably partial (or there may even be a complete misinterpretation of what has been shown). But the elements of narrative interest, suspense, and surprise are frequently determined by how this dynamic of knowledge and interpretation is played out across the length of the film.

Figure 2.5. *Spellbound* (1945): The doors of the mind (and of desire) opening.

This question of interpretation is central to Deleuze's argument that Hitchcock's development of the "mental image" allows him to be seen as either "the last of the classic directors, or the first of the moderns."[41] The mental image is a particular type of sign around which thought and interpretation circulates, framing and transforming the perceptions, actions, and affections of classical cinema rather than simply existing as autonomous entities within a causal chain of events. Working out of Charles Peirce's notions of thirdness as key for defining the philosophical tradition of relations, Deleuze writes that it is Hitchcock who introduces the notion of relations-through-thirdness into the cinema. Within thirdness we find not so much actions as symbolic acts in which we see a continual emphasis on interpretation and intellectual relations, on giving and exchanging in which crimes are not so much performed for the benefit and satisfaction of the criminal, but rather implicitly "offered up" to someone else.[42] A "perpetual tripling" is found in the structure of Hitchcock's films with relationships between characters often conceived in terms of triangles. These triangles are not simply romantic ones (although they often occur and even sometimes serve as a precondition for the element of thirdness). Virtually all relations between two characters will involve a crucial third partner who establishes a relation rather than the simple coupling, duel or doubling so central to classical cinema (as discussed in chapter 1). We find this repeated in *Marnie* in which virtually all of the major relations in the film are defined in terms of triangularity: Marnie/Mark/Lil; Marnie/Mrs. Edgar/Jessie; Marnie/Mark/Mrs. Edgar. Tripling in Hitchcock likewise spills over into objects, perceptions, and affections, creating a cinematic world in which "all is interpretation, from beginning to end."[43] Furthermore, thirdness in Hitchcock also serves to redefine the role of the spectator who becomes much more strongly implicated in the film's unfolding. In Hitchcock, characters frequently are spectators themselves, caught up in the chain of fascination over the relations being represented along with the viewers of the film.[44] The task of implicating the spectator in the sets of relations at the same time that the characters metaphorically become spectators results in a conception of the image that repeatedly seems to be examining its own operations. The element of thirdness creates a strong sense that the narrative is taking place under an almost constant field of perception, moving from the looks (and interpretations) of the characters, to the camera, to the spectator.

Throughout Hitchcock's work, the face (particularly in close-up) is a privileged vehicle through which thought and interpretation are articulated, faces that "do nothing extremely well," but through montage signify a wealth of emotion.[45] At the beginning of *Marnie*, however, we do not see our protagonist's face but the back of her head. We do not have a Hitchcock cool blonde here but a brunette. We must wait for this face and for the blonde hair, both of which are unveiled at the same moment. Why this withholding? As a potential star-making vehicle for Hedren, this opening shot is consistent with a tradition throughout film history of withholding the appearance of the star's face as long as possible, delaying the moment of unveiling, particularly if the face itself will become the site of some of the film's fundamental concerns. But this shot in *Marnie* exceeds both its relationship to the star system and to its more mundane narrative purpose. Throughout the film, Marnie's face will become a central terrain on which the camera will turn its fascinated gaze while her hair undergoes numerous changes as well, not only in terms of color, but also in terms of style. Both face and hair often become the indices of Marnie's fundamental elusiveness as a protagonist. A view of Marnie's face is withheld at the beginning of the film; her hair is the "wrong" color because the film has a different agenda for what it is attempting to do in relation to the face.

This results in Hitchcock having as his protagonist someone whose relationship to this cinema of interpretation is no longer stable. Marnie's stealing is a clearn symptom of something the source of which she does not know or understand. Her facial expressions and all of her activities that animate the narrative are nevertheless contaminated with her enigmatic visions, particularly those revolving around the color red. The film is split between these visions, the more mundane tracing of her thoughts through the point-of-view shot and the latter of these most often centering on the theft of money and changing of identities. Both of these looks, which are at the center of the film's operation, intensify the sense of displacement that runs throughout *Marnie* and to the sense that Hitchcock is here attempting to render visible what is, in fact, invisible. This invisible something is a mind that records and observes but does not fully understand and does not even primarily wish to but instead acts on unconscious desires. The operation of thought so vital to Hitchcock's cinema is present in a "neurotic" state here. She is not drawn by her visions but subject to them, so that when her vision is at its most acute, it does not take us closer into the heart of relations comprising the film but instead becomes an enigma. Mental processes are secondary in *Marnie* to the recording of a mental state that is blocked, unable to fully process, epitomized by the close-ups of Marnie whenever she sees the color red. As with so many of the close-ups of her face throughout the film, the face that we see is neither devoid of expression nor strongly marked by it, but poised somewhere between the expressive and the inexpressive.[46]

In this regard, the film is part of a tradition of postwar American and European cinema in which the face of the protagonist is marked by its inability or refusal to be expressive in any conventional sense. This tradition would include everything from the face of the boy in *Germany, Year Zero*, to the title character of *Gertrud*, to many of the actors who inhabit the films of directors as varied as Preminger, Bresson, and Georges Franju. These are faces that have exhausted their traditional ability to signify thought and emotion and instead become beautiful blanks onto which the spectator may project a multiplicity of meaning and emotion— or none at all.[47] If, as noted in chapter 1, the metaphoric figure of Mabuse seems to preside hypnotically over the cinema's first fifty years of existence, in the second half of the century of the cinema's development characters increasingly seem to behave as though they are engaged in forms of autohypnosis, their faces connoting states between alertness and sleepwalking. Literal hypnosis may sometimes exist along the margins of the film, as with the psychologist in *Gertrud* who speaks of the hypnosis he engages in with other psychologists, or Sèverine's confusing a magician with a hypnotist in Luis Buñuel's *Belle de jour* (1967), refusing to submit to the powers of the latter. Hypnosis may even be directly cited in a manner that is ironic but still does not completely discredit the hypnotic impulse, as in Fellini's *Nights of Cabiria* (1957) and *Juliet of the Spirits* (1965). The power of the hypnotic metaphor in relation to the filmed image, then, persists. But characters in this "new" cinema seemingly no longer require the intermediary of a Mabuse, and they may now simply behave as though they inherently embody the power of the mesmerizing filmed image through their movements, gestures, and facial expressions. However resistant Hitchcock's cinema may have been prior to this in terms of the hypnotic metaphor, *Marnie* partially belongs to this development (and certainly the mythology of Hitchcock's own Svengali-like behavior on the set of the film in relation to Hedren serves to reinforce this connection). The dreamlike, sleepwalking nature of Madeleine in *Vertigo* was finally only a pose, an act performed by a woman, Judy, who could not be more physical and earthbound. Marnie much more strongly exists as a character connected to mental states that operate beyond the rational and intellectual. (Her favorite racehorse is named Telepathy.)

Early in his career, Hitchcock treated hypnosis and the world of the paranormal, so central to Lang as both subject matter and in terms of his conception of the image, in only the most cursory manner. Hitchcock's spectators, whatever manipulations they are subjected to in the process of viewing, must function not as hypnotic subjects under the power of a presiding figure, but rather feel themselves to be continuously alert. Hitchcock asserts his authorial presence as strongly as Lang. But his inclusion of the spectator in the process of putting the film together as it unfolds is far removed from Lang's insistence on his authority (however sometimes ambivalently articulated) over his own images. Furthermore,

Hitchcock seldom shows any of Lang's fascination with large technological and ideological systems of vision and control. Although ultimately identifying with Lang's authorial position is possible, this cannot take place until one has seen the film in its entirety and then gone back and looked at it again. It is then that one is able to perceive the film's massive structure and take note of the knowledge that has been withheld from the spectator until the film's conclusion. Hitchcock, on the other hand, invites the spectator's participation on a first viewing. Knowledge is often withheld here as well (without it we have no suspense, no tension between the seen and unseen, between the known and unknown), but Hitchcock's attention to focalization and his complex use of identification and point-of-view works to mask what ever withholding does take place. The imaginary sense that the spectator is creating the film alongside of Hitchcock and that we are encouraged to identify not only with certain characters but also with Hitchcock-as-author gives the films a sense of frisson far removed from the systems of power and looking at work in Lang. Hitchcock's conception of the image is essentially nonparanoid. As Godard wrote in his review of *The Man Who Knew Too Much*, Hitchcock believes in destiny, but he does so "with a smile on his lips, [and] it is the smile that convinces me."[48]

One may see this sensibility as a profoundly English one, repeatedly drawn to irony, paradox and contrast.[49] Irony in Hitchcock establishes a form of critical distance, allowing for a foregrounding of the formal properties of cinema, one that establishes Hitchcock's authorial presence as both "serious" (in the rigorous attention to form and detail) and ironic (the frequent sense of formal playfulness, perfectly encapsulated in his cameo appearances). "Irony," writes Hayden White, "does not seek the ultimate metaphor, the metaphor of metaphors. . . . Irony tends in the end to turn upon word play, to become a language about language, so as to dissolve the bewitchment of consciousness caused by language itself."[50] Charles Barr has noted that such concerns with the operation of language itself are central to British cinema, which is full of examples of metacinema. He sees in British cinema a split between "modes of observation and interiority, of transparency and self-reflexivity, of sobriety and excess."[51]

However, by the early 1960s questions of interpretation and indeed many of the fundamental organizing principles of Hitchcock's cinema begin to be addressed in different ways. In *Psycho*, *The Birds*, and *Marnie* we see an increased lack of certainty in terms of how the characters should be interpreting what they see. *Psycho's* investigation in its second half, in which the answer to the mystery of Norman Bates and the question of Marion Crane's murder are divided among five characters (Sam, Lila, Arbogast, Sheriff Chambers, and the psychiatrist), represents a perverse reworking of the typical handling of such a process in Hitchcock's earlier films.[52] Throughout *The Birds*, the protagonists are continually engaged in acts of interpretation in terms of interpersonal relations among themselves. But the central crisis for the characters—and the central formal audacity of the film itself—is how these protagonists are unable to comprehend the reason for the bird attacks. The characters come up against a great, terrifying nothingness that blocks interpretation. Very much in the style of *L'avventura*, *The Birds* simply trails off at its conclusion, refusing to bring the moral journey the protagonists undertook to a fully rounded sense of closure in relation to the central narrative crisis.

Marnie presents a different set of problems in this regard. Certainly *Marnie* initially appears to be a film in which the structures of melodramatic and classical narrative are more in evidence than in *The Birds*. As Raymond Durgnat notes, *Marnie* is a film "preoccupied with secrets, with emotional refusals, with the past, with invisibles."[53] The film even periodically draws on the secret beyond the door trope, as does *Psycho* and *The Birds*: The taps at the door of the clients who come to visit the young Mrs. Edgar the adult Marnie repeatedly hears in her nightmares, displacing them as taps at the window, which function as one of the fundamental enigmas of the film until the resolution; and the ominous image of Mrs. Edgar's silhouette, positioned within the frame of the open bedroom door, links this sense of secrets and enigmas being tied to the door itself. "It's always when you come to the door," Marnie tells her mother as the mother awakens her from the nightmare, "That's when the cold starts." But while the film restores the explanatory resolution, reaching a state of closure and confirmation that *The Birds* resists, it continues on with the structure of displacement found in *Psycho* although here it occurs in a different manner.

As in *Psycho*, we find a displaced handling of the process of investigation even though the film restores certain more classical methods of uncovering. Mark handles the bulk of the investigation into Marnie's past rather than being split among five characters (although he is forced to rely on an unseen professional detective who discovers information about Marnie's past.) He is present at the film's resolution and helps Marnie to remember finally the traumatic event that led to her pathological state: her murdering the sailor client of her prostitute mother when Marnie was a child. The end of the film offers a tentative suggestion that Marnie is on the road to mental recovery and that her marriage to Mark will continue and perhaps even become a "real" marriage. But the film does not fully conform to either of the two primary modalities of investigation that dominate Hitchcock's pre-1960 cinema. In one, the protagonist attempts to uncover a secret (most often revolving around the question of mistaken identity) that has thrown his or her life into a state of crisis. Through the process of uncovering this secret, the protagonist enters into a romantic relationship of some kind and "grows up," ready to face adult hetero-sexual relations by the end of the film. In the other, an investigation takes place but the protagonist is denied full access to it and the uncovering most often occurs through the intervention of a third party.[54]

In *Marnie*, we find stray aspects of the second modality of investiga-tion through the presence of Lil. But this goes no further than Lil discov-ering one of Marnie's former employers, Strutt (a character from Marnie's past with whom the audience is already familiar, causing the audience to be ahead of Lil on this point), and presenting him at a party to Marnie's acute distress. It is this return of Strutt, however, which traumatizes Marnie and indirectly causes the death of her horse, Forio: Marnie undergoes an emo-tional crisis during a hunt at the Rutland estate on the morning after her attempted escape the night before, a crisis causing her to panic and forcing the horse to make a bad jump over a fence, fatally injuring him. This loss of her horse precipitates Marnie's almost total breakdown and renders her especially vulnerable to unlock her repressed memory. The film establishes the strong potential for Lil as a detective figure but then transfers this to Mark, who completes the investigation. Lil drops out of sight with neither her investigatory capacity fulfilled nor her function as a secondary female character hopelessly in love with the male protagonist ever permitted to play out its triangular function.[55] But this investigation is significantly post-poned in the film in that Mark's initial pursuit of Marnie is based purely around his fetishistic attraction for her as a thief while the "real" investi-gation initiated by one of her former employers, Strutt (and which could lead to Marnie being sent to prison), is delayed.

Hence the curious scene at the racetrack in which a man begins to harass Marnie about one of her possible identities as Peggy Nicholson. This incident is never referred to later nor is the name Peggy Nicholson ever again cited. The use of *Peggy* equally suggests that the man is mis-taken (since all of Marnie's other aliases begin with the letter M) or that he is right after all because Peggy is a nickname for Margaret, Marnie's real name, and that he met her in Detroit, one of the cities in which she later admits to committing robberies. The scene's narrative function largely appears to be one of providing a sense of urgency to the possibility of Marnie being pursued for her crimes, a situation that would not other-wise manifest itself due to the long delaying of Mark as investigator, a structural "problem" of which Hitchcock was well aware.[56] But the most interesting aspect to the sequence occurs in relation to its appendage-like presence, a clear sign of the film's difficulties in fully committing itself to the process of traditional investigation.

"I've often wondered," Hitchcock said to Truffaut, "whether I could do a suspense story within a looser form, in a form that's not so tight." Truffaut's response is that he feels Hitchcock has already experimented along those lines. Hitchcock then briefly turns the discussion to *Marnie*, whose story he feels is looser because it is driven by character as much as story while at the same time the more traditional "rising curve of interest" in narrative structure is still present.[57] In the case of *Marnie*, Hitchcock returns to a more conventional narrative with its "rising curve of interest" in relation to the central narrative enigmas of the film: Why does Marnie steal? What is the sexual problem she has in relation to men touching her?[58] The film ultimately supplies us with firm answers to both of these questions. But even with these answers given and a more classical sense of closure achieved, *Marnie* not only continues with the structural deviations of the two previous films, but also draws on and then reworks so many elements of Hitchcock's cinema that it may be seen as a "perverse" testament film.[59] The dialogue between Hitchcock and Truffaut on *Marnie* is indicative of the formal tensions at work in the film, as the two men alternately point out the flaws and defend certain aspects of *Marnie*. The film's looseness also results in what both men perceive to be structural errors: problems in story construction and character motivation and a rather hasty sense of compression in a film that seems to be trying to do too much.[60] All of this suggests a film that is not simply loose structurally, but a bit all over the map.

Of course Hitchcock's films have always been, quite literally, all over the map, dominated by narrative trajectories that take the protagonists out of their usual surroundings, thrown into situations beyond their control, across the landscapes of new and dangerous environments. Hitchcock's protagonists are fundamentally travelers, either by profession, choice (as tourists), or imposition, and the films often concern themselves with tracing a journey that is as much mental as physical. The journey becomes a kind of testing of the moral strength and integrity of the protagonists, most often played out through the formation of the couple. During the postwar period, however, what these protagonists begin to witness on their travels is a world that indirectly reflects back on their own mental states and perceptions and one in which the couple is increasingly marked by its troubled nature. In *Marnie*, we find this traveling protagonist once again as the series of jobs Marnie temporarily holds takes her to several East Coast locations in which she repeatedly changes her name and physical appearance. But the nature of this journey and how Marnie comes to form a romantic relationship with Mark Rutland are marked by some crucial changes. In *Marnie*, the movement from place to place occurs neither through direct physical action nor through the protagonist being caught up in events determined by their relationship to other forces and through events to which she must respond. Although Marnie does initiate actions through the various thefts, she also sets into motion a structure and a set of relations and movements marked by their highly displaced and "perverse" element. This results in making *Marnie* both a typical Hitchcock film (in that many of the basic structuring elements from his previous work are present here) and an atypical one (in that they are positioned in a much more idiosyncratic manner).

Perversions and Displacements

As noted, when *Marnie* opened, some of the criticism was based on the film's ties to gothic melodrama and the woman's film. In the aftermath of the historicizing of melodrama that has taken place since the 1970s, this "limitation" is no longer so apparent. Within this context, *Marnie* may partly be seen as a late variation on certain types of 1940s female-centered melodramas, often with an overt or implied psychoanalytic framework. But *Marnie* also clearly wants to be something more, to draw on some of melodrama's elements to create another example of this "new" kind of 1960s Hitchcock film. As we shall see, the film's relationship to the woman's film is not by any means aberrant within the context of sixties art house cinema.

Far from simply duplicating these generic forms, *Marnie* reworks certain components of what Mary Ann Doane has called "the medical discourse" film. Here we find a protagonist (usually a woman) who is mentally disturbed. Some sort of childhood trauma, long repressed, severely affects her mental and sexual development, its cause often traceable to an individual (most often a family member or some kind of parental figure, in *Marnie* the impoverished mother who had worked as a prostitute) and in which a single traumatic event often precipitates the neurosis (as in the mother's murder of the sailor). Her mental illness may be manifested in several ways, alternately or variously expressed through a life of crime, sometimes through a physical illness, sometimes through a total lack of interest in her appearance. A psychoanalyst, who also often functions as a lover or husband, investigates the source of this trauma, unlocks the repression, and leads the protagonist on the path to a well-adjusted life. The process of analysis is often eroticized and the woman eventually gives up her life of crime, or dies a beautiful death, or takes an interest in becoming attractive as part of the process of joining or rejoining society.[61] In *Marnie*, Mark assumes this role of psychotherapist as the film collapses his role as both husband of a persecuted wife and a nurturing romantic-partner-as-psychotherapist, although here his psychiatric skills are strictly amateur. In the medical discourse films, the body of the female protagonist assumes a central role in that it plays out a dialectic of surface and depth in relation to her mental illness. The male therapist in the medical discourse film is able to break through surface appearances and discover the essence of the woman underneath. The female protagonist's body is a "symptomatic" one in which "the visible becomes fully a signifier, pointing to an invisible signified."[62] The process of analysis makes visible what is otherwise hidden, the heroine's essential goodness, sanity and beauty: "The doctor's work is the transformation of the woman into a specular object."[63]

Marnie retains clear links with this strain. But in significant ways it also deviates from it. Marnie's central anxiety is ultimately located through a trauma that took place in her prostitute mother's apartment when Marnie accidentally murdered a client, an incident she repressed and one to which her mother never referred afterward. After the murder (for which the mother took the blame), Mrs. Edgar (Louise Latham) became devoutly religious but emotionally distant from her daughter as a result of Marnie's association with the mother's past, a distance that acutely manifests itself for Marnie in Mrs. Edgar's dislike of touching her. The centrality of the mother/daughter relationship as the culminating moment in unlocking the key to the narrative's central mystery strongly links *Marnie* with the earlier medical discourse films.

In *Marnie*, the tensions between the mother and daughter are established in a lengthy sequence in the mother's house early in the film. Even on a first viewing of the film, the mother's home clearly potentially contains the source of Marnie's problems: For the first time, we see her anxiety over the color red (when she spots the flowers on the television set) and that she has recurring nightmares in (and possibly in relation to) the space of the bedroom of her mother's house. But the film does not place this situation at the forefront of its narrative structure and instead transfers its interest afterward to the romance between Mark and Marnie. The mother disappears from the narrative afterward and does not return until the final sequence. By contrast, a more traditional medical discourse film such as Irving Rapper's *Now, Voyager* (1942) frequently returns to the mother's home (where the protagonist Charlotte lives) and Charlotte's gradual cure (which her psychiatrist initiated) is played out in several confrontations with her mother in which Charlotte begins to triumph over her mother's tyranny. In *Now, Voyager*, the woman's cure and her newfound emotional happiness apart from her mother provide the spectator with a more conventional sense of pleasure as we watch a victim triumph over her tormentor. After the death of her mother, Charlotte turns her mother's home into a positive social environment, giving the kinds of informal parties that would have horrified her straitlaced mother.

Marnie resists this temptation toward narrativizing the heroine's cure (especially because Charlotte's symptoms are less extreme than Marnie's and never manifest themselves in terms of criminal behavior), displacing the mother/daughter relationship from the narrative no sooner than it has established it.[64] Furthermore, a secondary displacement occurs in the film even when it returns to the mother's home at the end. The source of Marnie's neurosis does not lie within the mother's home, but in a small apartment the two of them shared in the past where Marnie murdered her mother's client. This type of melodrama traditionally insists on decor and the home as a physical externalization of the psychological dilemmas of the characters, an extension of the function of the castle or mansion in the gothic. As Peter Brooks notes, such a labyrinthine space becomes "an architectural approximation of the Freudian model of the mind, particularly the traps laid for the conscious by the unconscious and the repressed."[65] The fact that Marnie returns to a space that we initially believe to be associated with the traumatized heroine's past only for the film to tell us (through the visual evidence of Marnie's reawakened memory) that the key event from this past physically took place elsewhere is to invert a central process by which the woman-centered melodrama operates. The film lacks additional closure on this level because the heroine's cure does not take place within the space that initiated her trauma. Unlike most heroines of the woman's film, Marnie is defined in opposition to domestic space rather than through it.

Marnie also combines these variations on the persecuted-wife film with another type of female-centered melodrama of the period, the persecuted-wife melodrama of which Hitchcock's own *Rebecca* serves as the early prototype and of which both Minnelli's *Undercurrent* (1946) and Lang's *Secret Beyond the Door* are especially interesting later examples. This particular cycle of melodrama reached a peak of popularity in the 1940s, and Hitchcock made use of it on three later occasions during this decade: *Suspicion* (1941), *Notorious*, and *Under Capricorn*. Several aspects to the persecuted wife melodrama are crucial: (1) an insistence on a privileging of the heroine's point of view[66]; (2) an emphasis on the marriage, which takes place between the heroine and her new husband as one of impulse in which the heroine ultimately knows very little about the man she has just married; (3) the marriage itself is often based on strong class differences in which the woman is usually of lower-class origin who then marries into a much higher class; (4) once married, the man turns out to have a dark secret, which the heroine attempts to uncover and in the process of detective work her own life and mental well being are at stake;

and finally (5) within the home we often see a rival for the heroine, someone who has jealous and potentially murderous designs on her.[67]

Marnie's reworking of these elements is strongly bound up with the intervening years since the peak of the cycle's popularity in the 1940s. No longer is the heroine's point of view strongly privileged in Marnie. Although this point of view is still important, it enters into a much broader shifting network of relations. These relations are established through the act of looking and, equally central, through the role of knowledge and who is most firmly in possession of it. Central here is not only Marnie, but also Mark, Lil, Strutt, and Mrs. Edgar, the last of these being the one who ultimately knows, as she puts it, "the whole story." The film retains the class differences between husband and wife along with the device of the impulsive marriage. But the nature of the trauma for Marnie is not a dark secret that she discovers about Mark but rather that he will discover her dark secret in terms of her sexual problems (found out quickly enough on their wedding night) and her relationship with her mother. The impulsiveness of the marriage is not a sudden and intense attraction between the man and woman but something Mark put into action against Marnie's will. Instead of Marnie being the detective, Mark and Lil assume this function while Lil herself plays a less sinister version of the rival for the husband's affections. Mark retains only traces of the husband with the dark and violent secret, primarily through his insufficiently realized fetishistic attraction for a woman who is a compulsive thief. Furthermore, this hardly constitutes a dark secret for the heroine to uncover because Marnie herself is fully aware of this attraction Mark has for her. Not only is Mark not defined in terms of a dark past, but he is also repeatedly characterized as someone who resists the grip that such a past might have on him. He expresses no sadness over the destruction of the pre-Columbian art his dead wife collected that is destroyed during a storm even though these are the only items that had belonged to his wife that were still in his possession. He has not even a trace of melancholia. The strongest link Mark has with his brooding gothic predecessors is the action he performs during the infamous honeymoon sequence in which he rapes Marnie. This sequence will be dealt with in detail later. For now, however, the violent impulsiveness of this act may be seen as an unexpectedly manifested late symptom of Mark's relationship to the dark husband figure of the persecuted woman melodrama.

In Marnie, Wyckwyn Manor is a place where she is essentially held against her will. "It's not a house of correction," Mark tells her, but that is precisely how she experiences it. In this manner, the film appears to be a simple extension of the female gothic in which the home into which the heroine is taken becomes the source of psychological and sometimes physical violence. (Manderly in *Rebecca* is a contemporary updating of this.) But there is something particularly barren about Wyckwyn Manor. Unlike Manderly, it does not seem to have the weight of the past on it but exists as a shell of a gothic mansion, stripped down. When Marnie enters her bedroom for the first time, several point-of-view shots as she looks around the room define the space for her in terms of its remoteness and impersonality: empty cabinets and dressers, bare furnishings, a space without a past (we see no signs of Mark's first wife anywhere, he appears to have stripped the place of all of her belongings) or a future (Marnie does not belong here). Atypically for the protagonist of a woman's film, she is defined in terms of wandering, in this regard anticipating the title character of a more self-consciously modernist woman's film such as Chantal Akerman's *Les Rendez-vous d'Anna* (1978) with its own pivotal train station sequences, as much as she looks back to *Rebecca* or *Under Capricorn*. Domestic spaces become traumatic sites for Marnie in that they always exist in relation to absence, to a space apart from her mind rather than an extension of it. In writing of the Rio de Janeiro house of Alex Sebastian in *Notorious*, Bonitzer argues that the set of a Hitchcock film is invariably designed as a "labyrinth in which everyone—characters, director, and audience—loses and finds themselves, in the intensity of their emotions."[68] But in *Marnie*, no central setting is defined in this way. The key space for the heroine (the apartment in which she murdered her mother's client) is one that exists repressed in her memory and even after that memory is uncovered it refers to a space to which Marnie does not physically return.

Although Marnie's body here is indeed a symptomatic one, her process of analysis and transformation takes place in reverse of her 1940s predecessors. Marnie is a specular object from the very beginning of the film, presenting herself as such to men. She does not gain in physical attractiveness as analysis takes place but, by the end of the film, seems to lose interest in her physical appearance entirely. After the death of her beloved horse Forio, she suffers a type of breakdown, unsuccessfully attempts to rob from the Rutland safe before Mark drags her off to Baltimore to confront her mother about her past. Throughout these sequences, she is wearing the riding outfit, by now stained and dirty, that she wore at the time of Forio's death, and her hair hangs loose, wet, and bedraggled around her head. She breaks with her generic forebears here and joins ranks with other Hitchcock heroines, whose cool surface exterior must finally receive a form of literal and symbolic "dressing down" over the course of the film. This is certainly not unrelated to the analytic process of breaking through the surface of appearances to discover the "real" woman underneath. But within Hitchcock's body of work, Marnie's predecessors who undergo this process are not positioned as mentally unstable within the medical discourse that Doane describes. Rather, their contact with the world of crime or violence either directly or indirectly brings about this process of breaking the woman's surface glamour.

Finally, *Marnie* goes yet another step further by making use of certain developments in Hitchcock's thrillers from the postwar period that do not belong to either of these two cycles. This is the period in which protagonists in Hitchcock's cinema are predominately, as Žizek phrases it, "pathological narcissists." These protagonists are male (signifying an important shift from much of the female-centered work of the 1940s) and are often incapable of "normal" sexual relations with women, most often due to a problematic relationship with their mothers or with maternal figures, leading to a "blocked maternal superego":

> The narcissistic subject knows only the "rules of the (social) game" enabling him to manipulate others; social relations constitute for him a playing field in which he assumes "roles," not proper symbolic mandates; he stays clear of any kind of binding commitment that would imply a proper symbolic identification. He is a radical conformist who paradoxically experiences himself as an outlaw.[69]

Almost from the beginning of Hitchcock's cinema, the formation of the couple was a central element in his development of the espionage and detective thrillers, particularly as they began to crystallize during the 1930s. That there was always something perverse or uneasy about this coupling has often been noted even if the basic trajectory of these narratives was one in which the man and woman "matured" and discovered the benefits of romantic love through the adverse circumstances into which they find themselves. Although the specificity of these circumstances varied over Hitchcock's body of work, this function of the uneasy romantic couple persists from *The 39 Steps* (1935) through *North by Northwest*. The postwar period sees an increased tendency to situate the source of this fundamental uneasiness within the family situation itself, particularly as it relates to the mother's role in interfering with her son's "natural" sexual development. This shift is to a large extent the result of the increased influence of Freudian psychoanalysis in U.S. culture in which neurosis and any sense of an individual being a "maladjusted misfit" (to borrow the language of Thelma Ritter's Stella from *Rear Window* for a moment) is ultimately traceable to the family situation. Portions of Žizek's description of the pathological male would fit several postwar Hitchcock protagonists. But only one character fits it perfectly, Roger Thornhill in *North by Northwest*, whereas only one other character pushes this tendency to its logical and murderous culmination: Norman Bates in *Psycho*.

The mother/son situation is repeated in *The Birds*, through Mitch and Lydia Brenner, but in a muted and somewhat undeveloped way. By this point Hitchcock appears to have lost interest in this kind of male protagonist after having perfected the two poles of the character type through Thornhill and Bates. The shift may also be attributed to the general decline in this kind of approach to the family situation and to changes in the representation of neurosis and psychosis in general. Much of so-called modern cinema ignores or reacts against the confidence of a psychoanalytic discourse that traces neurosis to the family and childhood. This splintering effect in terms of the basic drive to know and interpret may be seen as the result of certain shifts taking place within these basic generic structures on which Hitchcock's cinema had drawn in the past.[70] By the time of *Marnie*, both the gothic, female-centered melodrama and the medical discourse film have given way to what Adrian Martin has termed "the poetic, mentally-disturbed woman films of the mid-1960s," which include not only *Marnie* but also *Red Desert, Lilith*, Roman Polanski's *Repulsion* (1965), and *Belle de jour*.[71] In *Repulsion*, for example, we have a female protagonist, Carol, who suffers a gradual mental breakdown over the course of the film. Like her 1940s medical discourse predecessors, she takes little interest in her physical appearance. As in *Marnie*, a recurring motif exists of her recoiling from the touch of men as a sign of her psychosis and Carol's relationship to her family is emphasized. She lives in an uncomfortably shared apartment with her sister and on several occasions the film cuts to a photo of Carol as a child, taken with her family, as though somehow this history provides a clue to the enigma of her psychosis. The film returns to this photo in the final shot of the film, as the camera slowly zooms into Carol's melancholy face, looking off-camera in a self-absorbed manner, in the snapshot. But the photo ultimately provides no definitive answers in terms of Carol's mental state. If, in fact, her problems are traceable to the family, the film never firmly pinpoints them as such. The photograph is situated in such a way that it carries the weight of evidence and yet what that evidence precisely consists of remains unclear.

In *The Birds* and *Marnie*, Hitchcock neither ignores nor reacts against the family situation in this way. The primary concern of *The Birds* in this regard is not the relationship between mother and son but the one between mother and daughter: Melanie Daniels and her absent mother, a mother who Lydia finally and symbolically replaces in the final sequence. In *Marnie*, Mark is a character primed to assume a position within the history of these 1950s male protagonists (in his elegant and ironic stance, he is in some ways a descendant of Thornhill), but this does not fully take place. He appears to have had no problematic relationship with his mother (a character who is never mentioned) and his pathologies are something the film has enormous difficulty in coherently addressing.[72] The burden then falls to Marnie to assume certain characteristics of this pathological protagonist, a character type who has, by this point, exhausted the various permutations possible as a male. Unlike her 1950s male counterparts, however, Marnie is not simply incapable of commitment to a romantic partner due to a repressive mother. In *Marnie*, the mother's repressiveness has assumed monumental proportions, partly resulting in Marnie's sexual frigidity and compulsive criminal acts. Like Norman Bates, Marnie resorts to crimes she is compelled to commit as a form of unconscious response to the problem of the mother. She assumes this Hitchcockian male pathology, then, but manifests it in a different way from her 1950s male counterparts. She is not a radical conformist who imagines herself an outlaw. She is an outlaw, understands this, and seems to derive actual pleasure from it, unlike either Norman Bates in relation to his crimes or the criminal women from the 1940s medical discourse films, who always clearly signal their desire to break from a life of crime early on.

The rules of the social game that allow Marnie to manipulate others are also played out in a much more deliberate and self-conscious way, through her various disguises and aliases. Unlike Thornhill, who "derails his narcissistic economy" when encountered with a "symbolic mandate that cannot be grounded in its properties" (his false identification as George Kaplan),[73] Marnie is in active control of a series of false identities. What threatens to derail her psychic economy are not symbolic mandates but certain specific properties that terrify her, a terror to which she cannot assign a definite source—the color red, thunder and lightning, the touch of a man. This causes her to regress as both a character within the fictional world of the film (these traumas often paralyze her emotionally to such an extent that she has mental blackouts) and as a fictional character within Hitchcock's cinema (she regresses to being an "old-fashioned" character out of a 1940s film with a set of symptoms waiting to be decoded by an analyst as the thunder and lighting outside rise up at the appropriate melodramatic moments).

At the same time, *Marnie* retains certain aspects to the role the female characters possessed in relation to the 1950s male protagonists. It was during the 1950s when the image of the Hitchcockian "cool blonde" crystallized, a crystallization that seemingly could not take place until the male protagonist had reached this "pathological" position. Here the woman is at her maximum state of desirability—beautiful, chic, intelligent, self-sufficient, and (cool surfaces to the contrary notwithstanding) sexually experienced and available. But for the male protagonist, she is perpetually caught up within a fantasy image of surface desirability that strongly attracts him. This protagonist is, at the same time, frightened and over-whelmed by the allure of these surfaces and of the implications of what lies beneath them, of the fantasy image giving way to reality, to flesh and blood desires. She is, as Jeff states explicitly about Lisa in *Rear Window*, "too perfect."

With the character of Marnie, all of Hitchcock's cool but neglected blondes seem to coalesce to enact a revenge against the pathological 1950s male protagonists. Ironically, however, Marnie only offers herself as a fantasy object to men as a brunette. To her mother, she presents herself as a slightly artificial blonde, an implied act of seduction for which the mother rebukes her. ("Too blonde o' hair looks like the woman's out to attract the man.") But this is also clearly an attempt on Marnie's part to return to the color of her hair she had as a child and that Jessie, the little girl Mrs. Edgar babysits and who is an active rival for Marnie in relation to the mother's affections, possesses. Marnie offers to men pure surface only—not coolness that masks a genuine eroticism but an almost total coldness and refusal to be, as she puts it, "handled." What lies beneath is not warmth and a desire for emotional commitment to a man but a pathol-ogy far more extreme than that of the film's male protagonist, Mark. Marnie, then, may be seen as the ultimate Hitchcock protagonist in that she col-lapses so many of the tendencies of both male and female characters in his work, being at once persecuted heroine, psychologically disturbed protago-nist, pathological narcissist, and the cool blonde object of desire.

Furthermore, the postponing of the investigative modality for the protagonists described earlier also creates a very different role for the formation of the couple in relation to the investigation itself. The couple here is not only already formed before the true investigation into Marnie's past begins, but formed under adverse circumstances in which the woman is both forced into marriage and also suffers from sexual frigidity. Hitchcock seemingly has taken the reluctant or skeptical blonde women from his earlier films—who initially refuse to believe in the innocence of the hero but who eventually come around to believing and then loving him—and turned this archetype on its head: The woman now truly and profoundly has no interest in the man on any level. As a result, the sense of the couple maturing through the process of investigation, although not deci-sively ruled out in the final sequence, is not one to which the film gives full voice. Indeed, Marnie's frequently quoted final words to Mark, "Oh Mark, I don't want to go to jail. I'd rather go home with you," fully sum up not only the ironies but also the difficulties inherent in the film's attempt at closure in relation to the formation of the couple.

The resolution in general plays itself out through a constant on-the-one-hand/on-the-other-hand structure. On the one hand, Marnie remembers the traumatic event and her mother confesses and tells the whole story; on the other, this appears not to resolve the central tension between mother and daughter; on the one hand, the mother tells her daughter that "she was the only thing I ever did love"; on the other, she still refuses to allow Marnie to be physically close to her ("Get up, Marnie. You're achin' my leg," a repetition of a line heard in their first sequence together.); on the one hand, when Mark tells the mother that Marnie will be returning for visits, there is a suggestion that a process of healing is under way; on the other, when the girls outside of the mother's house repeat their rhyme of "Mother, mother/I am ill," a possibility is raised that a healing is unlikely or at least will be a long and difficult process; on the one hand, the final two shots of the film (a shot of the closed door of the home followed by long shot of Mark and Marnie's car pulling away as we see the sun coming up and the great looming ship that had been there earlier is now gone) signifies a happy ending with the tensions resolved and pointing toward a brighter future; on the other, the music is rather somber and thematically unresolved and allows for a more pessimistic reading.[74]

The way that Marnie handles its resolution can be seen as being consistent with much of domestic melodrama, in which the happy ending is often a problem, frequently displaying contradictions that refuse to be resolved. "I just couldn't make a film like Hitchcock's *Marnie* as *Marnie* is told," Fassbinder has said, "because I don't have the courage for such naïveté, simply to make such a film and then at the end to give such an explanation. I don't have that something which *is* a natural part of courage, but maybe some day I will have it, and then I'll be just like Hollywood."[75] The ambivalent admiration that Fassbinder expresses for what he perceives to be a type of naiveté on the part of the film, and of which its resolution is particularly symptomatic, is something Fassbinder takes in another (but still related) direction in his own persecuted woman melodrama, *Martha* (1973). It is within the space left by the contradictory "happy endings" of Hollywood melodramas that an important aspect to Fassbinder's revision of the form may be understood. The resolution of a film such as *Martha* resists the "naïveté" of *Marnie* in that (like *Repulsion*) it never presumes to offer a cure for its heroine's problem or even to be able to point to any single traumatic event that would explain her predicament. The possibility is raised that Margit Carstensen's Martha Heyer (a name obviously a citation of Martha Hyer, the costar of *Some Came Running*, often typecast, as she is in Minnelli's film, in roles as sexually aloof or frigid women) is simply being paranoid in relation to her husband's behavior toward her: Like the heroine of a 1940s woman's film, she is convinced that he is trying to drive her insane. But the film never clarifies this for us (or for her), and Martha seems to be masochistically submitting to her husband's tyranny as much as she is a victim of it. The resolution shows Martha in a wheelchair, paralyzed from a car accident after trying to run away, her husband taking her out of the hospital, as two sets of elevator doors on either side of the couple close shut.[76]

Although one would be hard-pressed to call Fassbinder's resolution as naïve as Hitchcock's, I would argue that *Marnie*'s ambivalent drive toward a happy ending is one in which certain European art films of the 1960s were also participating. Among the several links between *Marnie* and *Red Desert* we may note that both films cautiously attempt to reintegrate their "neurotic" heroines into society. Like Hitchcock at the end of *Marnie*, in the final sequence of *Red Desert*, Antonioni works through a process of mixed signals. On the one hand, the dialogue Giuliana has with her son suggests that she has learned to accept the same symptoms of the modern world that had previously been such a source of neurosis for her (in particular, the pollution the factories near her home caused). As she explains to her son, the birds no longer die as a result of the emissions from the factory smoke stacks because they know that the fumes are poisonous and instead they now fly around them. But on the other hand, the visual and aural cues suggest the possibility of a return of Giuliana's neurosis: the electronic music building on the soundtrack in the final seconds of the film and the return of the indirect subjective use of unreal color for the fumes as indicative Giuliana's neurosis. We may see this ending as a vestige of the influence of melodrama and *Red Desert* does not "escape" its ties to the medical discourse film. Even the extreme visual style of the film (the use of unusually long lenses and of a very stylized and artificial approach to color) allows itself to be read in at least two ways: in melodramatic terms as a subjective symptom of Giuliana's neurosis; or in modernist terms in which the visual style resists a relationship to the purely analogical and representational.[77] Rather than ultimately choosing one approach over the other, seeing the latter approach as an extension of the former may be more productive. Like *Marnie*, *Red Desert* has, by its resolution, taken on more than it can effectively handle and can supply neither a firm happy ending nor an open-ended one. Nevertheless, this strain of tentative optimism in both films suggests not only a last gasp of melodramatic rhetoric, but also points toward the possibility of rethinking cinema's relation to the modern world itself.[78]

This was one of the topics raised in an interview Rivette and Michel Delahaye conducted with Roland Barthes published in *Cahiers du Cinéma* in September 1963 (and that also arose in a discussion of various critics and filmmakers of *Muriel* in the magazine two months later.) In relation to Buñuel's *The Exterminating Angel* (1962), Barthes complains that an

evasion of the story or of the psychological has too often become the
criterion of a work's modernity. He argues that modern works "have
ceased to have anything to say about interpersonal, inter-human relationships." Picking up on this, Rivette and Delahaye argue that "the one big
subject of modern art is really the possibility of happiness."[79] (One of the
most interesting features of *Muriel* was that, as Rivette put it, "failure 'is
not always a certainty.' "[80]) In a similar vein, Barthes would later write on
Antonioni not in conventional terms as a filmmaker dedicated to alienation but as "a utopian whose perception is seeking to pinpoint the new
world because he is eager for this world and already wants to be part of
it.[81] Antonioni's art is one of "always leaving the road of meaning open
and as if undecided. . . ."[82] In this regard, we may see the ending of *Red
Desert* as consistent with this strategy of vacillation in terms of fixed
meaning rather than a simple confusion or difficulty over how to resolve
the issues of the film. This notion of ambiguous hope is also as central
to Hitchcock as it is to Antonioni or Resnais. But although Antonioni and
Resnais take on ambitious social and political themes through which they
articulate this notion of ambiguous hope in relation to the modern world
(the ecological disasters of Italy during the 1960s in the case of *Red Desert*,
the Algerian war in the case of *Muriel*), Hitchcock's social agenda is comparatively modest. More in keeping with the traditions of the woman's
film, social conflicts and contradictions are played out through the dy-
namics of the family, whereas engagement with politics, economics, and
history is muted or handled indirectly. This is not, by any means, a neg-
ligible tradition or one that is oblivious to real social inequities. It does
suggest, however, that *Marnie's* relationship to the type of European
modernist cinema of the period Antonioni and Resnais epitomized,
although complex, is not one in which one may do simple one-to-one
equations.[83] But the fact that a woman stands at the center of these issues
is of some significance.

Possession and Loss

The purse that we see in the opening shot, whatever its relationship to
narrative hermeneutics, also clearly is meant to serve as a stand-in for the
body of Marnie herself, a fairly blunt vaginal symbol. Working through
the opening footage from *Marnie*, Bellour argues that Hitchcock's camera
is strongly connected to a form of "image power," particularly exercised
in relation to the female body in which voyeurism and fetishism play
fundamental roles. The male characters in Hitchcock's work, in their
desire for this female body, function as "nothing but doubles" of Hitchcock
who is always "the first among all his doubles, a matrix that generates

them. . . ."[84] Hitchcock's own look in *Marnie* is concisely embodied through the director's ritual cameo appearance, stepping out of a hotel door as the heroine passes by him at the beginning of the third sequence of the film—another shot of Marnie walking a straight path, this time down the corridor of the hotel, her face still hidden from us. As Hitchcock steps out of the door he "turns toward the spectator staring at the camera that he himself is and whose inscription he duplicates. The spectator in turn (re) duplicates this inscription through his identification with both Hitchcock and the camera."[85] Female characters are not by any means excluded from this structure of looking because Hitchcock's cinema depends "insistently and frequently" on the delegation of the look being handed over to the characters by the director.[86] But their look is often bound up with the ways in which it is finally returned to Hitchcock, particularly through the process of fetishization of the female body.

This desire for power as expressed through the camera is clearly present throughout *Marnie*, as Bellour's strong reading demonstrates. In fact, Hitchcock's articulation of the relationship between power and desire is unusually forceful here. But I would argue that this forcefulness is constantly marked by (and is even the result of) its own frustrated attempts to possess fully what it is filming. In spite of Bellour's contention that "a body is seized" in the opening shot, I see something much more ambivalent taking place here (and throughout the film as a whole) in which the woman is simultaneously possessed by the camera and attempts to escape from this possession. However, this escape by the woman, a site of frustration for the camera, is also bound up with the possibility of her

Figure 2.6. *Marnie:* Hitchcock steps out of the hotel door.

own erasure. As Marnie reaches the end of her walk along the line of the train platform, she is surrounded on both sides by sets of parallel lines (the trains on either side of her, the awning hanging over the platform itself) of which she forms the vanishing point at the receding end of the shot, an image into which she almost vanishes herself. What is being staged in this opening shot is not only the disappearance of the female protagonist, but also along with her the potential disappearance or erasure of the work itself.[87] Hence the centrality in the opening of Marnie not simply possessed by the camera but of her finally moving away from it, the camera ceasing to follow her and holding back, as though it realizes that it cannot get any closer to this body that is caught up in the camera's fascination.

That Hitchcock's long takes do not stand opposed to his conception of montage but instead articulate it in a different way is an issue that has been addressed on numerous occasions. What his extended takes most often highlight is the problematic assumption built into the notion of the single take's equivalence to either reality or to cinematic "innocence." Most often one is aware in these Hitchcock long takes of a forceful guiding of attention that can be as strong as it is during a montage set piece. In this regard, the opening shot of Marnie on the train platform is no less fetishistic than the brief sequences immediately following it.[88] If the opening shot is an image overdetermined in the intensity with which it is positioned as something to be looked at, the first shot of the sequence after the opening abruptly alters the allure of this spectatorial positioning. Hitchcock gives us a straight cut from the long shot of Marnie on the train platform to a close-up of Strutt (Martin Gabel) in his office, looking directly into the camera and saying, "Robbed!" He then turns to his right and says to the offscreen police officers, "Cleaned out!" The initial effect of this cut from Marnie in long shot to Strutt in close-up is as startling as the close-up of the purse at the beginning but its emotional effect stands in marked contrast to it. The opening shot of Marnie on the platform works by a process of seduction, luring the spectator into a state of suspended desire. But the cut to Strutt's face breaks the spell, shattering the reverie of both sound (through the harshness of his voice and the criminal content of the word *robbed* in relation to the relative silence of what precedes this) and image. His direct look into the camera not only implies that he is seeing this first image of Marnie, an image that initially appears to be addressing only the spectator, but also his direct look into the camera becomes a negative mirror image reflected back at us of our own gaze at the first shot of the film. Furthermore, because Marnie's face is concealed from us in the opening, our intense desire to see her face is doubly frustrated by suddenly having Strutt's face, blunt and unattractive, staring back at us instead.

In marked contrast to the opening, the sequence in Strutt's office consists of twenty-four shots in which he gives a statement to the police about the robbery committed by "Marion Holland," describing her face in detail before we actually see it with our own eyes. This statement is interrupted by the appearance of one of Strutt's clients, Mark Rutland. The sequence also stands in contrast to the opening in its visual starkness, comprised mainly of straightforward medium shots and medium close-ups, all in a high-key style, within the cramped space of Strutt's office, a sequence without any seductive component to it. During the formally rather ordinary sequence in Strutt's office the fetishistic impulse transfers over to language as the body of Marion Holland is verbally broken down and fetishized by Strutt through dialogue as he catalogues her body and features to the detectives: five feet five, 110 pounds, size eight dress, blue eyes, black wavy hair, even features, good teeth, a verbal description pre-paring us for the face that has yet to be unveiled for the camera. (Mark's fetishism is more economically expressed when he refers to her here as "the brunette with the legs.") In the following sequence, comprised of seven shots, the first shot maintains an explicit link with that of the film's opening: another close-up of the same purse with Marnie wearing the same outfit and again walking a straight path, the camera pulling back to reveal a hotel hallway. She is not alone but a porter carrying boxes and a new suitcase accompanies here. As in the opening, this is done in a single, brief take. We have yet to see Marnie's face but we do see Hitchcock's here.

The three shots of the following sequence show Marnie's hotel room, beginning with an overhead long shot and then two shots that show us her transferring her old belongings as Marion Holland into one suitcase while packing her new belongings as Margaret Edgar into an-other, each bit of framing and cutting working to conceal the appearance of her face. Instead, we see Marnie through a series of objects (items of clothing, bags, combs, makeup mirrors, and Social Security cards that she shuffles through, all but one containing her various aliases and all of them beginning with the letter M) and parts of her body (in particular, her hands), which stand in for a confirmed and whole identity that a close-up of her face would create. She then rinses the black dye out of her hair into the bathroom sink (two shots) to become—finally—a blonde Hitchcock heroine. It is also at this moment when her face is revealed, as she lifts her head up from the sink and faces the camera, her eyes not meeting the lens of the camera directly but instead look slightly up, just missing the possibility of an effect of direct address. But this shot is held very briefly and is taken away just as quickly before we cut to the inside of another train station, again showing Marnie from the rear, but this time surrounded by a great deal of activity. She is carrying both the old and new suitcases, this time wearing a pale green suit, the camera at a slightly elevated angle looking down at the suitcases and cutting Marnie off at the waist. The camera follows her to a locker into which she deposits the older suitcase, locks the door and then turns and faces the camera as it tilts up, offering our first sustained view of her face, her hair pinned up as she looks off camera. The cut that follows shows her point-of-view shot of a vent in the station floor. Hitchcock then cuts not back to her face but to a shot of her gloved hand, holding the key to the locker door as the hand stealthily moves toward the vent. A cut to a low-angled camera position near the vent shows the key being dropped down on top of it with the tip Marnie's high-heeled shoe gently prodding the key as it falls between the cracks.

Hitchcock's cinema contains numerous examples of fetishistic characters, from Mrs. Danvers in *Rebecca* to Scottie in *Vertigo*. But the fetishism in these earlier films was always framed within and mediated by the psychology of the characters. By the time of *Psycho* and *The Birds* we find violent set pieces (the shower murder of Marion Crane in the former, the attack on Melanie in the attic in the latter) in which not only is the woman's body brutally attacked within the diegetic world of the films, but also the editing and framing choices seem to break down the bodies of these women through the continuous cutting to hands, feet, legs, and waists. What is significant about *Marnie* within this development is the extent to which the film actively partakes of a fetishistic impulse toward the image of its female protagonist and on a scale that Hitchcock's cinema

Figure 2.7. *Marnie*: Suspended desire.

had never previously attempted. The intervention of the point of view of the fetishistic (and largely male) character is positioned differently in *Marnie* from Hitchcock's prior work and the film no longer waits for a violent set-piece before it begins cutting into the image of the woman. It can now take place within the context of more banal narrative events. Characters such as Strutt or Mark may fetishize, but their desires never directly animate the image in a one-to-one fashion (as, for example, Scottie's do in *Vertigo*). The images of Marnie on the train platform, in the hotel room, and in the second train station that surround the sequence in Strutt's office are something that Strutt responds to and they clearly seem to be activating his desires. But he remains within the confines of his drab office and his ordinary "classical segment in 24 shots."[89] The structure and mode of presentation of these images of Marnie are organized around a principle of elusiveness, of something that is just about to happen, of something that is just about to be revealed but either never is or (as in the display of Marnie's face at the bathroom sink) revealed very fleetingly, before spectators have had time to grasp fully what it is that they are seeing.

Even though for Hitchcock it was the "fetish idea" of Mark's desire for a woman who steals that inspired him to make the film, the final result shows enormous difficulty in articulating this: "To put it bluntly, we'd have had to have Sean Connery catching the girl robbing the safe and show that he felt like jumping at her and raping her on the spot."[90] The film does not come up with any visual concepts for this fetish (as *Vertigo* is able to do with Scottie's fundamental death-drive attraction toward Madeleine being displaced onto a variety of motifs, from the spiral in her hair to the ghostly gray and white colors with which she is associated); nor is this fully dramatized in the scenario through dialogue and dramatic situations (as happens in *To Catch a Thief* in which we find a similar kind of fetish for a criminal but this time with the genders reversed). In *Marnie* the idea of the male protagonist as fetishist is muted and instead the film as a whole seems to compensate for this by directly producing a fetishistic drive toward Marnie. Hitchcock's own camera becomes the primary desiring subject and has, in effect, replaced the male protagonist who is now reduced to being a kind of supporting player.

In this regard, the great "secret beyond" of the film becomes the body of the female protagonist, a film in which so many objects, so many items of clothing and aspects of the decor are eroticized, suggesting a connection back to Marnie herself. Throughout the opening as we see Marnie on the train platform, in the hotel room as she unpacks and exchanges identities, we are being brought into spaces for looking at Marnie that are denied Mark or Strutt. It is as though Hitchcock has taken us to the other side of the two-way mirror that Henry Travers wants to break through in *The Thousand Eyes of Dr. Mabuse*, allowing us intimately to glimpse the sort of thing that Travers can see only from a distance. These are highly private spaces in *Marnie* in which the texture of objects (the yellow leather purse, the tweed suit, the pink nail polish, the gold metal case holding her plastic identity cards, the pink satin lining of the suitcase, the tip of the high heeled shoe as it nudges the key down into the vent) are clearly meant to serve as displaced extensions of Marnie's body. All of this establishes a powerful environment in which the look generates the need to get even closer to the object of desire.

But this eroticism also extends to Marnie's stealing, as the film turns the process leading up to the theft of the Rutland safe into a displaced erotic spectacle, a type of striptease, of slight unveilings: the doors to the safe or to the drawer in the desk of the other secretary that keep getting open and closed, open and closed, most often under Marnie's watchful eye. So much of the film revolves around the possibility or act of getting into something private or remote—safes, suitcases, purses, desk drawers, the stall in the ladies' room in which Marnie hides, and ultimately the body of Marnie herself. That Marnie derives a displaced sexual thrill from her thefts is made explicit near the end of the film when, after the death of Forio, she attempts to rob the safe again with a look on her face approaching sexual bliss as she, in a low angle shot, slowly and lovingly turns the knob on the safe door. In one crucial sequence earlier in the film, the camera cranes around the office, lowering itself down to Marnie as she types at her desk. A cut to her point-of-view shot shows the office manager opening the safe. Cut back to a look of repressed pleasure on

Figure 2.8. *Marnie:* The importance of getting inside of things.

Figure 2.9. *Marnie:* Eroticizing the act of theft.

Marnie's face as she continues to type away. The camera then cranes up and shows Mark watching Marnie watching the office manager. This is not so much a Bellourian Hitchcock moment in which the woman's look is subsumed into the man's as one in which crime and desire become linked, from Marnie's explicit desire to get inside the safe, to Mark's desire to get inside Marnie, the criminal woman. Marnie's resistance to Mark takes the form of the bedroom door, the first of which is the one she aggressively slams on Mark on their honeymoon (precipitating the rape) and the other of which she more firmly closes on Mark when he brings her home to Wyckwyn Manor afterward.

A basic manifestation of the fetishistic impulse is its relationship not only to the partial object that stands in for the whole (particularly as it exists in relation to the body). It is also related to the attempt to represent something that has either been lost (and most likely is destined never to return) or something that never existed to begin with. The fetish becomes the sign of something both highly valuable and yet devoid of real substance. The sense of this potential loss or regression may account for the unusual intensity and directness with which fetishism is expressed in *Marnie.* The woman must be broken down into pieces because she is the focal point around which the film's transitional nature is most acutely embodied. She is the star of the film, the director's muse, the woman he wants to elevate to the status of a major actress. She is all substance, everything for which a director could wish.[91] But the film is also a star vehicle built around someone who did not become a star, someone who both rejected Hitchcock's camera and was rejected by it. Hence we have a film constructed around a void or around what is ultimately a refusal of the attentions being paid to it. The result is a character (and an actress) who becomes many things at once (a woman of multiple names and physical identities), but who is also a cipher, a woman who, as she explicitly tells Mark, believes in "nothing."

But this threat is something that many of Hitchcock's protagonists face time and again, in this cinema of vanishing ladies, of men whose identities become "crisscrossed," of the Roger Thornhills who are disastrously mistaken for nonexistent George Kaplans, of retired police detectives who fall passionately in love with women whose identities are "partly real and partly made up"? In this regard, the threat of nothingness that surrounds Hedren/Marnie may be seen as something that is accounted for within the actual narrative content of the film itself and is fully consistent with Hitchcock's body of work: In *Marnie*, the film perpetually offers up our protagonist's body in pieces because she herself is not psychologically "whole." The film's montage creates a fragmentation that is not so much a symptom of the problematic circumstances surrounding the production of the film as it is an inevitable outcome of the film's basic narrative situations and the psychological conflicts of its protagonist. Like Mabuse, Marnie is a criminal who operates under multiple aliases and disguises. But where Mabuse's multiplicity relates to issues of power, for Marnie, whatever power she attempts to exert over her male employers, this multiplicity also becomes another symptom of her lack of psychological wholeness. Putting it in this way, however, would place the film squarely within a tradition of film melodrama in which the hysterical symptoms of the body of the protagonist become displaced onto the text of the film itself. As has already been pointed out, the manner in which these situations and psychological conflicts are treated are also responses to the historical moment in which the film was made, as part of Hitchcock's ongoing project of rethinking his filmmaking.

Again the work of Antonioni is particularly central as a point of connection and contrast. Hitchcock's admiration for Antonioni is not only well known but eventually became the source of a certain amount of anxiety on Hitchcock's part. During the 1960s, Hitchcock began to sense that Antonioni was doing him one better, surpassing him in formal audacity and with narrative material similar to Hitchcock's own.[92] (In an early draft of the *Marnie* script, Marnie gets a job in a movie theater showing an Italian art film, a sequence that, regrettably was never shot.) Like Hitchcock, Antonioni's films are often detective stories in which the protagonists are not professional detectives but amateurs. The amateur nature of Hitchcock's detectives works to create a strong contrast between extraordinary events happening to otherwise ordinary individuals. In spite of their amateur standing, Hitchcock's protagonists usually uncover the film's basic narrative enigmas. But in Antonioni the aura of amateurishness surrounding the investigation ultimately works to diffuse a sense of urgency in uncovering these mysteries. Indeed, what often sets Antonioni's protagonists on their detective-like journeys is the search for an elusive or disappeared object or individual. But through this process the characters themselves often lose interest in the act of detection. Like children, they are easily distracted and incapable of truly sustained attention. As in Hitchcock, Antonioni's protagonists are haunted by the possibility of disappearance, of being erased from the landscape, but in Antonioni this idea is often taken to greater extremes, as in the final shot of *Blow-Up* in which the protagonist literally disappears or dissolves into the landscape. *Red Desert* also contains this idea as a distressed Giuliana looks at a group of her friends standing in the fog and the fog seems to erase them from the landscape. What we find here is not simply a disappearance alone but, as Bonitzer puts it in relation to *L'avventura*, "*the disappearance of the disappearance.*" Bonitzer describes Antonioni's world as one that is "plastically, narratively, and ontologically... a world in pieces" and one in which the restoration of the pieces is ultimately abandoned.[93]

This notion of a world in pieces clearly fascinates Hitchcock and one can see how increasingly drawn to it he is during the early 1960s, even before his acquaintance with the work of Antonioni. The shower sequence in *Psycho* is a defining moment, described in its original shooting script as a moment that "rips" the film into pieces, a metaphoric attack on the film screen itself.[94] This approach continues (although not so metaphorically charged) in the sequence of Melanie's attack in Cathy's bedroom at the end of *The Birds*. *Marnie* is less concerned with finding a set piece within which the female protagonist is violently attacked in this manner than in fragmenting her body and identity throughout the film. But what is crucial in all three of these films is the way in which female bodies serve as the pivots for a montage conception that is at once formally bold and violent. What is taking place here is not simply a heightened fetishistic response to female bodies as an end in itself. Rather, the films often articulate the struggle to give voice to a new kind of image, a new kind of cinema *through* the bodies of women, who serve as ambivalent sources of inspiration and (often) anxiety. For Hitchcock, as for much of the cinema of this period, the female body in pieces also represents a new kind of cinema as it attempts to depict a world it sees as shattering as well.

The cinema began to find relations between the bodies of women and the filmic apparatus and its various tools (camera movement, editing,

special effects) almost from the moment of its inception.[95] Dziga Vertov's
The Man with the Movie Camera (1929) may be seen as one of the primary
texts of the cinema's first fifty years of existence in this regard, from the
"awakening of a woman" with which the film opens to the recurring
images of women at work and at play with a central image occurring
roughly halfway through the film of a woman giving birth. The footage
of the film is at several points examined by the film's own female editor,
Yelizaveta Svilova, as Vertov repeatedly equates the camera and the process of film production with women and with the female body, symbol-
izing the great collective Soviet body politic. As much as Hitchcock may
have been influenced by 1920s Soviet montage, his cinema rarely (if ever)
showed this interest in filming great organic social collectives. Even his
wartime films have difficulty perceiving of democratic or antifascist collectives in this way. Hitchcock's filmmaking practice did not take root in
a culture strongly devoted to these kinds of collective principles and instead remained, if not entirely "obsessional, fetishistic and frozen," largely
concerned with the individual or the couple against which the social
world often functioned in an indifferent or destructive manner. Certainly
by the 1960s this kind of celebratory symbolic equation between women
and the camera seldom manifested itself to any strong degree. What
becomes common during the postwar period in general is a treatment of
women in which the camera becomes increasingly violent and aggressive,
as though the "from reverence to rape" trajectory that Molly Haskell has
famously outlined in relation to the depiction of women in films has
largely given itself over to the latter impulse. Michael Powell's *Peeping
Tom* is perhaps the purest instance of this in which the camera not only
films women but, through a weapon concealed in a leg of its tripod, also
murders them through the process of their being filmed. With *Marnie*,
Hitchcock likewise partakes of certain elements of this aggression although the full implications of this are far from being resolved.

The Touch

The rape scene on the ship in *Marnie* was key for Hitchcock. As is widely
known, the original screenwriter on the film, Evan Hunter, initially refused to write the scene, feeling that it was "unmotivated" and would turn
Mark into an unsympathetic character.[96] In fact, no evidence appears to
exist that audiences lose sympathy with Mark after the rape. We have
several explanations for this. Connery's romantic and sexual star persona
works to neutralize some of the more disturbing implications about the
rape: What "normal" heterosexual woman (although of course Marnie is
not normal) would refuse to have sex with Sean Connery?[97] After the

rape, the film very quickly works to restore Mark to his place as a romantic male protagonist, substitute psychotherapist for Marnie, and detective figure for the unraveling of the central narrative enigma. And because Mark assumes the role of psychotherapist in relation to Marnie, the rape on some level assumes a misplaced and horribly rushed therapeutic function. Furthermore, melodrama often shows an ostensibly sympathetic male figure raping a woman, provided the woman is his wife and that she, within the logic of the film, "deserves" this violent act performed against her.[98] But other factors also need to be taken into account.

First, let us take seriously Hitchcock's claim that *Marnie* was for him primarily a character study and only secondarily a thriller. What kind of character study is Hitchcock attempting? Major claims for the film in this regard should take their cue primarily from the scenes set in Mrs. Edgar's home. The art direction here is unusually detailed and naturalistic for this particular film with dirt and wear clearly visible on the walls and furniture, whereas the large yellow refrigerator (probably intended to suggest a gift from Marnie, its color matching her purse from the opening) stands out strongly for its newness and apparent expense. In a sense, the stage is set here for a psychological drama for which the details in decor will assume an important function, both in terms of general background and as props serving as an extension of the psychology of the characters. For example, in the kitchen sequence between Marnie and Mrs. Edgar they have a conversation centering on the possibility of Mrs. Edgar's neighbors, Mrs. Cotton and her young daughter Jessie, moving in. The sequence is initially comprised of a rather mundane medium two-shot of the women with a frontal medium close-up of Marnie as she cracks pecans sitting at the table alternating with two medium close-ups of her mother (one from her front, the other from her side) standing as she pours syrup. This configuration is suddenly broken as the camera position on Marnie shifts from the front to her side and moves in closer as she looks up at her mother and asks, "Why don't you love me, Mama? I've often wondered why you don't. Why you never give me one part of the love you give Jessie." We now return to the shot of her mother taken from the side but she now appears rather vulnerable in the shot, standing at the far right of the composition, in opposition to her daughter who sits center frame, unable to answer Marnie's question. Mrs. Edgar moves toward a salt shaker on the table and the film cuts to a close-up of Marnie's hand touching her mother's while uttering the word, "Mama." Mrs. Edgar pulls her hand away as the camera tilts up to her horrified face. A cut returns us to a medium two-shot as Marnie asks, "Why do you always move away from me. Why? What's wrong with me?" "Nothin," the mother says, "there's nothin' wrong with ya." "No, you've always thought that,

Figure 2.10. *Marnie:* Touching the mother.

haven't you? Always." A cut returns us to the centered close-up of Marnie looking at her mother as she continues accusing her mother of not loving her, detailing all the things she has done to make her mother love her. But this time, the close-up on Marnie is an almost imperceptibly slow tracking shot into her, while the reverse shots of her mother periodically interrupting those of Marnie's outburst, are still taken from the same slightly off-center position. Marnie's accusations build in intensity until Mrs. Edgar's hand enters the space of Marnie's close-up, slapping her. This is followed by a cut to Marnie's hand hitting the bowl of pecans as they fall to the floor, scattering.

Describing on paper the emotional quality of this scene is difficult. In the rigor of construction and the precision of cutting and framing it is recognizably Hitchcockian. But it has a raw, emotional quality that evokes not the European art cinema of the period, but the American cinema of a figure such as Kazan. Kazan's cinema epitomizes the postwar U.S. trend toward a strong character and actor-based cinema, insisting on close links between "inner" emotions and objects in the outer world. The canons of psychological realism prevalent by the 1950s (influenced in particular by the Method) insisted on what Christine Gledhill has termed "performance of the self as a source of truth."[99] This particularly U.S. transformation of melodrama strives for a collapsing of the relation between psychological realism and the external operations of melodrama in terms of performance and mise-en-scène. In Kazan's *Splendor in the Grass*, when Deanie returns home from a date with her boyfriend Bud, she flings herself onto the couch face down, embracing it with an almost masturbatory intensity, transferring her unconsummated desire for Bud onto an item of decor. When her mother comes down the stairs to talk to her, Deanie transfers her emotions onto a sea horn, which she handles more modestly, whereas her mother's lack of sexual drive is connoted through her naturalistic wolfing down of a sandwich.

Hitchcock somewhat uncharacteristically adopts this kind of visual and dramatic language for the kitchen scene in *Marnie*, although this is not the first time in his career in which Hitchcock attempted this kind of sequence: both the remake of *The Man Who Knew Too Much* (in which Ben McKenna tells his wife Jo about the kidnapping of their son) and *The Wrong Man* (1956; the sequences showing the mental breakdown of Rose, particularly the one in which she assaults her husband with a hairbrush) have comparable ambitions. This type of psychological cinema, pitched close to a level of hysteria, often demands a different conception of montage, one in which the physicality and emotions of the actor are not subordinated to either the design of the individual shot or the shot change itself but quite often the reverse: montage does not disappear but occurs after the fact, as it were, taking its cues from the actor. (The work of John Cassavetes, just beginning to emerge during this period, is central in this regard.)[100] In *The Man Who Knew Too Much*, montage is secondary to the dramatic and emotional content of the sequence, whereas in *The Wrong Man* Rose's hysteria is so extreme that the sequence ultimately builds to a moment of almost pure Expressionism, as Rose's assault against her husband culminates with a cut to a literal and metaphoric image of a mirror being cracked in a room dominated by heavy, Germanic shadows.

In *Marnie*, on the other hand, it is as though Hitchcock wants to continue to draw on the possibilities of montage as he has largely been practicing them throughout his career (which is to say that it functions as part of a prearranged design), but without sacrificing the possibilities of emotion being created within the shots as well and without the sequence falling back on the rhetoric of Expressionism, a sequence set in high key lighting, all contours sharp and clearly defined. The objects that we see here (the nuts that Marnie cracks, the bottle on the table that Mrs. Edgar reaches for, the syrup that she pours into a measuring cup) are not the standard Hitchcockian objects-turned-against-nature but expressive objects according to the codes of psychological realism. The centered close-ups of Marnie accusing her mother of insufficiently loving her just slightly avoid being direct addresses into the camera. But nevertheless a kind of naked emotional expression is at work here, so naked that, like Mrs. Edgar, one feels the impulse to recoil from what we are witnessing. Marnie is centered in the composition and is on the offensive, but she is seated and seems diminished in the shot; Mrs. Edgar is standing, but she is

shoved to the far right of the shot, finding moving difficult. The surprise
of the cut to the close-up of Marnie not only arises from its positioning
in contrast from the medium eye-level shots of the earlier set-ups to this
slightly high angle, but it also arises from the function of Marnie's face,
which is fully expressive here, connoting emotion both through facial
expression and through the sudden drop in the voice, which becomes
small and little-girl–like. (In the final sequence of the film this expressivity
of the face strongly returns when Marnie remembers the night she murdered the sailor.)

The close-up of two women's hands touching breaks this particular
tension but creates another more acute one, definitively establishing touch
as a motif that will recur throughout the film, but a touch that can only
be expressed in an indirect fashion. Mrs. Edgar cannot touch her daughter's
hand as an expression of love, but she can use the same hand to slap
Marnie's face, as Marnie's hand simultaneously hits the bowl of pecans
intended as part of a pie for Jessie. The bulk of emotional intensity here
occurs within the montage. The confrontation, the slap, the nuts spilling
to the floor—all of these occur in separate shots, a montage that is then
mentally "filled in" by the spectator as a continuous flow of emotion. But
the emotions themselves and the expressive use of objects belong more
strongly to a Kazan-style psychological realism. Within the traditions of
this kind of psychological cinema, what the sequence makes clear is that
Marnie's projection of herself in the world outside of her mother's home,
as an unavailable object of desire, is an unconscious response to this
situation with her mother. Because her mother, who originally "made her
living from the touch of men," will not touch her, will not love her, then
she will move in a world in which no one (particularly no man) will be
able to touch her. Out of this arises Marnie's (and the film's) drive toward
a world of surfaces, a drive that is nevertheless intimately related to the
need to unmask surfaces, to touch what is beneath the seductive and
remote exterior. This then may be seen as another factor in the neutral-
ization of Mark as a rapist in that he is not simply Marnie's antagonist nor
her romantic opposite, but a kind of double of her in relation to the film's
motif of touch and desire. Mark's relationship with Marnie duplicates her
relationship with her mother, with Mark assuming Marnie's role and
Marnie assuming her mother's.

As a set piece, the rape sequence not only joins ranks with the
shower sequence from *Psycho* and the bedroom attack from *The Birds*, but
it also belongs to a major group of sequences from 1960s art house and
Hollywood films in which a woman's rape becomes a pivotal dramatic
moment and, quite often, a formal tour de force for the auteur: the
murder and symbolic rape of Nadia by Simone crosscut with Rocco fighting

in the boxing ring in Luchino Visconti's *Rocco and His Brothers* (1960); the rape and murder of the teenage Karin in *The Virgin Spring* (1960); the gang rape of Naomi in *The Chapman Report*, the fantasy rape of Sèverine at the beginning of *Belle de jour*, and so forth. But the recurrence of sequences of this nature also extends beyond spectacle. A group of French soldiers in Algeria performed the assault and torture of the title character of *Muriel*, an event that took place prior to the narrative events directly depicted within the film itself, is never shown, only described by Bernard, who participated in the violence against her. The images we see as he narrates this are documentary footage of Algerian soldiers engaged not in battle but in various forms of horseplay. In many ways following the logic of dealing with the Holocaust in *Night and Fog*, the full horror of this action is one that cannot be directly represented, threatening to become a form of obscenity—one with enormous political implications. But the problem of interpretation in relation to the rape of a female protagonist is central to another film in which, as so many commentators on the film have noted, Hitchcock's figure is shown as a cardboard cutout: *Last Year at Marienbad*. In that film one of the central questions addressed is whether Delphine Seyrig's nameless heroine was raped by her lover in a hotel room. The film frequently goes over the possibility of this occurring and in one notable moment, through a jarring series of cuts, the camera repeatedly and quickly tracks forward into Seyrig's open arms, the image looking slightly overexposed. The camera seems to be symbolically penetrating her—or at least attempting to, the repetition of the movements and overexposure of the image connoting frustration or failure in this regard as much as it signifies true culmination. Hitchcock's own language to Evan Hunter in his description of the rape scene from *Marnie* is symptomatic of this approach: "Evan when he sticks it in her, I want that camera right on her face!"[101]

One of the most interesting aspects of this rape sequence from *Marnie*, then, is how the issue of interpretation itself arises. What exactly does happen here? Is it a rape at all? Jay Presson Allen, for example, claims that she never saw the sequence in those terms and that Hitchcock never used the word *rape* itself during their script conferences.[102] Robin Wood has made the intriguing argument that although Marnie experiences this moment as a rape, Mark does not.[103] (And, in fact, Mark only apologizes to Marnie for ripping off her nightgown, not for the act of sexual penetration.) My purpose here, however, is not to argue whether a rape technically is supposed to be taking place. Instead I would like to discuss how the issue of interpretation itself arises in this sequence. If this is a split within the diegetic world of the film between two conflicting interpretations of a single event (Marnie sees it as rape, Mark sees it simply as sex), what are the implications of this in terms of Hitchcock's cinema and of the spectator's relationship to it?

The rape sequence itself does not stand alone in *Marnie* but needs to be understood in relation to at least three other sequences. One is the flashback near the end of the film in which we see Marnie killing the sailor (Bruce Dern) whom she believes to be hurting her mother. If the construction of the rape scene complicates the question of either the spectator or the protagonists having a unified interpretation of what is taking place, the flashback does this in yet another way.[104] A gap appears to exist between Marnie's narration of these events from her past (the events that established her pathology) and what is taking place within the images themselves. A real possibility is raised that both Marnie and her mother are misinterpreting the sailor's intentions here. The child Marnie's repulsion at the odor of the liquor on the sailor's breath causes her to pull away from his attempts to comfort her after her nightmare. Are his actions of kissing her and stroking her hair merely meant to console the child or does he have sexual intentions as well? Marnie's mother certainly reads the latter into them, but whether this is a hysterical response or an entirely valid one is not clear. (The sailor behaves as though he has done nothing wrong: A defensive measure or a legitimate one?) The sailor's resistance to the mother beating him with a poker from the fireplace causes him to fall over on to the mother, injuring her leg. The close-up that confirms this action (the sailor's leg caught between the open legs of the mother) suggests, if not rape, certainly violent sexual penetration. Marnie misinterprets the accident of the fall as a deliberate physical attack against her mother, leading to the fateful moment of Marnie beating the sailor to death with the poker. Hitchcock certainly made many films in which characters misinterpret the actions or emotions of others, often in relation to criminal acts. But most frequently this involved a split between what appears to be the truth of a character or situation on the surface and the reality that lies beneath this surface: In *Vertigo*, Scottie (as well as the spectator) is duped into believing the image of Madeleine before the truth is revealed, first to the spectator (via Judy's letter to Scottie) and then to Scottie himself (through Judy's slip of putting on Madeleine's necklace). But *Marnie* does not unambiguously clarify the acts of interpretation (or misinterpretation), which stand at the center of the film. Within the tradition of the medical discourse film, Marnie's repressed memory is uncovered. But what is not clear is whether Marnie and her mother fully understand what took place on that night in which the sailor was killed. As with Mark's rape of Marnie, the spectator is given "too much" material to interpret, is in possession of more knowledge than the characters and a sense of closure in relation to the issues being raised is not fully achieved. I do not necessarily disagree with those who argue that this ambiguity is part of the film's intention. But it does suggest that Hitchcock is rethinking certain possibilities for handling the question of interpretation so central to his cinema.

Another sequence is the opening shot itself, the action of Marnie walking away from the camera's hold on her discussed earlier. The rape scene is a response to this opening shot, a moment in which the camera at last seems to have its moment of conquest. Marnie can no longer escape, can no longer walk away, and is held captive by Mark and by the camera, both lowering themselves on to her. Even here, however, the camera must finally look away and, without a cut, pans over and tilts up to a porthole with a view of the sea as Mark completes the sexual act off-camera. Most obviously, this is a response to possible censorship. Even in 1964 one still cannot "show everything," and so we have this movement away to a symbolic image, a reverse of the cliché of Production Code Hollywood of the pan to the fireplace as a symbol for the couple making love. Here we get an image of water instead of fire as the heroine is sexually assaulted. But we may also see this as a type of self-censorship and, as in the opening image of the film, the camera must pull back or look away from the image with which it is so clearly fascinated but realizes that it can never fully possess.

The final sequence the rape relates to is the one set in Mark's office when Marnie comes to work for him on a Saturday. It is at the end of the sequence when the tree crashes through the window, frightening Marnie and sending her into the arms of Mark who kisses her. With great relish, Donald Spoto describes how Hitchcock gave incredibly precise directions to his cinematographer, Robert Burks, for filming Hedren's face in which "the camera was to come as close as possible, the lenses were almost to make love to her." Specifically citing the shot in which Mark kisses Marnie in his office, Spoto labels this image as being "nearly pornographic."[105] Indeed the camera does come extremely close to these two faces, particularly through the zoom that is executed at the moment of the kiss. The image in question is, in fact, a very close two-shot of Mark and Marnie, even though Marnie's face dominates slightly more than Mark's here. In this regard, the shot fits in with several famous extreme close-up love scenes that run throughout Hitchcock's work. Far from being pornographic, the image has a stunning tactility to it, producing a heightened awareness of the texture and color of the flesh of the faces of both Connery and Hedren.

One of the major differences of *Marnie*, however, from these earlier films is how the female character is positioned within this erotic moment. Marnie's pathology in relation to being touched by men has not been firmly established at this point and will not be until the honeymoon. But even on a first viewing, something is clearly slightly "off" about this erotic encounter. Unlike, for example, the extended kissing scene from *Notorious*, no reciprocity seems to occur on the part of the woman for the man. Her eyes are closed and her fears of thunder and lightning appear to have caused her to become less than entirely conscious. Is this what Mark is responding to? He looks down at her face, sees the closed eyes and either misinterprets this as an invitation to kiss her; or he sees a woman in a helpless and possibly unconscious state and decides to take full advantage of the moment. The latter interpretation would be of particular relevance to the dialogue earlier in this sequence that revolves around instinctual behavior in animals and Mark's clear equation of Marnie with female predators. In this regard, the kiss anticipates and in many ways prepares the spectator for the rape. Mark does not seem to so much kiss Marnie as run his mouth along her face and then places his mouth on hers, as though grazing its surface, reinforcing a strong sense of the tactile that the image communicates. The woman achieves a status as a pure image or surface setting desire into play but never reciprocating the emotions that her physical presence gives rise to—hence the need on Mark's part on their honeymoon to break that surface, to force it into responding to him.

The desire to touch another human being who does not want to be touched animates the system of looking, desiring, and knowing, which always determined Hitchcock's cinema. But in *Marnie*, the relationship of the look—that of the camera, of the characters, of the spectators—to desire has seldom been as intense as it is here because it now introduces touch, the presence of a hand against an object, another human being, an animal (and Marnie's physical response to her horse, Forio, is far more intimate and sexual than with any human being in the film) as the culmination of the chain of desire and process of perception. In the midst of a montage sequence on board the honeymoon cruise ship in *Marnie*, Mark describes to Marnie an object in Africa that, to the naked eye appears to be a flower. But not until one reaches out and touches this object is one able to perceive that the flower is in fact a conglomeration of tiny insects, fattid bugs, gathered together in the shape of a flower as a form of protection from the forces of nature. This brief monologue (almost tossed away by the film) is nevertheless crucial for understanding the relationship between touching and looking, which structures much of *Marnie*.[106] *Marnie* demonstrates a desire to break through certain classical conventions of representation and to enter a realm of 'pure touching' in which the hand both feels and sees and in which images are offered to the spectator almost as though they were tactile and not purely visual. Again, the opening shot of the film is central. The camera's initial closeness to the woman's body—almost hugging it—creates a tactile atmosphere in which the texture of the yellow leather purse and the gray tweed jacket creates such a strong affective response that issues of narrative hermeneutics are arguably secondary. And Strutt's description of Marnie's features for the police officers is not simply verbal. He also gestures as he speaks, as though attempting to touch those features that he is describing or mold them into a form equal to his desire.

The film is replete with images of hands (from the dream images of the sailors' hands tapping Marnie's bedroom window to the shot of Marnie's gloved hand dropping the key down into the vent) although in itself this recurrence is not unusual for Hitchcock. The discovery of the hand and of the expressive possibilities of gesture was as crucial to the early history of cinema as the face. Lang's work, for example, represents one of the most important examples of this history. Unlike Hitchcock, Lang was able both to draw on the fascination with the fragmented body via the close-up while incorporating this within a strongly gestural cinema. Furthermore, the hand in Lang is often bound up with the very concept of the imprint, of a strong physical trace being left behind, a fascination that in itself suggests a strong link to Lang's own authorial hand marking itself on the work. Lang's work is dominated by the fingerprint, the footprint, the mark, the index. In Hitchcock, the hand's gestural power is more elusive, barely concerned at all with the concept of the imprint. Instead, the hand is most often channeled into close-ups in which gesture assumes an immediate and precise function in relation to an object; or gesture will often assume a function suspended between life and death itself, simultaneously a gesture of connection and of violence, as in the gesture of the policeman who attempts to save Scottie's life at the beginning of *Vertigo* by reaching out to him, but in the process only falls to his death, an image that, as Scottie says in the second sequence, continues to haunt him. In either case, we have a recurrence of the idea of a light grazing of the hands toward objects or bodies. This is not so much a world of the overdetermined indexical sign of Lang (simultaneously traceable to the site of its origins and to death) as a world of slightly suspended desire, in which often only the lightest of touches is required, such as the slight accidental grazing of the tips of their shoes that the two male protagonists of *Strangers on a Train* (1951) engage in just prior to their first meeting.

Delezue writes of the impulse toward a tactile cinema as one of the preconditions for the breakdown of the "traditional sensory-motor situations" so central to classical cinema.[107] What is important about *Marnie* within this more recent history is the intensity of expression given to the possibilities of a tactile cinema, the desire to move to a deeper level, to somehow break through some of the conventions of the earlier Hitchcock films. It is especially symptomatic of the film that, like its heroine, it both offers up seductive images and then will just as quickly pull away, that *Marnie* is both a "character study" and a kind of art film fascinated with pure surface. The touch can no longer be a light one. It is extreme, heavy, confused, violent, not always certain why it needs to touch in the way that it does, hence the repeated need to pull away, such as Marnie quickly pulling herself together after her mother has slapped her face. But as the film repeatedly demonstrates, once these powerful and seductive images have been offered, once the fantasy has been put into place, the very act of pulling away carries enormously complex implications: for the camera subject, for the spectator, and especially for the auteur.

3

Staging the Death of the Director

Two Weeks in Another Town

I don't know what you're waiting for. I've got nothing to say... unless you want to talk about Vincente Minnelli.

—*David Holzman's Diary*

⟨⟩

T WO WEEKS IN ANOTHER TOWN was made by artists whose careers were bound up with the heyday of the Hollywood studio system and who enjoyed enormous financial and critical success within it: the director Vincente Minnelli, the producer John Houseman, the screenwriter Charles Schnee, and the film's principal male star Kirk Douglas. Adapted from a 1960 Irwin Shaw novel, the film bears little relation to its source material, relying on only the most basic situation of the novel out of which it constructs a work with very different implications.

If a prior text haunts the film of *Two Weeks* it is not Shaw's novel but another film. Ten years prior to making *Two Weeks in Another Town*, Houseman, Minnelli, Schnee, and Douglas (as well as the film's composer, David Raksin) had collaborated on a financially and critically successful film about Hollywood, *The Bad and the Beautiful*. In *Two Weeks in Another Town*, they again tell a story about Hollywood filmmaking, here transplanted largely to

141

Rome and—unlike *The Bad and the Beautiful*—set entirely in the present day. At the start of the film, a washed-up Hollywood movie star named Jack Andrus (Douglas) is in Connecticut, attempting to recover from years of decadent living, from the humiliation of a devastated career, and from a tortured relationship with his sexually promiscuous former wife Carlotta (Cyd Charisse). Although doctors tell him he is now fit to be released, Andrus still feels psychologically unequipped to face "reality" again. Only when director and former friend Maurice Kruger (Edward G. Robinson) summons him to play a small role in a film Kruger is shooting at Cinecittà is Andrus able to walk out of the sanitarium. But Kruger is likewise plagued by troubles. Unable to get work in Hollywood any longer, he has been reduced to working on an international coproduction financed by an "international peddler," an Italian producer whose sole concern is that the film be shot on schedule and within its allotted budget. Kruger's Hollywood-trained methods are beginning to run the film behind schedule and the producer is now calmly threatening to shut the project down as part of a strange business maneuver that allows him to turn a profit even if the work is never released. Kruger enlists Andrus to help him with the dubbing, against the advice of Kruger's obsessively jealous and possessive wife, Cora (Claire Trevor). Kruger eventually collapses from a heart attack and Andrus steps in to finish the shooting for him. Although he initially attempts to remain faithful to Kruger's script, he begins to deviate from it, even shooting retakes of Kruger's footage, a move that causes Kruger to denounce him. After plunging into a psychological tailspin as a result of Kruger's rejection, Andrus reaches a moment of catharsis and decides to return to Hollywood, uncertain about his future but determined to begin again.

In attempting to dramatize this story, however, Minnelli and his collaborators found themselves caught up in the same kinds of dilemmas *Two Weeks* was documenting. They had numerous production and postproduction problems and the final cut of the film was taken out of their hands, a turn of events that prompted all participants to disown the released version. That version was not only a critical and financial failure, but was widely taken to be a primary instance of Hollywood's irrelevance as it now attempted to model itself on the fashionable and "decadent" European art cinema of the early 1960s. The *New York Times* headline for Bosley Crowther's negative review consisted of a single word: DEGRADATION. Thus, *Two Weeks in Another Town* is a film characterized by failure, decline, and decadence—both in its subject and in its essence. It has posed problems not only to critics and spectators, but also to the artists responsible for the film. It is an unclaimed "bad" object in which the artists' intentions were altered, compromised, or eliminated. Indeed, in his memoir *Final Dress*, Houseman describes the film's production as being doomed from the start:

In the years that had passed [since *The Bad and the Beautiful*] we had all undergone great personal changes: I was no longer the frightened, desperately eager producer I had been in 1952; Charlie Schnee, increasingly beset by bad health and domestic troubles, was not the flexible, fresh, imaginative writer he had been nine years before; Minnelli, grinding out film after film for MGM, had begun to tire. Kirk, finally, was now an established major star, no longer at the stage in his career where his intense, tireless drive for success and recognition coincided perfectly with the roles he was playing for us. . . .[1]

Two Weeks in Another Town was the first film in ten years in which Houseman took "neither pleasure nor pride."[2] In subsequent years, Minnelli attempted to position *Two Weeks* as a "profound" film made "shallow" by the studio's interference.[3] But Houseman more perceptibly points out that it is a film in which creative impotence and exhaustion are at the very core of the project. What Houseman fails to note, however, is that impotence and exhaustion are also the film's subjects. Far from diminishing interest in the work, the atmosphere of failure that has surrounded *Two Weeks in Another Town* foregrounds the film's importance as a document of the end of a certain practice of Hollywood cinema.

Houseman also complained that *Two Weeks* lacked "the invention and irony" of *The Bad and the Beautiful*.[4] For him, much of the failure of *Two Weeks* was related to the lack of firsthand knowledge that he, Minnelli, and Schnee had of the international film scene in Rome. This was particularly fatal in Minnelli's case because he was so overwhelmed by the city and the situations he found there that it "diverted him from the dramatic flow and personal relationships of the film he was making."[5] Here again, Houseman grasps an essential point about the film's problematic nature but without fully understanding its full importance. The title of the film already suggests that what we are viewing is an "outsider's" look at this environment—two weeks, a standard sojourn for a tourist. And while the reediting of *Two Weeks* at the hands of MGM is sometimes apparent, the film is certainly not the fragmented and incoherent viewing experience that those who worked on the project would have us believe. At 107 minutes, it is shorter than any of the Minnelli melodramas preceding it, several of which run approximately two and a half hours. Perhaps as a result of the studio's interference, *Two Weeks* does not have the precise, stately rhythm and structure of Minnelli's later melodramas. If this makes for a sometimes awkward viewing experience, it also gives the film its distinction, as though the crisis it is attempting to dramatize cannot be encompassed fully within the forms it is employing.

Essentially two critical approaches have been taken toward *Two Weeks in Another Town*. The first is a mainstream critical discourse derived from the reviews at the time of the original release. As noted, this attitude is not simply negative but dominated by a tone of shock and dismay at the decline in standards (aesthetic and moral) both in the work of Minnelli and Houseman and in Hollywood filmmaking in general.[6] The second approach, also largely from the period of the film's original release, is much more positive. Focusing on Minnelli as auteur, it can be found, predictably, primarily in the pages of periodicals such as *Cahiers du Cinéma* and *Movie*: The film was on Godard's Ten Best list for *Cahiers* in 1963 and placed twenty-first in the magazine's critics poll for that year, tying with Godard's own *Le Petit soldat* (1960). In *Movie*, Paul Mayersberg's essay on the film was titled "The Testament of Vincente Minnelli." For Mayersberg, the film was a "personal statement" about the process of filmmaking, comparable to Hitchcock's *Rear Window*, Renoir's *The Testament of Dr. Cordelier*, and Lang's *The Thousand Eyes of Dr. Mabuse*.[7] And Peter Bogdanovich's review in *Film Culture* declared that *Two Weeks* was "the ballsiest, the most vibrant picture [Minnelli] has signed."[8]

As a film about the creative impotence of filmmaking, *Two Weeks* emerges on the international scene one year before two other cinematic works that also deal with this matter: Godard's *Contempt* and Fellini's *8½* (1963) In comparison with these two films, *Two Weeks* might seem like a minor exercise in metacinema. But as I will argue in this chapter, *Two Weeks in Another Town* has its own kind of integrity and interest. If Minnelli's film lacks some of the assurance of these other modernist works, if it does not pursue certain issues in the same manner, it also addresses issues that these other films avoid. While Hollywood had been making films about its own working environment for almost as long as it had been in existence, these films had largely concerned themselves with presenting Hollywood as an occasionally troubled but largely regenerative community devoted to principles of hard work and self-sacrifice for the sake of the benevolent production of entertainment.

But during the postwar era, the entertainment to be had from these Hollywood-on-Hollywood films was in observing the replacement of one kind of mythical and iconographic power that this cinema once held over its spectators (that it could generate a highly idealized, magical, and glamorous world) being replaced by another kind of power, one built on the spectacle of decadence, violence, and corruption. During this period, the symbolic importance of Hollywood cinema as the great repository of ritualistic and mythical thought began to fade, the result of a combination of economic and social changes taking place both within the industry and outside of it. Especially notable here was the break up of the studio system and the de-centralization of Hollywood as a community. As early as 1951 David O. Selznick equated Hollywood with Egypt, "full of crumbling pyramids. It'll never come back. It'll just keep crumbling until finally the wind blows the last studio prop across the sands."⁹ This sense of Hollywood as a crumbling ruin began to manifest itself in films about the process of Hollywood filmmaking. *Sunset Boulevard* (Billy Wilder, 1950), *In a Lonely Place* (Nicholas Ray, 1950), *The Star* (Stuart Heisler, 1952), *The Barefoot Contessa* (Joseph L. Mankiewicz, 1954), *A Star Is Born* (George Cukor, 1954), *The Big Knife* (Robert Aldrich, 1955), and *What Ever Happened to Baby Jane?* (Aldrich, 1962) are all indicative of a tendency on the part of Hollywood to view its environment as one dominated by violence and chaos, as a community with apparently little conscious memory but everywhere marked by the onslaught of time. Far from being an aberration, *Two Weeks in Another Town* is of a piece with Hollywood's tendency to now look back on itself and take its own internal disintegration as the starting point for a reconceived notion of the kind of cinema it feels the need to produce.

In the years since *Two Weeks'* initial release, auteurist approaches have remained the only ones that have attempted to make a case for the film.¹⁰ But as auteurism itself was in a process of decline and revision during much of the 1960s and 1970s, these defenses of the film feel as though they are coming at the end of something rather than marking the beginning of a process of revisionism. In the two most recent books on Minnelli published in English, Stephen Harvey's *Directed by Vincente Minnelli* (1989) and James Naremore's *The Films of Vincente Minnelli* (1993), *Two Weeks in Another Town* is not a film around which significant arguments revolve—something that would have been unthinkable during Minnelli's testament days of the early 1960s. Naremore scarcely mentions the film; there is one brief negative evaluation of a sequence from it in relation to a comparable sequence in the (for Naremore) clearly superior *The Bad and the Beautiful*. And Harvey's approach takes us right back to Bosley Crowther. For Harvey, the film is a "fiasco"; it is "lurid" and "a stubborn lesson in the law of diminishing returns."¹¹

The cinema of Minnelli is one of the numerous intertexts cited in *Contempt*: Aside from the obvious reference to *Some Came Running*, *The Bad and the Beautiful*, and *Two Weeks in Another Town* also circulate within Godard's films as possible reference points (although I am not aware of Godard ever publicly acknowledging this relationship to these last two Minnelli films). As with Godard's other citations of favorite auteurs, Minnelli's work symbolizes the lost plenitude of classical film language for Godard rather than the source of a vital, living intertext. Both *The Bad and the Beautiful* and *Contempt* plunge us into their respective worlds of filmmaking through highly seductive opening shots in which a diegetic camera moves toward the nondiegetic moving camera filming this action (a crane in Minnelli, a tracking shot in Godard). In Minnelli's film, this camera movement is an ecstatic one, as within the diegetic world of the film we see a camera crane self-confidently glide across a soundstage while Minnelli's own camera crane moves forward to meet it, both of them meeting up with a beautiful woman lying across some cushions. Here we observe the full, glamorous panoply of filmmaking in a Hollywood studio, accompanied by the jubilant strains of Raksin's score. But in Godard's film, the camera is an almost achingly slow forward tracking shot through the deserted back lot of Cinecittà. The camera crew is small, almost invisible. Offscreen is the mournful sound of Georges Delerue's score and Godard's own voice as he reads the credits. Minnelli's cinema becomes the site of the multiplicity of petrifications that structure *Contempt*'s allegorical impulse, allowing Godard to build his modernity on the "ruined" remains of classical cinema.

Two Weeks in Another Town, on the other hand, is the ruin itself. This occurs as the film attempts to maintain the formal systems at work in Hollywood cinema, systems that the film knows on some level to be no longer valid (a situation that it indirectly dramatizes), but that it feels compelled to perpetuate in some ways. At the same time, it cites and incorporates those cinemas that at the moment of the film's appearance are documenting the increased irrelevance of Hollywood. By the early 1960s, it was a generally held belief that a particular practice of Hollywood cinema prevalent since the 1920s had effectively passed out of existence. Hollywood's production and distribution methods were reflecting this by now as well because the structure of the studio system of the previous three decades ended and the major studios converted their assets into television and alternative methods of production and distribution, and stars, producers, and directors began to operate independently rather than contractually. Furthermore, competition from cinemas outside of Hollywood began to pose a significant challenge to Hollywood's methods. Whereas none of these films could be considered as a significant source of domestic economic competition, they often posed a threat to U.S. economic dominance in overseas markets. In Italy in 1960, for example, Italian films dominated the domestic scene for the first time since 1946, surpassing Hollywood in popularity, while Hollywood was also increasingly filming in Rome to the point where Cinecittà studios had earned the nickname of "Hollywood on the Tiber."

During this period even *Cahiers* was beginning to be disillusioned about what they regarded as the decline of Hollywood. The enthusiasm the group had expressed toward Hollywood (as well as Italian) cinema during the 1950s was strongly related to the ways in which the cinema of these two countries was able to vividly express the social reality of their respective cultures, something felt to be lacking in most French cinema.[12] Through a combination of Hollywood's decline and the sharpened ideological and economic understanding of the industrial operation of the cinema, however, the magazine's contributors had become disenchanted. In a 1963 roundtable discussion with several prominent filmmakers and critics (including Godard, Rivette, and Truffaut), the emphasis is now on Hollywood's collapse. As its economic structure begins to change, so do its production and distribution methods. Its filmmakers now attempt to incorporate the latest European developments in cinema, leading to synthetic films that fail to have any relevant social meaning or context within American culture. Furthermore, its aping of European developments is ultimately timid and pale in comparison with the European vanguard. Luc Moullet complains, "instead of creating a new American cinema on the same basis but with a different character from the one that existed ten years ago, they made a copy of European cinema, except that they only kept its most superficial aspects."[13]

Still, these writers did not constitute a homogeneous group and the early 1960s was a strongly divisive period at the magazine with some critics still defending more traditional cinemas. The reception of some of Minnelli's films during this period is especially symptomatic of the split at the magazine between old guard positions, which still defend traditional Hollywood and those which question its formal methods and ideological workings. Minnelli's 1960 melodrama *Home from the Hill* was the official U.S. entry at the Cannes Film Festival that year and Jean Domarchi's report for the festival published in *Cahiers* praised the film for its "perfection." But the film received no awards. The Golden Palm that year went to Fellini's *La dolce vita*, the International Critics Prize went to Bergman's *The Virgin Spring*, and the Special Jury Prize was awarded to Antonioni's *L'avventura*, the last of these films "irritating" and "pretentious" to Domarchi.[14] This opinion was not shared by his colleagues at the magazine: *L'avventura* placed second in their annual poll for 1960; the "perfect" *Home from the Hill* did not even make the list.[15] At about the same time Minnelli was shooting *Two Weeks in Another Town*, Fellini was nominated for an Academy Award for Best Director for *La dolce vita* along with of people such as Stanley Kramer, Robert Wise, and J. Lee Thompson.

Furthermore, Hollywood's declining power as an aesthetic force was now also declining within the purview of the popular press of the period. When Minnelli's 1962 remake of the silent classic *Four Horsemen of the Apocalypse* was released to uniformly bad reviews in the United States, some critics referred to the grandiose, old-Hollywood irrelevancy of the project in relation to the more important contemporary developments in cinema. "It hardly seems possible," one reviewer wrote, "that at the same time Resnais was making [*Last Year at Marienbad*], MGM was working on a remake of *Four Horsemen of the Apocalypse*."[16] Within this context of inexorable decline, a polished and self-confident film such as *The Bad and the Beautiful*, although only ten years old at the time *Two Weeks* was released, comes to represent a long-lost golden age in the history of Hollywood. Excerpts from the film are screened in *Two Weeks* as a fictional (unnamed) film the director Maurice Kruger and the actor Jack Andrus had made together sometime in the past at the peak of their success in Hollywood. For contemporary reviewers of *Two Weeks in Another Town*, this act of self-citation made the failure of the current film even more obvious: "This inside joke is enough to remind us that these people have done better, and know better. Shame on them.[17] This "done better" is clearly the efficient professionalism of the Hollywood studio film that Minnelli and his collaborators are no longer able to provide.

In *The Classical Hollywood Cinema*, David Bordwell and Janet Staiger note that Hollywood has had a long history of appropriating important developments in European art cinema.[18] Throughout Minnelli's earlier career (including his work as a designer and director of Broadway musicals before he came to Hollywood), he often took advantage of European modernist developments within the arts and synthesized them into a distinctly American product that could theoretically be enjoyed and understood by anyone: Modernism as entertainment. As Naremore has pointed out, Minnelli's "historical importance lies in his ability to modernize entertainment, drawing on both 'high class' and bohemian domains of art."[19] What this most often involved was a form of citation or appropriation from modernist or avant-garde art, using them to transform his mass cultural products into something more significant than "mere" entertainment. But with *Two Weeks in Another Town*, this desire for a successful appropriation of European art cinema into a Hollywood narrative fails (at least within the popular perception) and consequently the power of this art cinema threatens to render Hollywood obsolete.

Like all of Minnelli's films, *Two Weeks in Another Town* was produced with all of the resources MGM could throw at a production of this nature. But it is also a victim of that largesse, an example of a lavish Hollywood studio entertainment and a melancholic reminder of those days, an auteurist testament of the postwar era and the shattered remains of a work uncomfortably situated between the era of Hollywood's heyday, the period of its postwar breakdown and the European cinema emerging and yet to come that challenged it.

Vincente Minnelli or the Interior

The first images of *Two Weeks* establish a sense of movement and space central throughout much of the film. Prior to the credits, we see an open road surrounded by woods. Out of the left of the frame, Andrus slowly emerges and looks left and down the road. The camera then tracks backward to reveal that a massive white iron gate blocks his path to the right. The road that initially suggested a journey is, in fact, a driveway, a contained "natural" space. At this point the music and credits begin. He turns away from the gate and slowly walks down the drive, the locked gate carefully circumscribing his freedom of movement. Throughout the credits, we see Jack slowly walking through the grounds of an estate, grounds that are at once luxurious and confined. A series of dissolves links Jack's movements as he walks along the outside of a cement pond, then through some carefully tended lawns, followed by a shot of him in a garden taken from a moderately high angle, the garden constructed of several footpaths. Jack stops in the midst of this and strokes the back of his head, as though he is not sure which direction to go in, before finally turning left. Another dissolve shows Jack walking past two men playing croquet before we get the film's first straight cut, which shows not Jack but a waiter emerging from what appears to be a large house, bringing a tray to two men playing chess on the terrace. As the waiter sets the tray down, Jack is visible in the left rear of the shot moving forward. Another straight cut takes us to the other side of the terrace as we see a shuffleboard diagram on the lawn and Jack picks up a cue and begins playing alone as the waiter brings a cablegram over to him. Jack does not read the cablegram but

Figure 3.1. The opening of *Two Weeks in Another Town* (1962): The journey of Jack Andrus, open.

Figure 3.2. The opening of *Two Weeks in Another Town*: The journey of Jack Andrus, closed.

merely walks away as we dissolve to a medium shot of him sitting on a bed, his hand visibly shaking.

This opening initially set us up to believe that Jack Andrus is a wealthy and powerful man taking a melancholy stroll over grounds that belong to him. Although certain details (in particular, the curious appearance of the other men who do not acknowledge Jack) already hint at a different reading of this opening, not until the second sequence is the sense of melancholic confinement confirmed as we discover that the estate is, in fact, a sanitarium and Andrus is a patient there. Several issues this opening raises are worth isolating. First, the importance of movement itself, not so much camera movement here (it will become central later in the film) but movement within the frame, the way that Andrus is positioned within the shots and the way that he moves through them. Second, even though this is an outdoor setting, design and decor play crucial roles in relation to the framing of the protagonist within his environment, a natural world that is also a controlled natural one, establishing a crucial relationship between confinement and freedom. And finally, in culmination, all of these elements lead toward the revelation that this is a sanitarium, situating many of the formal elements of this opening in relation to the psychological and the neurotic and between spaces that are private and those that are public.

As Andrus moves through the grounds of the sanitarium, he primarily keeps his hands in his pockets. His most significant gesture is stroking the back of his head as he looks around the paths of the garden, uncertain as to a direction. When he plays shuffleboard, he does so alone; it becomes a game without a purpose. Minnelli's protagonists are often slightly detached from their surroundings, like Andrus narcissistically moving in a sleepwalking or dreamlike fashion. Several of his early films contain explicit dream sequences (and in the case of his 1943 debut film, *Cabin in the Sky*, a *Wizard of Oz*–like dream frames the entire narrative). But these dream elements only make explicit the link between the ways that his characters behave and respond to the stimuli around them and the world of sleep, dreams, and—what this most often translates into—the visionary. One may then see this opening in *Two Weeks* as a typical Minnelli opening dealing with "the self-in-exile" out of which emerges the basic desire for movement and action.[20] But the intensity of Jack's neurosis that is established at the beginning of *Two Weeks* and the resulting enormous difficulty he has in spurring himself into action is unusually strong for Minnelli. In the second sequence of the film, which confirms that Jack is in a sanitarium and not his own home, the nurse asks him if he wants a one-and-a-half- or three-grain sleeping pill that night, placing Jack not so much within the company of dreamers as in the company of those who simply wish to withdraw entirely. The result is that we have a protagonist who has enormous difficulty in moving at all, whose every gesture connotes a relationship to an extreme form of neurosis, and who exists within a world in which space and decor seem to be utterly detached from his being.

The issue of mise-en-scène has, for better or worse, dominated much of the discourse on Minnelli. The fundamental debate surrounding his work in auteurist circles in the 1950s and 1960s was whether he was an auteur at all or simply a gifted metteur en scène, a minor artist strongly dependent on input from his collaborators and often preoccupied with decor to the exclusion of all other elements. This issue continues to crop up in the literature, even when the approach is sympathetic to the possibility of Minnelli as auteur. Naremore's argument that the authorship of Minnelli's films is "in the last analysis multiple or collaborative" is typical.[21] But the auteur/metteur en scène distinctions so important to debates about authorship in the 1960s were inadequate in coming to grips with Minnelli in that they failed to perceive the manner in which his cinema derives much of its energy from collapsing these distinctions. In 1961 Rivette referred to Minnelli as a "talented 'director' [who] has never been and never will be an auteur. When you talk about Minnelli, the first thing to do is to talk about the screenplay, because he always subordinates his talent to something else. Whereas when you talk about Fritz Lang, the first thing is to talk about Fritz Lang, then about the screenplay. . . ."[22] Such an attitude is completely misplaced and subordinating himself to the screenplay is precisely what Minnelli does not do. As with Lang and Hitchcock, Minnelli is more profitably understood in relation to obsessional filmmakers.[23] Repeatedly to the point of obsession, Minnelli's films do not simply represent a mise-en-scène–based cinema of decor, but they dramatize its very conflicts. Minnelli's protagonists are not simply frustrated artists (as has been pointed out time and again), but frustrated metteurs en scène who must arrange the settings of their lives in accordance with their own desires. However, what the films most often dramatize is a battle of wills between artists with conflicting visions. If Mabuse becomes the alluring and powerful double of Lang's own position of auteur, these metteurs en scène dominating Minnelli's cinema may be seen as an extension of Minnelli's own position as a director. Whereas the Mabuse films show that the master criminal ultimately self-destructs through his own megalomania, in Minnelli the need of the characters to create through the decorative arrangement of their own environments is often so strong that it likewise pushes them to the point of destruction—of themselves, of the decor, and of others around them. With Minnelli, a sense that his characters are actively engaging with the decor of their homes and work spaces rather than simply being determined by it, is something that occurs time and again.

In this manner, Minnelli's work captures in a unique way one of the historical moments of passage into modernity Walter Benjamin described: the rise of the bourgeois private citizen in the aftermath of the July Revolution, in which domestic spaces increasingly become distinct from work spaces and in which the insides of homes become expressions of the taste and sensibility of their inhabitants, "phantasmagorias of the interior."[24] On the one hand, Minnelli shows family homes, often ornate and clearly designed for public display, such as the Smith house in *Meet Me in St. Louis* (1944) or the Hirsch house in *Some Came Running*; on the other, we see rooms within these larger spaces that are more directly shaped by the sensibility of the individual who inhabits them: Emma's bedroom in *Madame Bovary* (1949) before her marriage to Charles, cluttered with prints and books devoted to erotic images of seduction, or Georgia Lorrison's rented room in *The Bad and the Beautiful* with its shrine dedicated to the memory of her dead father. The room becomes not so much an unconscious projection of the individual psyche as a conscious projection of a basic aesthetic impulse, a form of presentation of the self, "a box in the world theatre."[25] That such presentations of the self do not ultimately escape the social but are strongly determined by it is an issue Minnelli's films address. Hence the repeated action of the destruction of this decor, either because it does not adequately live up to the artist's vision, or because a conflict arises between two (or more) types of decor leading to the destruction of one in favor of the other, as in that bitterest of domestic comedies *The Long, Long Trailer* (1954), when the Collini mobile home accidentally destroys the garage, front porch, and lovingly tended rose bush of the aunt's home while her pathologically shy daughter looks on with an expression of barely repressed glee.[26]

Figure 3.3. *The Bad and the Beautiful* (1952): Georgia's shrine to her father, a "phantasmagoria of the interior."

Minnelli's characters are not only decorators but collectors, their interior spaces literally stuffed with objects. Georgia's shrine to her father chaotically overflows with items (scrapbooks, portraits, recordings) that evoke the memory and physical presence of her dead father. "Living," writes Benjamin, "means leaving traces."[27] The impulse to collect and display in this manner becomes a form of leaving behind such traces. This impulse is one Benjamin also connects with the rise of the detective story, a genre that in itself is strongly determined by its fascination with traces, clues, and indices. Minnelli is clearly invested in the possibilities of domestic traces and the intensity with which he invests in this creates a response in which, as Elsaesser has argued, spectators are encouraged to empathize not simply with the characters, but also with the setting, "which no longer functions as an objective point of correlation, but becomes wholly absorbed into the action as the natural extension of the protagonist's being."[28]

Furthermore, in the enormous sense they always communicate of a very deliberately and artificially composed frame, held up and presented for our perusal, they suggest the strong visual imprint of the auteur, equally committed to the collector's impulse as he leaves his own traces behind. Naremore has written that Minnelli tends to use the screen "as a window onto a colorful, expensive, and slightly heightened world,"[29] a manner of seeing that undoubtedly has much of its roots in at least one of Minnelli's professions prior to becoming a film director, a window dresser for Marshall Field's department store in Chicago. In Lang's *Fury*, Joe and Katherine walk in front of a series of shop windows looking at carefully designed fantasy rooms (of the sort Minnelli himself may have once created) and planning their future together. However, ultimately Minnelli—not Lang—becomes the central filmmaker for giving cinematic life to these windows. Although Lang's more distanced and critical eye generally keeps his protagonists and the spectator on the other side of this window, Minnelli moves directly into it, replacing Lang's mannequins with flesh-and-blood actors while introducing narrative into his highly mobile frames.

As with Lang and Hitchcock, doors often assume important functions in Minnelli, but the fascination with the gothic secret beyond the door has little hold. Space in Minnelli is almost invariably public, something on display rather than hidden. Consequently, it has little use for the door as a metaphoric marking for something hidden or repressed.[30] This is true even in his gothic melodrama, *Undercurrent*. In this film, Ann Garroway enters the home of a brother-in-law she believes to be dead. She walks around this living room and marvels at the design and decor. It is neither death nor the body that are primarily being represented here but rather a sensibility exercised through the arrangement of the decor in a public area of the house rather than in the private space of the bedroom. "It looks as though it was waiting for someone," she says of the room, "It's a home. It's someone's home." She attempts to open the bedroom door, asking for the key from the caretaker (in reality, her brother-in-law although she does not yet realize this) who informs her that the door is not locked but merely stuck. When she enters the bedroom, she briefly looks around but the place clearly does not have the same power for her as the living room.

Whereas both *The Thousand Eyes of Dr. Mabuse* and *Two Weeks in Another Town* are set in hotels with doors that never seem to be firmly locked, in *Two Weeks* the relative openness of the spaces and their lack of privacy is not connected (as it is in the Lang) to deeper, more paranoid visions of an all-seeing eye. If a door possesses any kind of residual qualities of mystery or magic in Minnelli, if it continues to mark a passage from one space or world into another, it is because what it ultimately opens onto is not a sinister private world in need of decoding, but a public space designed for presentation and performance: The preeminent examples here are the different, brilliantly colored doors in Jeffrey

Cordova's apartment in *The Band Wagon* (1953) as various characters open each of these doors to look into the room in which Cordova is extravagantly acting out a play for his potential backers. This emphasis on the door in relation to the public and in relation to spaces of performance may be seen as the result of both Minnelli's origins in the world of musical theater (doors as the opportunity for making a spectacular entrance and exit) and his status as a filmmaker of American origin in which transparency and openness serve as ideals within the context of a democratic nation-state. In terms of the latter of these, however, Minnelli's work is part of a complex postwar manifestation of this tendency that will be discussed in the following section.

Gaston Bachelard links the door to two basic manifestations of the daydream. In one of these, the door is tightly closed and padlocked; in the other it is wide open.[31] In Minnelli's cinema, with its fascination with the dream, we find neither of these examples in clear-cut form but instead we see the recurring motifs of doors that are seldom fully closed or fully open. The final shot of *The Long, Long Trailer* shows us not the door to the trailer closing, its married couple embracing on the other side of it, but instead the door incessantly opening and closing shut. The opening

Figure 3.4. *The Band Wagon* (1953): Doors opening onto a space of performance.

and closing shots of *Two Weeks in Another Town* are framed by two doors (or doorlike) images: the closed iron gate to the sanitarium and the closed door of the airplane that will return Jack to Hollywood. Both of these images, however, are marked by a certain hesitation, as though the film cannot offer clear images of entrapment or freedom. Instead the film is, like the flapping door at the end of *The Long, Long Trailer*, caught within a structure of ambivalence that, as the next section of this chapter argues, shapes so much of Minnelli's cinema.

Beyond this, however, the repeated use of the door or, to be more precise, the door frame becomes part of a much larger fascination with the very idea of the frame itself: doors, windows, mirrors, and portraits situated within frames, which are often filled with items of decor. The enormous attention to decorative clutter in Minnelli is a pointed rejection of a major strain of functional and streamlined modernist architecture. (And the Smith family house in *Meet Me in St. Louis* is precisely the type of American home space Frank Lloyd Wright reacts against.) Even in Minnelli films with contemporary settings one searches in vain for any spaces that strongly suggest a relationship to this type of architectural modernism, something that cannot be said of either Lang or Hitchcock. Both of these directors, whatever fascinations they had with premodern or gothic spaces, showed an equally strong fascination with more stream-lined types of modern design. But as David Gerstner has shown, Minnelli's visual aesthetic is in itself a type of modernist one, a visual language a diverse group of sources from James McNeill Whistler and Aubrey Beardsley to the post-Impressionists and the Surrealists formed. Although Gerstner applies no precise term to Minnelli's visual style, he uses such words as *excessive* and *chaotic*, ultimately situating this style within a "queer" modernist aesthetic and the tradition of the dandy.

In this manner, Minnelli's visual sensibility is not simply a style but also a site of ideological struggle, a resistance to the strongly (hetero-sexual) masculine aesthetics so central to much of modernist design in the early twentieth century.[32] *Undercurrent* has a sequence in which Ann visits the office of her husband, the office designed in a modified version of a modern streamlined style (with a large mural of airplanes and other modern vehicles painted on the wall). She expresses disappointment over this particular interior because it contains no "personality," the lack of person-ality here clearly connoting an excessive display of generalized virility through the sparseness of decorative elements that will stand in particular contrast to the home of her brother-in-law, which she will see in the sequence immediately following this. The very impulse to decorate, to fill a room, or to fill the frame with objects is, within this context, neither completely feminine nor completely masculine but a combination of the two. This tension between the masculine and feminine will ultimately acquire enormous significance in *Two Weeks in Another Town*.

However, if Minnelli's cinema represents a particular high point in this approach to the question of decor has it, by 1962, reached its limit, no longer able to carry the same kind of expressive weight it once had? Andrew Sarris's statement that Minnelli "has always required relatively luxurious projects upon which to lavish his taste"[33] more immediately suggests that within the context of the cinema of the 1960s, Minnelli's approach has begun to lack its former urgency. Minnelli's conception of the image implies a relationship to the expensive resources of the Hollywood studio system because this system is able to provide the kind of detailed and often sumptuous work on decor that Minnelli often requires. By 1962, this reliance on studio machinery begins to connote a relationship to what is increasingly perceived to be an anachronistic practice of cinema (one that, as noted in the previous chapter, Hitchcock also faced on *Marnie*). While mise-en-scène had been a primary terrain on which discussions of the auteur had taken place throughout the 1950s, by the early 1960s we are in a period in which mise-en-scène, as Godard stated in 1965, "doesn't exist." That statement specifically arose in relation to a brief discussion of Minnelli's latest film, *The Sandpiper*, which Godard dismisses as "an amateur film on a Hollywood scale."[34] Two years after this, André S. Labarthe wrote a brief piece for *Cahiers*, "Mort d'un mot," in which he recommended dispensing with traditional uses of the term mise-en-scène entirely.[35] Concerns now began to shift to cinemas that more strongly interrogate the very nature of filmmaking itself and that become increasingly and overtly political—a change from the idealist approach of the 1950s to the more materialist approach of the 1960s and after. Arguably more than any other U.S. director, Minnelli's reputation began to suffer during this period. His films not only appeared to be steeped in the artificial settings of Hollywood, but also presupposed (however ambivalently articulated) the idea of an expressive will in which individuals have the ability to shape and control the spaces around them as an extension of a visionary dynamism.[36] The bourgeois apartment of Hélène in *Muriel* is at the opposite extreme of a Minnelli space. Like a Minnelli space, it is filled with items of decor. But these items are mainly antiques that Hélène displays not as a form of personal expression but for the sake of selling them because she is a dealer. The decor gives the room a "personal touch," which is effectively a false one, always nervously in a state of transition, never permanently marked by its inhabitants. And although Minnelli lovingly films his decors in fluid camera movements and extended long takes, Resnais violently cuts into the objects of Hélène's apartment, disrupting any possibility of the spectator becoming acclimated to the space.

Furthermore, Minnelli's almost total lack of interest in realism had caused his work during this period increasingly to seem like so much cardboard and glitter, an evasion or pasting over of reality rather than a confrontation with it.[37] The year after Minnelli shot his penultimate musical *Bells Are Ringing* (1960), Godard released his "neo-realist musical," *A Woman Is a Woman*. Its interiors were largely shot on a soundstage, the type of film that (for Godard) should theoretically have been made "with a taste for details. A set designer's film" but instead was shot in a loose, improvisational manner.[38] What becomes urgent now is not so much the question of shooting entirely on location, of rejecting the very concept of sets and decor but rather of much more acutely measuring these stylized or fantasy elements against particular conceptions of realism. Jacques Demy's use of color and decor in *The Umbrellas of Cherbourg* (1964) is a perfect example of this. Demy's primary colors and stylized decor are, if anything, more extreme than Minnelli's. As in Minnelli, we are often meant to read this stylization in terms of a split between reality and how the self-absorbed, dreaming protagonists perceive the world around them. But Demy's film seems much more concretely steeped in its middle or working-class world. If Minnelli animates the shop window, Demy literally takes us inside the shop where the primary struggle is not between one dream or decor and another but rather how various historical, cultural, and economic factors interfere with a single romantic dream of the protagonists.

Nevertheless, *Two Weeks in Another Town* presents a particularly complicated variation on Minnelli's basic approach to the expressive possibilities of decor. It is a film whose interior spaces are almost entirely those of transience—hotels, sanitariums, and restaurants—spaces not marked by a relationship to the protagonists but by their alienation from them, spaces that refuse to allow the protagonists to project on to them. Although the mirror traditionally played a major role in Minnelli's work, functioning as everything from the passage from one world into another to emblems of the narcissism of the protagonists, here the protagonists barely respond to mirrors at all. Jack does not even look back at his own reflection in the sanitarium and barely makes any eye contact with himself in the hotel room mirror.

Although both *The Thousand Eyes of Dr. Mabuse* and *Two Weeks in Another Town* contain key moments in which a large hotel mirror is smashed, the fragments of the mirror in the Minnelli are divorced from the grandiose metaphoric signification that they have in the Lang. In the Minnelli, the mirror smashes because Cora has locked herself in her hotel bathroom, attempting to commit suicide by taking too many sleeping pills, and Kruger breaks down the door, inadvertently breaking the mirror in the process. The smashed mirror here may be read as a traditional psychological symbol of Cora's own shattered ego in the face of Kruger's rampant and public infidelities. Typically for Minnelli, if characters such as these are to become true artists, they must finally learn to, in a sense, turn away from the mirror and project this eye out on the world, allowing their vision to circulate. Jack keeps only two personal artifacts (an Oscar statuette and a photograph of Carlotta) and these he tucks away in drawers, only occasionally taking them out. It is as though his own neurosis is so extreme that he is incapable of collecting and arranging decor, of displaying anything. (Compare this behavior to the sequence early in *Some Came Running* when Dave Hirsch settles into his hotel and immediately begins establishing the room as his by taking out books by revered authors, stroking the books lovingly as he removes them from his bag, and then carefully arranges their placement on a dresser, thereby refusing the anonymity of the hotel room.)

Bachelard has referred to the house as a space that "protects the dreamer," a space that "allows one to dream in peace." When the subject is banished from the house or cast out, he is faced with "a circumstance in which the hostility of men and of the universe accumulates."[39] This is the kind of dilemma Andrus is now facing, banished from the house in the Hollywood Hills he shared with Carlotta, which serves as a primary space of memory for his neurosis. If Andrus is now incapable of projecting on his environment, if he cannot move through a world arranged in accordance with his own desires, then he (and the film) is in a situation close to death. Indeed, one character early in the film refers to him as "that face from the dead."[40] A central problem the film gives itself is how to restore movement to Andrus, for him no longer to be a "face from the dead." The answer, not surprisingly for Minnelli, is for Jack to become, literally, a metteur en scène, a film director. This will prove to be not quite enough, however, for either Andrus or for the film.

Ambivalent Utopias

Although only five years younger than Hitchcock, Minnelli belongs to a later group of Hollywood filmmakers who emerge not during the silent era but during the 1940s. This group (which also includes Ray, Mann, Preminger, Aldrich, Kazan, Fuller, and Losey) has a relationship to Hollywood's practice of classical narrative and to genre conventions that is transitional in nature, neither completely belonging to earlier paradigms nor completely shattering them.[41] Although remaining in many ways a cinema of action and spectacle, it is also one in which these actions seem to be entering what Deleuze has called their "final agony."[42] Largely operating within the mode of melodrama, they also differ from earlier American conceptions of melodrama that most often bore some relationship to the transcendent or to an emphasis on the individual or the couple being absorbed into the community. If, has been argued to the point of cliché, the American Dream becomes bitter after World War II, its melodramas likewise reflect an increased skepticism about both the transcendent and a belief in the possibilities of a forceful and dynamic energy to alter circumstances. As Elsaesser has phrased it in his seminal study of postwar melodrama, "the linear trajectory of self-fulfillment so potent in American ideology is twisted into the downward spiral of a self-destructive urge seemingly possessing a whole social class."[43] Throughout this later period, the narratives of these films become increasingly marked by violence and ambiguous motivations in which the most vital actions seem to be happening "inside" the characters and that they cannot fully articulate or resolve by putting into action.

Minnelli's dramatic films are part of a specific manifestation of this development, the family and small-town melodrama. Within this type of melodrama, the characters are frequently blocked, and the films repeatedly deal with the inability of characters to change or shape their own environments. The visual style of these films often takes place through the establishment of visual metaphors or tropes, a mise-en-scène, which reflects what characters are feeling, their emotions more than their thoughts. The performances of the actors, their movements, facial expressions, and manner of speaking likewise reflect this basic drive toward not only melodrama, but often also quite literally emotional breakdown and hysteria. The overwrought physicality of Kirk Douglas in the three films he did for Minnelli are primary examples of this performance style in which Douglas's clinched-teeth facial expressions and taut body language (performances always on the verge of caricature) seem to dominate the films. Although this style may not be radically different from what much of bourgeois melodrama has always done, the approach itself reaches a state of particular intensity in Hollywood during the postwar period. (As noted in chapter 2, even Hitchcock began to be affected by it in parts of *Marnie*.)

However, the emotional and physical violence in Minnelli's films is positioned in a somewhat different manner from that of most of the other directors who emerge during this period. These other directors made films in which the violence seemed to permeate almost every formal aspect of the films, a strongly kinetic cinema in which a sometimes fragmented decoupage and often angular and deep space compositions became major identifying formal traits and a significant extension of the violence of the films.[44] In the films of Kazan, Losey, and Ray, setting and decor are primarily social, reflecting less the desire of the protagonists to impose a vision on their immediate environments than a reflection of how that social world initially frames and articulates those desires. Decor, costuming, and the blocking and staging of action are crucial to this kind of cinema in that emotions are so often directly projected onto the spaces within the films and on to the bodies of the actors in an extreme and sometimes violent manner: the wife breaking the bathroom mirror in Ray's *Bigger Than Life* or the older son hysterically smashing his head against the glass of the train window in Kazan's *East of Eden* (1955). In both cases these violent gestures become external forms of acting out the basic psychological conflicts and repressions that the films dramatize. Minnelli's own melodramas take part in this, but certain aspects of his work also stand apart from that of other American filmmakers of his generation who work within this mode. Although the family melodrama typically plays out its conflicts within domestic spaces, Minnelli's films avoid the larger architectural approach to space found in the work of Ray, Losey, and Douglas Sirk, in which massive and cold interiors seem alternately to overwhelm or stifle the protagonists—the mausoleum-like home of the widow in Sirk's *All That Heaven Allows* (1955) being a prime example of this.

But Minnelli (like Preminger) tends to draw on a much more polished style comprised of fluid camera movements, complex staging of action, generally discreet cutting, and shot durations that, while often on the long side, rarely achieve extreme lengths. Close-ups are used sparingly and the camera seldom seems to be as closely tied to the bodies of the actors as it is in the films of Minnelli's colleagues. The camera eye in Minnelli is more consistent with the transparency on which classical Hollywood constructed itself and Minnelli's cinema partakes of neither the panoptic eye of Lang nor an image of thought in the manner of Hitchcock. And yet Elsaesser has linked Minnelli with Lang (as well as with Jean Renoir and Max Ophuls) for their exemplary nature in that in their work, "the act of seeing, the constraints and power-relations it gave rise to, appeared so uncannily foregrounded that the action always tended to become an adumbration or metaphor of the more fundamental relation between spectator, mise-en-scène, audience and (invisible, because reified) director."[45]

Let us look closely at a sequence from *Two Weeks in Another Town* in this regard. In this sequence, Jack and Veronica (Dahlia Lavi) are sitting at a table in a restaurant in Rome. In the midst of this chaotic, noisy public space, Jack quietly tells Veronica of his obsession with his wife Carlotta and of the night he discovered her in bed with another man—a traumatic event causing Jack to jump behind the wheel of a car and take a calamitous and drunken ride down the Hollywood Hills until the car crashed into a wall, thereby scarring his face. The sequence is about three minutes long and is done in a single take. This take is not static, but the camera movements in the sequence are not continuous either. Minnelli's cinema is not primarily one of the face or of the object seen in isolation, but a cinema of the body in motion, in which the face and the object are constantly linked up with this moving body. The body itself, however, does not give the appearance of enjoying unrestricted freedom but frequently seems to be moving in a choreographed fashion, the action carefully staged in accordance with the precise framing and movements of the camera. In this manner, one could argue that Minnelli's actors are no "freer" than Hitchcock's or Lang's in that they still seem to be part of a precise formal arrangement.

The sequence begins with the camera pulling back from a shot of a bickering young couple, tracks past a single man eating a plate of spaghetti, and then tracks back and to the right where Jack and Veronica are sitting. Whereas Jack and Veronica remain in the foreground and center of the shot throughout the remainder of the sequence, by the end the camera eventually tracks an almost 90-degree path around their table. In each case, the movements appear to be dictated by the movements of the extras around Jack and Veronica. For example, a couple sitting on Jack and Veronica's right get up and leave the restaurant early in the sequence, exiting to the left of the frame as the camera tracks to the right of Jack and Veronica's table. The classical logic behind this camera movement is clear: if the camera did not move, then the exiting couple would leave an "empty" space at their table to the left of the frame, throwing off the balance of the composition. Minnelli's camera then gently moves to the right as a waiter in the background of the shot moves in this direction as well and the camera more tightly frames Jack and Veronica. The waiter stops at a table at the far right of the frame and takes an order as Jack continues to narrate to Veronica. The camera then moves again, now slowly tracking forward, moving more closely in toward the couple as Jack's description of his violent evening reaches its conclusion, eventually framing the couple in a close CinemaScope two-shot.

The movements of the camera in this sequence do not simply follow the movements of the extras around the restaurant. They also follow an "internal" movement here, that of Jack's psychological state as he describes an evening in which he came across his former wife Carlotta engaged in what was a presumably bizarre sexual activity (he stops before getting to specifics as though what he saw was unspeakable) in the bed-

Figure 3.5. *Two Weeks in Another Town*: The restaurant sequence, shot in one extended take, within a mobile frame, culminating with Veronica touching the scar on Jack's face.

room they had once shared. The camera's tracking movement around the table until it finally reaches a state of relative intimacy with the two-shot of Jack and Veronica are clearly intended to correspond to Jack's increased withdrawal from the present situation he is in with Veronica, pushing him psychologically back into his past with Carlotta. Not until the final moments of the sequence, as Veronica reaches out to touch the scar on his face and tells him that she is glad he was not killed, does the movement of the camera completely center the couple in a comfortable two-shot. The staging of this sequence is cluttered, with waiters darting back and forth behind Jack and Veronica and patrons entering and exiting the restaurant. Initially, the soundtrack is cluttered as well with the sounds of the fighting couple spilling over into Jack and Veronica's conversation. All of this creates an important level of verisimilitude, at least within a tourist's sensibility: we are in Rome and everybody knows that Romans are noisy and excitable.

However, the bickering couple functions not simply as local color but as a variation on the "neurotic" and possessive relationship between both Jack and Carlotta and Kruger and Clara. In place of obsession and violence we have in the young Roman couple a relationship defined by its theatrical nature: Veronica translates the argument for Jack and tells him that they are actually expressing their devoted love toward one another, which she says is "very Roman." The sounds of the couple eventually go away, replaced by nondiegetic music for Jack's narration. The entrance of this music and the camera movement circling closer around the table signify Jack's withdrawal from the world around him. The sequence in general may be seen as engaging in a struggle between a representation of a moment in the present (space and movement conceived of in terms of a rejuvenative reciprocity with Jack and Veronica enjoying one another's company at a restaurant full of happy, active people) with one in the past (Jack's memory of Carlotta, which affects his response to Veronica and to the sights and sounds around him and also "contaminate" the movements of the camera, now also determined by the role of memory as much as by movement in the present). Furthermore, the sequence looks and moves in the way that it does because it has a prophetic function. The gliding camera movements have a vaguely ominous quality to them. Not until the end of the film does this fully manifest itself as Jack replays his violent night in the Hollywood Hills from five years earlier, this time through the streets of Rome. And finally, the sequence also has a heavily authorial feel to it: the elaborate blockings of the extras as they move around the couple and the camera movements that are there to be noticed, partly because of their psychological function (they are movements that trace Jack's mental state and consequently noticing them is vital to a full understanding of the sequence), but also because, like the movements of the extras, they create a strongly choreographed environment, a sense of performance and presentation. And Jack's body is extremely stiff here, as though physically paralyzed by his own memories. The camera movements supply the necessary rhythm and movement the actor is not permitted to.

However melodramatic the content of this sequence is, its choreographed quality undoubtedly evokes the genre with which Minnelli's name is most strongly associated, the musical. The musical genre traditionally presents an ideal image of both the cinema and of the real world to which it refers. This is largely a question of song and dance, of movement, and how these become magical, transformative acts. Elsaesser has gone as far as to argue that "all of Minnelli's films aspire to the condition of the musical,"[46] and that the melodramas "are musicals turned inside out."[47] He sees the paradoxical nature of the musical as Minnelli's metaphor for the cinema in general, in that it is a genre that is highly disciplined and controlled but at the same time geared toward producing an overall impression of spontaneity and fluidity. Although Minnelli's protagonists are still goal oriented in accordance with classical Hollywood, this drive is "only superficially concerned with a quest, a desire to get somewhere in life, i.e., with any of the forms by which this dynamism rationalizes or sublimates itself."[48] Instead, his characters are concerned with a gratification of their senses, with a desire to see the world around them brought into line with their own conception of how that world should look, behave, and function, moments that frequently reach maximum moments of intensity through song and dance.

For Elsaesser the characters in the Minnelli musicals are largely able to achieve gratification through song and dance. This basic level of conflict, however, is often not completely transcended. The classical musical's utopian impulse, its investment in the values of community, of collective effort, of a belief in the transcendent value of the romantic couple, all of this ideally expressed through song and dance, is still present in Minnelli, but in a much more ambivalent fashion. One character's gratification in the Minnelli musicals usually takes place at the expense of another individual or group; someone must pay a price (emotionally speaking) for someone else's happiness. Space in Minnelli often becomes, as Deleuze terms it, "absorbent," invested with the dreams, the visions, the subjective states of several characters moving through them rather than as the ultimate site of a collective or romantic transformation through song and dance. Dance is not simply movement within space for Minnelli but a "passage from one world to another, entry into another world, breaking in and exploring."[49] As in Hitchcock in relation to the question of thought addressed in the previous chapter, the doors of Minnelli's cinema must, to some degree, always be open or at least flexible enough to allow such a passage to take place. This peculiar drive may partly explain the unresolved tone to many of Minnelli's musicals, which seldom fully give themselves over to the utopian impulses one most commonly associates with more traditional practices within the genre.[50]

In a larger sense, however, one may see the musical's emphasis on collectivity as a metaphor for Hollywood cinema as a whole and for Minnelli's position as a filmmaker within that system. Minnelli creates genre pieces that allow themselves to be read as, in many ways, traditional Hollywood films, while at the same time frequently dramatizing and representing the possibility of a rupture or breakdown of that form. Perhaps much of the frequently detected strain of melancholia that runs through Minnelli's work is the result of what he imagines his own role as auteur in this process to be—at once an artist with a strong and recognizable style and a contract director for hire, working in a strongly collaborative environment in which individual traces of authorship are frequently submerged by the conditions of production in a major Hollywood studio.[51] In a sequence from Minnelli's 1955 melodrama *The Cobweb*, Stevie violently rips up his designs for the curtains of the sanitarium in which he is a patient only to be reprimanded by an employee, Meg, who tells him that those designs do not belong simply to him. Even though he designed them, they now also belong to the sanitarium and to the patients. In other words, Stevie must learn that his art is fundamentally collaborative (other patients and employees of the sanitarium made contributions to the designs and to the production of the curtains), and once his designs are finished they will hang and be displayed in such a way that they will also enter into the needs and desires of those who will look at them. This process is clearly analogous to working in a large industrial apparatus such as Hollywood, in which art is produced in collaboration and in which that art must likewise speak to the needs of a wide range of individuals with the result ideally existing as both art and entertainment.

In *Two Weeks in Another Town*, Jack and Veronica walk down the steps of the Via Veneto and come across a painter surrounded by various portraits he is selling of people sitting on these same steps. Everything has been finished in these portraits except the face of the sitter, who in this particular case is about to be Veronica. Paintings being mechanically turned out, made to order, no point of view taken, the only mark of distinction and humanity coming at the very end of the process as a specific individual comes along—the accidental subject of the portrait—and intervenes in the process. It is this portrait that becomes the only object that Jack later displays in his hotel suite, the single mark he attempts to make on it. But it is a work that is ironically devoid of a strong personal style and it is a portrait of a woman he is ultimately not in love with. Moments like this recur in Minnelli, in which art is caught between the forces of mass production and the needs of the individuals who both make and consume this art.[52]

In both *Two Weeks in Another Town* and *The Band Wagon*, a washed-up movie star leaves Hollywood and attempts to revive his career elsewhere but instead finds himself suffering at the hands of an egomaniacal director. Only by replacing this director and creating a sense of a supportive community of people working together on the project (something that had been absent before) does the star begin to regain his footing and the project come to life. *Two Weeks in Another Town*, then, becomes a partial reworking of not only *The Bad and the Beautiful*, but also *The Band Wagon*, which it turns "inside out." Like *The Bad and the Beautiful*, *The Band Wagon* was produced as the Hollywood studio system was declining. But Minnelli and his collaborators were still doing quite well within that system in spite of the obvious signs of change around them. Both films touch on the idea of failure and decline, but only to come back around to the idea of renewal (complete in *The Band Wagon*, tentative in *The Bad and the Beautiful*). Like *The Bad and the Beautiful*, *The Band Wagon* places a strong belief in the collaborative value of art. This connection between the two films is reinforced throughout *The Band Wagon* as the marquees on the various theaters in Times Square advertise the films Jonathan Shields made in *The Bad and the Beautiful*, as though both films inhabit the same fictional world. As much as *The Bad and the Beautiful*, *The Band*

Wagon is a film about Hollywood. Against those who might charge Hollywood with producing anonymous entertainments turned out on an assembly-line basis, both films stress the positive values of working in collaboration and of the magical entertainments that are produced as a result of the lavish resources of the major studios. But by the time of *Two Weeks in Another Town*, we find an absence of any kind of positive community within the narrative world of film, a symptom of a similar absence surrounding the production of the film itself. MGM (now under the head of Joseph Vogel) is actively antagonistic toward the film, a far cry from the relationship of the Dore Schary regime to *The Bad and the Beautiful* ten years earlier. The disappearance of this community from *Two Weeks* not only intensifies the isolation of Andrus and Kruger as protagonists, but it also gives the film an uncertainty as to where its social parameters are.

The film in general seems to be marked by a certain stridency of tone unusual for Minnelli. In particular, the confrontations between Kruger and Cora are played at almost the same hysterical pitch from beginning to end, while moments such as Davie Drew (George Hamilton) suddenly bursting into Jack's room with a knife in his hand become almost parodies of melodrama. (The latter sequence even quickly switches to a comic mode when Kruger walks in and quickly removes the knife from Drew's "limp wrist.") Although the expressive use of gesture is crucial to Minnelli's cinema and often serves to replace the limits of spoken language, in *Two Weeks* gesture becomes uncharacteristically violent. If the hand in *Marnie* becomes caught up in a system of unrealizable tactility, the hand in *Two Weeks* becomes almost entirely shaped by violence and neurotic behavior. Jack's shaking hand becomes the clearest sign of his neurosis (it is the first significant gesture he makes when we see him in his room in the sanitarium), and when Kruger's hostile assistant, Janet Bark (Joanna Roos), taunts Jack she says, "Some day you won't be able to keep that hand from shaking." When the hand is not shaking, it is lashing out at others, from the slap across the face that Jack gives to Lew Jordan (George Macready) at the airport, the slap that Barzelli gives to Davie in the film-within-the-film, Davie slapping Veronica across the face in the screening room, Clara and Barzelli slapping one another at the anniversary party after Barzelli attempts to fondle Kruger ("Tell that hand to stop working under the table!"), and finally Jack slapping Carlotta during the orgy sequence. It becomes the ultimate mark of Kruger's powerlessness as a director after his heart attack when, unable any longer to gesture at all, his entire body is tightly wrapped up in his hospital bed, mummy-like. But it is crucial to Jack's success as a director in replacing Kruger that his "taming" of Barzelli takes place centrally through the hands. Barzelli cannot understand why Jack will not allow a hand double for the shot of her pulling jewels out of a jewelry box, and she begins to throw a hysterical fit over the matter, causing Jack to kick her in the rear end, a gesture that causes her to return obediently to the box and obey all of Jack's instructions.

The faces of the protagonists become marked by this violence as well: the black eye that Davie gives Veronica, the cut on Kruger's face from Davie's knife attack, and the scar on Jack's cheek, the last of these almost playing as the last vestige of the heavily marked body of melodrama. At the time of the film's release, Manny Farber complained that Douglas here is simply "a body on display, one now shrinking in middle age while the mind of his employer is fixed on other things."[53] To whom Farber is referring here when he writes of a disinterested employer is not clear. Is it Kruger or Minnelli? Essentially it does not really matter. What is important is this physical impression of an actor "shrinking in middle age." Minnelli continues to use (either through habit or necessity) more traditional film actors in a context that renders their presence problematic or anachronistic. These actors are being asked to give something new, something different of themselves that they must struggle to do. The fact that it is clearly a struggle and that their presence embodies what Minnelli is likewise experiencing toward his own project creates a situation in which the actor becomes a constant reminder of the inadequacy in fully realizing a vision and which is doubled within the film itself, as Kruger struggles to deal with Davie and Barzelli. The violence of the actors here becomes an embodiment of the intense struggle on the part of the film to give birth to something new. (It will later become this motif of the slap as the principal of film production and of the personal relationships that develop out of this situation Fassbinder will likewise take up in his 1970 film *Beware of a Holy Whore* in which the slap is repeated so often that it becomes ritualistic.)

Figure 3.6. *Two Weeks in Another Town*: The struggle to control gesture.

Minnelli's musicals had always sought to reconcile (if only tentatively at times) the conflicts within its world of battling visionaries. Of the melodramas, this aspect of art as compromise is clearest in *The Bad and the Beautiful* where Georgia Lorrison, Fred Amiel, and James Lee Bartlow endure numerous personal sacrifices and tragedies at the hands of Jonathan Shields (betrayals, lies, infidelities, personal humiliations, and, in one case, the death of a spouse Shields's intervention indirectly caused) but who all go on afterward to extremely successful Hollywood careers as a result of their contact with him. To what extent this constitutes an optimistic picture of the production of Hollywood cinema is debatable. I do not agree with Jacques Aumont's contention (in comparing the film unfavorably with *Contempt*) that *The Bad and the Beautiful* indulges in "totally mythical self-congratulation" in its treatment of the tortured producer as Serious Artist.[54] While the film certainly engages in its own share of mythologizing, it is best seen as a deeply ambivalent film about Hollywood and the structures and the desires it sets into motion and in which this ambivalence becomes a structuring element. The film frequently seems to be engaging in a dialogue with itself, moving between accepting the conventions of Hollywood and treating them ironically.

This ambivalence is very strongly bound up with *The Bad and the Beautiful*'s historical position as a big-budget star film MGM produced, but at a moment when Hollywood was in a state of economic decline. In its sumptuousness, the film (like so much of Minnelli's work throughout the decade) represents a throwback to the earlier, more profitable days of the studio. But it is also a film affected by the formal changes at work in the cinema (in Hollywood and elsewhere) during this period. It no longer completely believes in its own structures and meanings but rather than thoroughly question those structures it reproduces, complicates, and subjects them to irony. The ambivalent structure of *The Bad and the Beautiful* is a perfect realization of the desire to still retain some investment in the values of community and of action but in a highly displaced and fragmented manner. Jonathan Shields is indeed an active, goal-oriented protagonist in the classical sense—a strong leader. But the film does not place him at the very center of its narrative structure. Instead, the three flashbacks, the memories that set the film's narrative into motion, belong to essentially passive characters who only become dynamized into action through their contact with Jonathan: When Amiel denounces Shields near the end of Amiel's flashback for stealing his idea for a film, Shields responds by telling him, "With you it would have stayed an idea." Amiel's own status as a goal-oriented protagonist, his rise to the top of the industry after his breakup with Jonathan is something the film does not dramatize because it is essentially not interested in this more classical form of representation.

Jonathan always seems to be on the set, immaculately dressed, just behind a director who waits for his final okay on the sequence. He is, as the director Von Ellstein puts it, a producer who "thinks like a director."[55] Throughout Amiel's flashback, he rarely seems to have a creative idea of his own. Where would this Academy Award–winning director Amiel be, the film asks, without this producer? More to the point, the film implicitly asks where would Hollywood cinema be without great producers in general during a time when the "great" producers (such as David O. Selznick and Sam Goldwyn) were becoming so many "crumbling pyramids." (When Prokosch invites Lang to lunch in *Contempt*, Lang declines saying, "Include me out, as Goldwyn, a *real* producer, used to say.") *The Bad and the Beautiful* does, in fact, show us a director at work but that director is Jonathan and not Amiel or Von Ellstein or any of the other minor figures who dot this narrative. The director function in this film is simply displaced onto Jonathan, as though the film must call the director something other than what he is. *The Bad and the Beautiful* is both a work of mourning for the creative producer of the past while pointing toward the creative director of the present and future—all embodied in the character of Jonathan. Only when Jonathan begins firing directors and completely dominating productions does his downfall begin (a clear parallel with Selznick). At the same time, the film cannot present us with a new conception of the director emerging out of this with the result that the character of Amiel remains somewhat shadowy and undeveloped.

In *Two Weeks*, the characterization of Kruger is far more compelling than Amiel, not only due to the sharper writing, but also due to the performance of Edward G. Robinson, whose star persona brings with it here an inevitable association from his past roles with crime films, their motifs of gangsterism and corruption completely in keeping with the way in which Kruger is characterized.[56] While in Shaw's novel the character is named Maurice Delaney, the film not only supplies him with a different last name, but also in the casting and rewriting gives him a certain German/Jewish Teutonic quality carrying inevitable associations with a similarly exiled figure such as Lang, particularly given Robinson's association with Lang through two of their most successful Hollywood films, *The Woman in the Window* and *Scarlet Street*.[57] As with Lang, Kruger exhibits, in the one sequence that shows him directing, strong-willed and almost sadistic behavior on the set, particularly toward Davie Drew, whom he regularly insults with homophobic remarks. As with Lang, Kruger is not a team player and shows little concern for the feelings of others. He tells Andrus that he is "the only actor I ever made a friend of," evoking Lang's history of brutalizing and alienating his own actors. As a Hollywood film director, he is (also like Lang) unacceptable and the film must eliminate him in some way, remove him from the set of his own film so the more democratic figure of Andrus can replace him. But it is this very act of replacing Kruger, of the need to replace him, which has enormous symbolic importance.

What Does a Director Do?

The problem the Minnelli films exhibit in giving full legitimacy to the role of the all-powerful director is something which cannot be ascribed to the limitations of his films alone, nor even to distinctions between modernist and classical cinema. The cinema in general has had enormous difficulty in representing the film director, in demonstrating what a director specifically does. Films have been made in which the act of filming by a solitary individual, a lone filmmaker or cameraman, is represented: *The Man with the Movie Camera*, *Peeping Tom*, or Jim McBride's *David Holzman's Diary* (1969); or films that show the film director at work, but in more "primitive" forms of production: the early days of silent film: Peter Bogdanovich's *Nickelodeon* (1976) and Paolo and Vittorio Taviani's *Good Morning, Babylon* (1987), or the shooting of pornography: Shohei Imamura's *The Pornographers* (1966) and Paul Thomas Anderson's *Boogie Nights* (1997). But with regard to representing the production of cinema within a larger industrial apparatus, the specific act of directing itself is most often pushed to the margins of the narrative and becomes virtually unrepresentable. Many films take us on movie sets, showing us productions under way. But the director characters are often continually prevented from directing or directing effectively, from Lowell Sherman's alcoholic director in Cukor's *What Price Hollywood?* (1932) to Truffaut's mild-mannered traffic manager in *La nuit américaine* (1973). In a way, most films on filmmaking continually insist on the "the death of the director," not only in the extent to which directors in these films tend to die a literal or symbolic death, but also that they show that the act of direction does not fully exist or at least not through a single individual. For cinemas that emerge within a large industrial form of production, the director pushes the representation of filmmaking to the breaking point. What, after all, does a film director do? One may show the screenwriter at work (*Sunset Boulevard* and *In a Lonely Place*) because that profession is bound up with narrating, and the act of writing can be easily represented. But if that writer is also a director (as in *The Barefoot Contessa*) then neither activities are directly shown and the act of labor becomes veiled.

In this regard, Minnelli's art film successors (or contemporaries) do not completely solve this problem of how to represent the film director either. In *8½*, Fellini spectacularizes Guido's inability to direct his latest film in which, through its mirroring structure, $8^{1}/_{2}$ itself becomes the film-within-the film. Although this strategy allows Fellini to treat the subject of filmmaking in a much more audacious manner than if had he literally shown Guido directing (an impossibility anyway, given the nature of Fellini's project here), we still have another film that does not show us, in a concrete fashion, what *directing* specifically means. Indeed, the very subject of much of modern cinema when it turns to the topic of filmmaking is not so much to foreground the material process of film direction as to further problematize and delay this subject, which classical cinema has already had such difficulty in facing. Even *Contempt* shows us very little of Lang actually directing *The Odyssey*. Instead, he spends much of the film pontificating, watching tests, concerning himself with the margins of production while Godard's own film reproduces (albeit in a different way) the standard producer/director/writer conflict *The Bad and the Beautiful* already addressed. By the time of *The State of Things* in 1982, Wim Wenders merely intensifies all of these conflicts. Almost the entire running time of the film is concerned with the director, cast, and crew waiting for the film to be made, waiting in a hotel on the Portuguese coast for the funds to arrive. The producer is not shown offering a lot of hot tips to the director (as in *The Bad and the Beautiful* or *Contempt*) but is in another country, living on the run out of his mobile home as he tries to avoid the mobsters from whom he has borrowed money. At the end of the film, the producer meets a fate that surely must be the dream of so many directors, past, present and future: he is killed, gunned down by the mob. But the director (alternately called Fredrich or Fritz, a combination of the first names of two of the leading Weimar cinema filmmakers, Murnau and Lang, the latter's star on Hollywood Boulevard shown near the end of the film) shoots this process and as a result he is also gunned down. Whether he actually dies at the end is unclear, but the final images of the film are of those that can be seen through the viewfinder of his camera as it lies on the ground in a parking lot in Los Angeles. If at the end of *Two Weeks in Another Town*, the death of the director is metaphoric in *The State of Things*, it is both literal and metaphoric—the director dies in the line of duty. But the camera runs uninterrupted without him and images continue to be produced.[58]

Deleuze pinpoints the fundamental problem facing film production itself as being that of money, of capital: "[W]hat defines industrial art is not mechanical reproduction but the internalized relation with money."[59] This is an issue that postwar cinema often addresses when it takes film production as its subject, but that classical cinema has largely avoided. For the classical Hollywood film about filmmaking, money is rarely an issue explicitly addressed because within the self-mythologizing context of the studio system, money is plentiful. In *The Bad and the Beautiful,* all the rises and falls of the various careers we see, all the production difficulties are primarily personal and psychological in nature. Even when Shields and Amiel work for the notoriously stingy B-film studio executive Harry Pebble, Pebble is ultimately willing to finance the A budget production idea Shields and Amiel have for their breakthrough film, *The Faraway Mountain.* Where a B-film studio was able to get the financing for this project does not matter: The money is always there, somewhere, it is simply a question of wresting it out of the proper hands. *Two Weeks* marks an important break in this regard in that it does acknowledge the flow of capital as being fundamental to production in a way that its predecessor (nor, to my knowledge, any Hollywood film prior to this) does not. (For that matter, the flow of capital is not addressed by *8 1/2* in which, as Aumont notes, "the anxiety of creation seems in the end to shake off all material constraints."[60]) The producer character in *Two Weeks,* Tucino (played by Mino Doro of *La dolce vita*), lacks even the reptilian charm of Prokosch in *Contempt.* He is solely concerned with turning a profit, does not even offer negative input on Kruger's film (as his impassive response to *The Bad and the Beautiful* during the screening room sequence shows, he has no response to the cinema as such), and is happily willing to completely shut down the project rather than allow Kruger to go over budget. It is money that threatens to erase the director, destroying or compromising the images, either by closing down production or by re-placing the director with someone else. As the director Harry Dawes notes with bitter irony in *The Barefoot Contessa,* his own profession is "not important" in comparison with that of a wealthy producer such as Kirk Edwards. The ultimate betrayal for Kruger, however, comes from Andrus, not so much when Andrus shoots scenes that Kruger was not able to shoot after his heart attack as when Andrus does retakes of Kruger's own footage that Kruger "shot with his blood." Andrus, in a sense, writes *over* Kruger's images, "improving" them.

In noting the difficulty that most films about filmmaking have in adequately dealing with the production of cinema, Rivette argues that a film crew is a "conspiracy, completely closed in on itself, and no one has managed to film the reality of the conspiracy." There is "something infamous, something profoundly debauched about cinema work," while at the same time he adds that this debauchery is something that is very difficult to represent. For Rivette, theater becomes the cinema's great subject, in fact the subject in which cinema most fully deals with its own inner workings although in a somewhat displaced form, theater as cinema's "elder brother . . . another way of looking at itself in a mirror. . . ."[61] Whatever his antipathy toward Minnelli, Rivette's comments have some bearing on understanding what is at stake in *Two Weeks in Another Town*. First, this notion that theater is a way of looking at the cinema "in a mirror" becomes a way of addressing "the subject of truth and lies, and there is no other in the cinema."[62] The very artificiality of Minnelli's images, the ways that they seem to redress and decorate over the real world, suggests a cinema that has, at the very least, a complicated relationship to the idea of cinematic "truth." One of the interests of Minnelli's cinema on this matter has not to do with moments in which a language of visual artifice interacts with a language of realism (as in Renoir, Visconti, or Demy), but rather with how this artificial world repeatedly dramatizes its own implicit limitations. "I've been faking so long," says Kruger, "I don't think I can feel what's real anymore," a line Guido repeats almost verbatim in *8½*. Drawing on the world of theater and performance becomes crucial here, both for pointing up the limitation of this approach to filmmaking and for celebrating its own particular strengths.

Throughout Minnelli's work the theater and theatricality become ideal states (in ways that the circus often functions for Fellini), sites of play in which the difficulties of the real world (or of creation) are successfully reworked as public performance, as in *8½*'s famous final sequence in which the characters out of Guido's life step down from rafters hidden behind a curtain, join hands and dance in a circle around a circus arena. The sequence from *The Bad and the Beautiful* screened in *Two Weeks* is entirely built around issues of theatricality, irony, and decay. We hear Jonathan play a recording of Georgia's father reciting a famous soliloquy from *Macbeth* ("A poor player who struts and frets his hour upon the stage"), and he tells her that she is, in fact, giving a performance for him right now but that it is the performance of a bit player and not a star: "You can't be a star in a cemetery." For Jonathan, the essential difference between Georgia's excesses and her father's (in both cases, alcoholism and promiscuity) essentially boil down to a question of "style": her father had it and she does not. Jonathan draws a mustache on a portrait of her father and tells her that she must learn to do likewise "and laugh the way he would have laughed." Georgia lacks the necessary ironic distance from her situation and consequently is unable to keep death at bay. Like a sleeping princess, she must be awakened from her deathlike withdrawal (here, exacerbated by alcohol) to rejoin the film's definition of reality in which one continually must maintain the proper balance between irony ("laugh the way he would have laughed") and theatricality (her "acting isn't good enough" because it is that of a bit player and not a star). Truth and reality are not givens, waiting to be discovered, but neither are they inherently unknowable concepts. Instead, they are continually shifting, determined by context and subjectivity in which performance becomes the central method by which one may continually balance this shifting nature of reality.

In *The Band Wagon*, such a transformation into the world of the theatrical is complete: the musical Tony Hunter takes from Cordova is a huge success, his career is revived, he is adored by the company, and the leading lady falls in love with him. Hollywood rejects Hunter but he finds an alternative community in the theater world. "The show's going to run a long time," says Gaby to Tony at the end of the film; "And as far as I'm concerned it's going to run forever." It is a declaration of love but one that draws on theatrical metaphors and is stated in front of the entire company who then circle around the two of them to sing. Life is turned into one long theatrical performance. In *Two Weeks in Another Town*, Andrus, like Hunter, revives a demoralized cast and crew working on Kruger's film. In opposition to Kruger, Andrus has a rapport with them, asks for their help and suggestions, and seems to be far more skilled in getting performances out of the actors than Kruger. For the first time, the film seems to be taking shape. Furthermore, Minnelli's method of filming Jack's takeover of the production of the film has a strongly theatrical feel. The concern here is not with the finished film or particularly with the technical apparatuses of filmmaking: We are never even permitted to look behind the lens of the camera let alone glimpse a frame of the footage shot by Andrus and the actual narrative content of the film-within-the-film is unclear. Instead, Minnelli invites us to observe the act of filming itself as theatrical spectacle—actors being temperamental or directors and crew members darting about. We have no suggestion that Andrus has had even the slightest experience in directing films before this, but the implication seems to be that, as an actor, he is more qualified to give life to images than Kruger. In *Two Weeks*, the act of filmmaking reaches its highest state when it becomes performance, a theatrical mode rather than a purely cinematic one and happily produced in an atmosphere of collaboration.

Second, this notion that the production of a film is fundamentally a conspiracy, a closed world, is something that *Two Weeks* addresses. If *The Thousand Eyes of Dr. Mabuse* creates a paranoid environment through its typically Langian narrative structure based on duplicity and withholding of story information, much of it taking place within the surveillance space of the hotel, *Two Weeks* creates an environment that, while not producing a paranoid spectator, certainly establishes the sense of a closed world turned against itself very strongly.[63] Taking a large urban setting for a film and characterizing it in such a way that rather than a firm opposition being established between urban and small town environments close relations are established instead is typical of Minnelli (as perhaps it is of much of American cinema and American culture). The small town may be characterized negatively in terms of its provincial nature against which a large urban space (never seen but frequently discussed) becomes the site of a desired-for escape (Paris in relation to the small towns of *The Pirate* (1948) and *Madame Bovary*, or Chicago in relation to the small town of *The Cobweb*). At the same time, the big city is characterized in such a way that an impression of a small town is created (*Meet Me in St. Louis, An American in Paris* [1951], and *Bells Are Ringing*). Urban space as such is secondary in Minnelli to a conception of community that links the characters (positively or negatively, depending on the context) and is most often defined in terms of the aestheticism of a small group of its inhabitants. If Minnelli's cinema is so dominated by space (including and especially domestic space) being public, then the concept of privacy inevitably will have little weight. Although the disappearance of the private in Lang relates to larger notions of technological apparatuses of ideological power and control, in Minnelli it takes place on a more immediate human scale. Gossip, central to the small-town melodrama and domestic comedy in general (the tone of the gossip sequence in *Fury* combines both genres), becomes a fundamental discourse in Minnelli's films set in large cities as well, both for linking the community and potentially tearing it apart, and for doing away with the possibility of the private.

By the time of *Two Weeks in Another Town*, we have an environment dominated by an almost complete failure of the characters to communicate with one another in which most verbal and written forms of discourse are destructive. Jack moves from the sanitarium in which news of the arrival of the cablegram from Kruger spreads quickly and is known by the psychiatrist on night duty ("You don't miss much around here, do you?" Jack says to him), to the world of Rome and Cinecittà, dominated by gossip, publicity and life as public spectacle. When Kruger and Tucino have a conversation in a hotel lobby, the (mostly female) extras visible behind Kruger are constantly looking in the direction of Tucino, attempting to catch his eye, this "private" conversation becoming as public as the activities of the gossiping habitués of Maxim's in *Gigi* (1958). A brief private conversation on the set between Davie and the agent Lew Jordan, filmed in long shot and that we never hear, is described as one whose content will spread to the Via Veneto in ten minutes and within an hour to Hollywood. Gossip and publicity here are marked by an alternation between total falseness and a destructive type of "truth": Kruger wants to plant a story about Barzelli and the homosexual Davie Drew having an affair, which the journalist Brad Byrd (James Gregory) refuses to run because it is a lie; instead, Byrd unexpectedly runs a true story about Kruger's affair with Barzelli in which Kruger is characterized as the "prototype of the obsolete talent now flourishing in Rome. Once imitated by all, now only Kruger imitates Kruger." Kruger's style has now become "a museum of directorial clichés." The sense of conspiracy in relation to the production of Kruger's film arises largely through the destructive nature of these discourses. Janet Bark, whose last name is self explanatory within this context, becomes a primary vehicle through which false stories about Andrus's behavior on the set filter back to Kruger, resulting in Kruger telling Andrus, "Get off my set." This, in turn, results in Kruger and Clara planting a false story about Andrus being "washed up" with the intent of forever killing Andrus's chance at a comeback.

Anxiety about the spoken word is also addressed in relation to the multiplicity of languages heard in the film. The kind of international coproduction that Kruger is working on necessitates cast members of diverse nationalities speaking in their native tongue to one another on the set, as we see in the hilarious scene early in the film in which Barzelli and Davie play a stilted love scene to one another in two languages. This, in turn, later requires dubbing (as we saw in relation to the final result of *The Thousand Eyes of Dr. Mabuse* in chapter 1). If Rivette is correct in his description of the shooting of a film being a kind of conspiracy, then the international coproduction may be seen as a particularly acute example of this, in which actors and crew members often do not understand one another, an atmosphere that surely must only feed on the sense of isolation and paranoia. Godard and Fellini take this issue that *Two Weeks* raises in terms of language in the two major directions possible under the circumstances: In the case of Fellini and *8½*, the international cast becomes part of a great expressive sound tapestry of dubbed voices, musical in its implications, whereas with Godard and *Contempt* it is a question of exposing even further the internationalism at work through a dizzying multiplicity of languages heard in the film, from English and French to German to Italian, with the crucial role of Prokosch's translator positioned in the midst of all this.

In *Two Weeks*, the primary battle Tucino and Kruger have over control of the final cut of the film is not so much on the set as in the dubbing room. As Kruger notes, "Dubbing makes or breaks you," and Kruger ultimately wants Andrus to supervise the dubbing: Rather than acting in the film as a physical presence, Andrus becomes a ghostlike presence in the dubbing booth. Minnelli's musicals depend on the standard playback system that, as Michel Chion states, "marshals the image in the effort to embody." Judy Garland in *Meet Me in St. Louis* or Fred Astaire in *The Band Wagon* hear their own voices over this system during the shooting and attempt to, in effect, live up to the power of this sound. Dubbing, on the other hand, is a process in which "someone is hiding in order to stick his voice onto a body that has already acted for the camera," a process in which "no emotion arises" and which "produces only indirect effects."[64] Dubbing itself may even be seen as a kind of conspiracy against the actor, taking his or her voice away and substituting it with the voice of another.[65] However, we may also see this as part of Andrus's gradual recovery ("a chance to live again," as he puts it) as though to become an actor once more he must first work on the voice (not his own initially, the voices of others). Before he ultimately comes to control the image (or Kruger's images, at any rate) he must first learn to control the voice. In the midst of Andrus's successful takeover of Kruger's film, he solves a dispute with a hysterical Barzelli over the script by pulling her aside and whispering in her ear. While Andrus is told by an assistant that Barzelli speaks no English, Andrus continues whispering until Barzelli not only calms down but kisses Andrus passionately on the mouth. Andrus has (at least temporarily) not only conquered the voice, but also language differences as well.

Throughout Minnelli's work the emphasis on the voice receives its most privileged moment in his famous party sequences, so often built around gossip and idle chatter as spectacle in terms of both image (these sequences are always designed as elaborate visual set pieces) and sound because the gossip and chatter themselves are often given a rhythmically chaotic sound quality approaching that of song. (In the musicals, the party sequences often literally become musical numbers as in the "Gossip" number from *Gigi* or "Drop That Name" from *Bells Are Ringing*.) In *The Bad and the Beautiful*, Jonathan, Amiel, their publicist, and Amiel's wife crash a glamorous Hollywood party. The sequence is shot in a single take with the camera first tracking backward and then right as it follows the four characters through a large room in a Hollywood home, crowded with people, hordes of extras milling about and chattering at once. Although the camera movement essentially follows the movements of the four major characters of the narrative as they move through the room, they also get a bit lost in the shuffle as our eyes are diverted by other, more interesting bits of business: a director babbling with a woman about films that are overedited ("Montage, montage, montage! But where's your story?" a statement particularly apt in a sequence that partly derives its force by being shot in a single take) or a starlet in a corner of the room holding court over the right of her fans to see her in the flesh once in a while. In the foreground of the frame and to the right, a woman is seated at a piano bench singing "Don't Blame Me," but no one seems to be listening to her. Although what we are shown here reflects a chaotic environment, it is far from being a chaotic sequence. Minnelli is in firm control of what he is filming: The elaborate camera movement across the

room and Minnelli's direction of the extras in which he gives them individual personalities, dialogue, and bits of business—all of this creates a
lively sense of staged chaos.

In *Two Weeks in Another Town*, Minnelli revisits this sequence. If
within the film's narrative "Kruger imitates Kruger" here we find Minnelli
imitates Minnelli. That the sequence actively invites comparison with the
one just described from *The Bad and the Beautiful* is apparent from its
opening shot of a woman (Leslie Uggams) once again singing "Don't
Blame Me." But here she is moved from the far right of the frame to the
far left and her skin color is reversed as well: she is black. The partygoers
are not actively moving about as they were in the earlier film. Here, they
are literally frozen, their faces elaborately made up to resemble ghosts,
zombies. The camera does not track fluidly through the space in a single
movement, but repeatedly cuts from extra to extra. In the original conception for the sequence, these extras were supposed to be observing a live
sex show.[66] As it stands now, the only suggestion of sexual activity is when
we see Andrus being passed around from Carlotta to two other women.
But ironically, this removal of the live sex show renders the sequence even

Figure 3.7. The party sequence in *The Bad and the Beautiful*.

more abstract. And whereas in the previous party sequence, this sense of nonstop chatter and gossip seemed to animate the image, here there is no talk at all, only an inarticulate murmur from Jack as he is passed between the two women. The emphasis on decadence and corruption here reverses what we find in *The Bad and the Beautiful*, in which chaos is transcended to become choreographed movement. But in the world of *Two Weeks*, the characters reach a state of paralyzing and decadent immobility.

While the orgy sequence is partly a revision and a freezing of the party from *The Bad and the Beautiful*, it is also just as clearly a citation of Fellini's orgy sequence from the end of *La dolce vita*. Minnelli's citation of an art film such as *La dolce vita* is, on one level, nothing especially remarkable for him. As already noted, his work in musical theater and film had always freely borrowed from or parodied the realm of "high art" for quotation although this citation of an "art" film is fairly new.[67] What is interesting about this Fellini citation is how Minnelli simultaneously cites his own work within it, implicitly measuring it against Fellini's. It is as though Minnelli wants to reimagine his earlier cinema, trying to expose what had been repressed in the earlier film: decadence, ruin, corruption. The embracing of chaos in Minnelli in the past was a matter of embracing movement in all of its lack of coordination and centerdness, of the protagonists being lost in the vertiginous swirl of bodies becoming space and decor. Whatever its moral intentions, *La dolce vita* (as with Fellini's work in general) is also a cinema of spectacle. Like Minnelli, Fellini revels in the swirl and movement of elaborate costumes and scenery; his characters and his camera seem to be in perpetual motion and in *La dolce vita* Fellini is drawn to the decadent spectacle that he also attempts to criticize. But Fellini's decadent revelers dance whereas Minnelli's, regardless of his formation in musical comedy, stand still. What Fellini is doing

Figure 3.8. *Two Weeks in Another Town:* The orgy sequence as a "decadent" and immobile rewriting of the party in *The Bad and the Beautiful*.

during this period (and *8¹/₂* pushes this even further) is creating a cinema in which chaos becomes the (paradoxical) structuring principle of the film itself. While Minnelli is unquestionably drawn to the possibilities of this state, he clearly finds making this kind of total leap into structural chaos, fully embracing decadence and setting it in motion much more difficult. In this regard, Minnelli remains not only a type of "classical" filmmaker, but also perhaps too conventionally American, still somewhat tied to a type of Puritanism that can only see the activities at the orgy in the negative because they represent a type of "sick organism," a corruption of American innocence abroad.[68]

If money is a key concern in terms of the modern cinema filming itself at work, the other concern is that of the representation of sexuality and its relationship to power and creativity. This largely seems to be an issue in relation to cinema after the breakup of the conventional studio systems in the United States and Europe. For this reason making a distinction between the classical film about filmmaking, particularly Hollywood's, which refuses to see this degree of infamy about film production (being products of a situation in which both the working methods and the content of the films are carefully controlled) with modern cinema, which in its comparative freedom of production and censorship circumstances, more easily lends itself to this atmosphere of creative "infamy" is important. A recurring strategy in these films is to show protagonists who suffer from various forms of emotional and sexual excess, for example, alcoholism, promiscuity, homosexuality, drug addiction, psychosis, and paranoia, presenting them not as special problems but as symptomatic of a fundamental illness at the very core of the production environment itself and, by extension, with the production of cinema in general. On the rare occasions when this cinema has attempted to represent the film director directly

Figure 3.9. Dancing revelers from the orgy sequence of Federico Fellini's *La dolce vita* (1960).

and show him as a major protagonist, he is most often characterized as an overtly sadistic and destructive individual: Aldrich's *The Legend of Lylah Clare* (1968), *Beware of a Holy Whore*, Abel Ferrara's *Dangerous Game* (1993), or as someone on the brink of physical and emotional collapse, as in Olivier Assayas's *Irma Vep* (1996).

In the first three of these films, the act of the director having sex with actors and crew members becomes a kind of overstepping of boundaries, a violation of the bodies and the integrities of the collaborators and an assertion of power over them that leads to more wholesale forms of destruction often far in excess of the need for getting the film to conform to the director's vision. Romance and the couple are effectively removed from the films as viable and regenerative entities to be replaced by characters incapable of sexual fidelity—Guido in *8½*, for example, whereas in *Contempt* Javal seems actively to encourage Camille to have sex with Prokosch, offering his wife to his producer as a fair object of exchange. Sexual desire freely circulates in these films but divorced from strong emotional attachments or commitments. The various emotional and sexual problems of the characters effectively prevent the sense of a regenerative community from forming. The sense of the physical and emotional displacement of the protagonists is often played out through the film being shot on location rather than in the comfort of a studio (or, in the case of *Two Weeks*, the studio being one that is not in Hollywood) and in which the hotel becomes a primary setting. Both *Beware of a Holy Whore* and *The State of Things* are representative of this strain in which the hotel serves as a festering ground of resentment and pent up emotions, but one can also see it in *8½*, *Dangerous Game*, and Godard's *Passion* (1986).

Two Weeks in Another Town is historically important for the manner in which it anticipates (and slightly overlaps with) this move toward filmmaking as a form of debauchery. A brief catalogue of the various "disorders" affecting the protagonists: promiscuity (Carlotta), homosexuality and drug addiction (Davie Drew), paranoiac and suicidal (Clara), and Andrus exhibiting the widest range of all of them. At the beginning of the film we are told that he suffers from "manic depression, psychosis, compulsive violence, delusional episodes, alcoholism acute and chronic"). Kruger's own sexual promiscuity and his wife's extreme reactions to it strikingly anticipates the response of Guido's wife to his own chronic infidelities in *8½*. Although this partly relates to certain Romantic clichés about the intensity of the desires and emotions of the strong artist being equal to the intensity of the work, it also suggests that the production of certain kinds of cinematic images are, in themselves, extensions of the erotic impulse. *The Bad and the Beautiful* could not be clearer about this when Jonathan explicitly equates the making of a film with the courting of a woman while describing the moment when the film is finished as a kind of postorgasmic letdown in which both the film and the woman are abandoned. Likewise in *Two Weeks*, Kruger refers to Andrus's first sighting of a motion picture camera on his set as one of "pure lust." Hence the importance of Andrus-as-director calming down Barzelli by implicitly seducing her, as well as the importance of the moment when he is able to handle successfully an actress having difficulty in dubbing Barzelli by eroticizing the dubbing process, albeit a displaced form of eroticism: He tells the actress to think about the "luscious" banana splits from her favorite ice cream parlor in Hollywood while she recites the lines. Film-making, then, is designed as a form of seduction in which the creator of the images (and sounds) is himself a type of seducer who is often bored with the object of desire once it has been created or conquered.

Nevertheless, the problem with Kruger and the consequent need to eliminate him as a director in the film is symptomatic of a strong ambivalence toward the role of the all-powerful artist seducer in Minnelli. This power is largely male and is often an expression not only of a strong aesthetic impulse, but also of an expression of virility. As in Lang, hypnosis may become the metaphoric extreme of this position of power, treated explicitly in *The Pirate*, as the actor/metteur en scène Serafin handles a spinning hypnotic mirror, which he uses to seduce and control Manuela and to unmask the false pretensions of Macoco, the black pirate masquerading as a bourgeois citizen (in both cases, the act of hypnosis takes place in a theatrical space). In *The Band Wagon*, Cordova is initially situated as an almost Mabuse-like figure; Lily Martin, the librettist of the show-within-the show (also called "The Band Wagon"), is even described by her husband at one point as being under Cordova's hypnotic influence. The first time we see Cordova he is playing in his own production of *Oedipus Rex*, whereas the libretto of the new musical he plans to stage with Tony Hunter is one in which he wants to bring out more fully the Faustian subtext and in which he will play Mephistopheles to Hunter's Faust. These two master narratives of Western culture, endlessly recycled and reworked, preside over not only the show-within-the-show of *The Band Wagon*, but also over the central narrative of the film. As *The Band Wagon* turned inside out, *Two Weeks in Another Town* reworks these basic situations with Andrus playing Faust and Oedipus to Kruger's Mephistopheles and Polybus.

Oedipal situations are very common in a postwar U.S. cinema strongly influenced by Freudian psychoanalysis, either through overt subject matter or through the ways in which the relationships among characters, particularly within the family, are defined. In this regard, nothing is particularly unique about their presence in Minnelli. But several aspects to the way that Minnelli's films draw on Oedipal situations are worth isolating. One is that they sometimes overlap with Faustian ones, the function of the latter clearly emerging out of the enormous degree to which Oedipal conflicts in Minnelli are also aesthetic. In Minnelli, the Faustian desire to "fly among the stars" has less to do with the desire for youth or material goods than to fly among the stars of aestheticism. This repetition of Oedipal situations in Minnelli results in the sense that many of his films, regardless of their ostensible dramatic situations, are essentially films about the family, literal or symbolic, with the creation of art itself being a type of family affair. Furthermore, they tend to show only marginal interest in the figure of the mother as the vehicle through whom the passage to "adult" sexuality will ultimately take place. The strongest incest taboo in Minnelli is not the possibility of sex with the mother but sex with the father around whom revolves the fundamentally ambivalent drives of the characters, male and female: The father not only as a source of identification and (sometimes) sexual attraction, but also as a figure around whom powerful feelings of both love and hate are expressed because the father does not live up to the child's fantasy.[69] Because drives of this nature in Minnelli so often concern themselves with the aesthetic impulse this also affects the tone and structure of the films that become marked by these ambivalent drives. In *The Bad and the Beautiful*, Georgia Lorrison does not identify with her mother (a character who is never mentioned) but with her father, whose alcoholism and sexual excesses she imitates (her own first name is derived from his, George), while simultaneously maintaining a fetishistic shrine to him in her apartment. Jonathan's primary goal in the same film is to redeem the reputation of his father, a powerful Hollywood figure who died in poverty: Jonathan wants to "ram the name of Shields" down Hollywood's throat by becoming successful. At the same time, he and his father "couldn't stand to be in the same room together," the father's one fundamental redeeming quality being that he made "great pictures." Furthermore, George Lorrison also assumes a patriarchal function for Jonathan because Lorrison taught him "the facts of life" and gave him his first drink, assuming the fatherly duties of initiating him into adulthood at which presumably Jonathan's own father failed. (Hanging in Jonathan's office is a caricature that Lorrison drew of Jonathan's father as a Mephistopheles-like devil figure, clutching a dagger.) This results in Jonathan and Georgia's affair having a quasi-incestuous nature also typical of many of the relationships in Minnelli's films. (The relationship between Theo and Vincent Van Gogh in *Lust for Life* [1956] brings both repressed homosexual and incestuous desires together.) But it also suggests that Georgia more closely enacts the desire for the father that Jonathan represses.

As noted in chapter 2, by the 1960s standard depictions of Freudian psychoanalysis had lost much of their explanatory and mythic power. *Two Weeks in Another Town* shows a film in which its protagonist's extended stay in a sanitarium produces no significant improvement in his psychological state and merely becomes a place where, as Andrus says near the end of the film, all he learned were words such as "transference and sublimation." The standard Oedipal conflicts persist but this ambivalence toward the father also spills over into how virtually all relationships among the characters are defined. In the sanitarium sequence, Andrus describes his personal and professional relationship with Kruger as one based on "hate . . . and love, mixed together with lots of ice and an onion, the Kruger way." Here we see a cut from the word *hate* in medium long shot to a close-up of Andrus as he says the word *love* tenderly. The first glimpse we see of Kruger's film shows Davie and Barzelli engaged in a struggle in which Barzelli keeps telling Davie how much she hates him, a struggle that nevertheless culminates in an embrace, a moment repeated in the bickering couple in the restaurant sequence described earlier who are, as Veronica says, "screaming about how much they love each other." Likewise Janet Bark's own relationship to Kruger is one in which, as Andrus says to her, "After all these years you still don't know whether you love him or hate him." But not only is this something that has spilled over from *The Bad and the Beautiful*, but *Two Weeks in Another Town* also actively draws comparisons between the two films in this regard. During the screening room sequence showing *The Bad and the Beautiful* described earlier, we hear Jonathan instruct Georgia to make up her mind about her father: "You say you hate him yet you build this shrine to him." Whereas the characters in *Two Weeks* seem intent on duplicating the love/hate relations already present in the earlier film at least one crucial difference exists: There does not seem to be any great film being made to compensate for personal suffering. Significantly, what Kruger watches with Andrus are not the rushes from his most recent film but a much earlier collaboration with Andrus. Because *Two Weeks* is dealing with protagonists undergoing a state of creative and emotional crisis, the film-within-the film that is in production resists becoming a desired object. All that is left (at least initially) for Kruger and Andrus to project onto is a work from the past—*The Bad and the Beautiful*.

In the sequence when Andrus and Kruger watch the earlier film, it simply looks like a more traditional Hollywood product in glossy black-and-white and academy ratio, evoking a lost world of (to borrow a phrase from Albert Valentin) black-and-white magic, in marked contrast to *Two Weeks*, in CinemaScope and color. In the later film, the violent primary reds of the leather chairs of the projection room, spread out across the composition of the widescreen frame with Andrus wearing a matching red sweater in contrast to his idealized self onscreen ten years earlier in an immaculate white suit, a blatant color symbolism suggesting a decadent or "fallen" state, one far removed from the one contained within the small black and white frame image in the projection room. *The Bad and the Beautiful* functions here as a text of memory, in Proustian terms as an example of *mémoire volontaire*, which freezes its subjects. Within the context of *Two Weeks in Another Town*, *The Bad and the Beautiful* represents the site of the lost plenitude of Hollywood cinema. These earlier images that Kruger watches for motivation are inaccessible to him. He can no longer make films like this, and he knows it: "Yes, I *was* great," the significance of which Minnelli underlines by one his rarely employed close-ups. Desire in *Two Weeks* becomes largely something that exists in the past tense and the film has enormous difficulty in animating its narrative through the twin articulations of desire for a body/desire for the creative work that had dominated Minnelli's earlier films.

Masculine/Feminine

The characters of Davie Drew and Carlotta are especially significant in terms of the increasingly problematic nature of sexual desire in Minnelli. Davie is the first and only attempt in these films to present a homosexual character directly, an embodiment of the repressed tensions between the two creative male figures and a crucial element of what is at stake in terms of this particular Oedipal fantasy. Davie becomes, for Kruger, the man who "isn't a man." At the same time, this failure to be a "man" also ties into an aesthetic problem for Kruger because Davie's love scenes with Barzelli clearly lack the necessary passion. "Pretend you're a man," Kruger says to Drew, "Don't kiss Barzelli like she was your mother, your sister or your gym teacher." Kruger's remark suggests a wider-ranging sexual repression on Davie's part, locating his homosexuality initially within the family situation but also implying that Davie has difficulty in giving full voice to his homosexual desires as well: Kruger as the Mephistopheles who knows all and Kruger as the tyrannical father who berates his son for his failed masculinity.[70]

To present Davie in this way, however, the film immediately backs off from the implications of his character. It heterosexualizes him, giving him a female love interest in Veronica. Veronica, the film would have us believe, is the only woman he has ever loved after years of, as he puts it, "all the filth," that is, homosexuality. Veronica essentially exists within the film as a potential object of redemption for both Andrus and Davie as she is passed back and forth between them over the course of the narrative in which Andrus assumes a symbolic role playing the "big brother bit" to Davie, the two of them ultimately working together on the film both for Kruger and against him. In *Beware of a Holy Whore*, Fassbinder brings this homosexual element much more strongly forward. The director is himself bisexual while the cast and crew of the film seem to be dominated by gay or sexually ambiguous men: "The place is crawling with them," complains one female character. The director here, however, is not so much a patriarchal figure such as Kruger, but the perpetual adolescent son so central to New German Cinema in an ambiguous revolt against the father. However, my concern with *Two Weeks* has less to do with the banality of Davie's redemption through heterosexual love than with the basic ineffectualness with which it is presented. The Davie/Veronica love affair is something that the film cannot even bring itself to show us. In their first scene together in the screening room they have no dialogue and they do not even sit together: Veronica sits alone while Davie stands huddled against the wall. Aside from a brief moment of hands touching, the only physical contact they have here is when he slaps her face and gives her a black eye while showing absolutely no embarrassment at having done so. Otherwise, they spend the bulk of the film apart and the film never makes a coherent case for them as a couple. Naremore notes that Minnelli, while never treating homosexuality directly in his films, "flirted" with it on occasion.[71] To have an explicitly homosexual character in a Minnelli film, to cease "flirting," upsets the precarious sexual order on which this cinema is based. It assigns a fixed meaning to a world that depends on a constant tension between masculine and feminine drives and sensibilities, a world in which, as Gerstner states, "hyper-masculinized bodies are ironically placed within [an] over-aestheticized frame."[72] In this regard, Davie's heterosexuality is perhaps not as stable as it might initially suggest because his hysterical possessiveness toward Veronica is based on his awareness that she represents a unique case for him.

While Davie points toward one possibility for a breakdown of the sexual order of Minnelli's cinema, Carlotta's promiscuity represents the other. Like all of the female characters in the film, we have less a fully nuanced psychological portrait than a blunt image of Woman. Harvey is superficially correct in his observation that "such wholesale misogyny has no precedent in Minnelli's movies" and that this results in "one-note caricatures."[73] It seems to me, however, that it is not simply caricature at work here but an impulse toward a kind of primitivism that in itself is a modernist gesture, particularly if we recall that primitivism is often a response to or an embracing of the possibility of an aesthetic form falling into a decadent state. Again most likely taking a cue from *La dolce vita* and from the implications of their shared Roman setting, we see a fascination with archetypal images of strident women (Clara, Janet, and Barzelli) and with an image of woman as a figure of Madonna-like redemption, Veronica, who stands opposed to the world of artifice and aesthetics: "I hate films," she says in her first scene. Mayersberg notes Minnelli's increased tendency in the early 1960s to create not so much characters as "figures—almost a mythology of his own."[74] Submitting the film's treatment of women to classical psychoanalytic categories of the phallic mother, the harlot, or the pure image of woman is entirely possible. But while still retaining links to psychoanalytic methods of interpreting character, the film seems to want to draw on some of the myths that underpin certain fundamental Freudian concepts and that have always strongly shaped Minnelli's own cinema. This links the film not only with *La dolce vita*, but also with *Contempt* in the parallels that are drawn between the ancient and the modern, citing the ancient to understand the modern, although for Godard, Rome functions as the modern world whereas Capri functions as the ancient, "nature before civilization and its neuroses."[75]

According to Houseman, Minnelli insisted on casting Charisse in the role of Carlotta against Houseman's own strong reservations: "Dressed to the nines in [Pierre] Balmain's flashiest creations, she was gorgeous to look at but never entirely convincing as the Queen of the Jet Set."[76] But Minnelli's insistence on this matter allows one to pursue yet another way in which *Two Weeks in Another Town* is *The Band Wagon* turned inside out and that Charisse's appearance in both films encourages. At the beginning of both films the women are the site of enormous anxiety on the part of the male protagonists. In *The Band Wagon*, Tony Hunter calls Charisse's Gabrielle Gerard a "monster." In *Two Weeks* this argument is extended even further when Kruger claims that "all women are pure monster." But *The Band Wagon* works to resolve Hunter's anxiety successfully by: (1) showing this to be based on an initial misunderstanding—Gaby is not really a monster; and (2) allowing these anxieties to be played out in theatrical terms, through song and dance. In the film's big musical piece, "Girl Hunt," Gerard plays a dual role, a blonde and a brunette, the first a "bad" girl with the appearance of good and the latter a "bad" woman who remains bad at the end but is attractive precisely because of this: "She was bad, she was dangerous, I wouldn't trust her any farther than I could throw her. But she was my kind of woman."

Two Weeks, on the other hand, works to intensify and confirm Jack's anxiety about Carlotta. If Houseman is correct that Charisse is not convincing as the Queen of the Jet Set it may be because that is ultimately not her function in the film. On the one hand, her style of dress and hair and her languorous movements evoke Delphine Seyrig in *Last Year at*

Marienbad.[77] Two years after Anna Karina expressed her (impossible) desire in *A Woman is A Woman* to star in a Hollywood musical "avec Cyd Charisse," Charisse now less overtly expresses a desire to be the star of an art film. Minnelli's decision to cast a dancer strongly associated with his past musicals rather than an experienced dramatic actress in the role is but one indication of his need to revise his own work. Indeed, Minnelli's fascination with luxurious immobility and languorous movement in *Two Weeks* is probably as influenced by Resnais's film as it is by *La dolce vita.* Resnais's comment that *Marienbad* for him was "a musical comedy, without songs" only strengthens the possible linkage between the two directors.[78] The recourse to decor and stylized movement in *Marienbad*, the emphasis on theatricality as the possible search for meaning in life are present here but emptied of concrete meaning. In *Marienbad*, we are in "this mournful mansion from another age," one "encrusted with ornamentation," a seductive and beautiful world but one that no longer supplies the film with the coherence it does in Minnelli. "Girl Hunt" is replete with images of statuary and mannequins, of characters freezing in action, but Astair's and Charisse's dancing repeatedly overcomes and transcends the threat of immobility. In *Marienbad*, Resnais never releases his characters into this state because they never had it to begin with. And in *Two Weeks*, dance does not complete Charisse as it did in *The Band Wagon.* Instead, like Seyrig, she is a vehicle in fetishistic high-fashion evening gowns, in perpetual slow motion, gliding across rooms but never completely giving herself over to dance. A brief montage of Jack and Carlotta going out on the town to various clubs immediately precedes the orgy sequence. But Jack is always the one who is dancing here while Carlotta remains at her table.

Figure 3.10. Delphine Seyrig, iconic art film star, in *Last Year at Marienbad.*

Figure 3.11. Cyd Charisse, iconic musical comedy star as art film star in *Two Weeks in Another Town*.

However, Carlotta's movements and style of dress go beyond Seyrig's in *Marienbad*. In a way, Carlotta is simply Kruger's female counterpart. Both are active seducers, Carlotta less hypocritically than Kruger because the man she is living with accepts and is sexually aroused by her infidelities. Furthermore, Kruger and Carlotta are linked in another way in that they had sex one evening in a motel while Carlotta was still married to Jack. This is Kruger's (possibly dying) confession to Jack as he is lying in Barzelli's bed waiting for the ambulance. The confession is traumatic for Jack: It seems to function as both a betrayal from a friend and as a peculiar reworking of the primal scene between an Oedipal father and a devouring harlotlike mother, but in this case one that the child only hears about and does not witness. This confession works to motivate Jack to replace Kruger, a gesture at once profoundly generous but also destructive in terms of Kruger's own work when Jack begins to do retakes, an ambiguity lost on Andrus but not missed by Kruger.

Kruger uses the metaphor of "prowling" to describe Carlotta's techniques of seduction, implying a link between Carlotta and the animal world that her costumes, usually making prominent use of feathers or fur, reinforce. But the word *prowling* could equally apply to her movements in general throughout the film, which evoke a stealthy, catlike searching for prey. The same type of prowling movement becomes a dance in "Girl Hunt" when Charisse's "bad" woman emerges from within a three-way mirror and moves across the floor to the detective, Rod Riley, her arms waving through the air like a 1920s vamp. "Girl Hunt" is a parody of the private-eye genre, the type of fiction whose emergence, as already noted, Benjamin has traced to the simultaneous emergence of the bourgeoisie and its concept of private space. Furthermore, because the Oedipus narrative has, in its search for origins, often been described as the original detective story, a private-eye musical number allows this thematic to be subjected to a simultaneous parody and reworking as popular culture, drawing a comic moustache on its symbolic cultural hold. The traces left behind for the detective in the ballet to investigate are "a rag, a bone, and a hank of hair," a citation of Rudyard Kipling's poem "The Vampire." Carlotta takes this element of the "bad" woman in "Girl Hunt" and pushes it to an extreme, becoming at once a vampire in the sense of a seductress as well as in the sense of "pure monster," such as the classic Fatal Woman out of Romantic thought. It is not a rag, a bone, and a hank of hair that she leaves behind for Jack to find but a green chiffon scarf, placed on his bed, a talismanic object that evokes their past sexual life: "We always had a thing for green." In *Vertigo*, the retired detective Scottie is in love with a woman named Madeleine, possessed by the ghost of her suicidal great-grandmother, Carlotta. Scottie's obsession takes the form of trailing Madeleine (unseen by her) through the streets of San Francisco. In *Two Weeks*, we have a Carlotta who openly and explicitly seems to stalk and trail the male protagonist, a creature who is all sexuality and no romance, but who seems to exert a hypnotic hold over Jack, who is powerless to resist her influence.

This equation of Carlotta with the animal could not be clearer during the orgy sequence as she steps away from Jack and passes him on to two other women and then leans against a sphinxlike statue of a creature. This direct expression of her sexual drives most strongly evokes the world of the animal because she appears to have no censoring mechanism, no conventional social repression. Jack describes to Veronica the large dog Carlotta was devoted to during their marriage that was always in her attendance. Jack eventually poisoned the dog, which he perceived as a sexual rival, thereby suggesting a relationship to bestiality. Throughout the film, there are repeated equations of the animal and the human: Kruger, for example, refers to Tucino's technique of dubbing as one in which actors are "mouthing their words like mother guppies gobbling their young," whereas the world of the press agent becomes "the voice of the vulture." The presence of Carlotta, then, crystallizes this motif. If we recall Georges Bataille's observation that human beings fundamentally derive their bodily and sexual prohibitions (including incest) from a denial and repression of their relationship to the animal world,[79] then Carlotta represents the force of this animal world coming into the film. When Bataille writes that full social humanity "allows only the clean space of a house, of polished floors, furniture, window panes, a space inhabited by venerable persons, at once naïve and inviolable, tender and inaccessible,"[80] he could almost be writing about Minnelli. As immaculately and stunningly dressed as Carlotta is, she also threatens to disrupt the fragile social equilibrium of this world.

Dennis Giles has argued that Gaby in *The Band Wagon* functions as a type of maestro who ultimately leads Tony Hunter through the Other world and toward the happy ending of the successful show.[81] In *Two Weeks*, consequently, we see Carlotta as fulfilling the same kind of function, turned "inside out." If in her sexual promiscuity she is linked with Kruger, she also finishes the job of Mephistopheles to Andrus's Faust, which the hospitalized Kruger is unable to continue performing. Carlotta must lead Jack through his evening of damnation, culminating with the orgy and their cataclysmic car ride together. The orgy, then, is not simply *La dolce vita* revisited, but also a Faustian Walpurgis Night in which sphinxes (and other archetypal female creatures) traditionally assume major roles. By this point in the film, Minnelli begins to take the spectator on its own flight through the stars.

The Exorcism

Virtually all of the Minnelli melodramas have a spectacular sequence of some kind in which a realist system of representation breaks down and for several minutes the film gives itself over to a chaotic universe of movement and theatrical hysteria. All of these sequences come about because the protagonists are caught up in situations in which their emotions are too large for their environments and a battle of wills occurs between those emotions and the reality of that environment. Although such a strategy is hardly unprecedented in melodrama (and most likely has its origins in the theatrical melodrama of sensation), Minnelli's realization of these moments has an intensity and power unmatched by any other Hollywood filmmaker during this period. These sequences seem to be moments of culmination while at the same time stand they slightly apart from the rest of the film.

In *Two Weeks in Another Town*, the set piece occurs near the end of the film in which Jack and Carlotta take a drunken and hysterical ride in a sports car. The sequence is one of the most elaborate of its kind in this director's work and directly follows the orgy sequence. But something about it sets it apart from the other Minnelli set pieces and this difference points toward the complicated situation in which the film is caught. The sports car that that they ride in evokes the convertible of *La dolce vita*, although that car never spins out of control as this one does. Furthermore, the importance of the problematic car ride in the midst of a film about filmmaking also anticipates *8 1/2* (the traffic jam dream opening) and *Contempt* (the car crash) as well as, much later, Fellini's "Toby Dammit" episode of *Spirits of the Dead* (1968).[82] The resolutions to both *Contempt* and *Two Weeks* revolve around a tumultuous and violent car ride. But in *Contempt*, the car crashes, killing both of the protagonists while the crash itself takes place off camera, the melodrama elided. It is the remains of the wreck itself, as an aestheticized object of destruction and ruin, which interests Godard and not the melodramatic blood and thunder of the disaster. Minnelli puts us in the car and is on the verge of taking us to the point of crashing but just narrowly avoids it, leading his protagonist on the possible road to redemption, in itself a gesture that suggests a difference between a filmmaker poised between classical and modernist impulses and a filmmaker who much more fully feels himself to part of a modernist tradition.

As with the opening sequence of *The Thousand Eyes of Dr. Mabuse*, the ride Carlotta and Jack take together is a blatant attempt to cite and recycle another earlier and well-known set piece from the director's work: in this case, Georgia's car ride from *The Bad and the Beautiful*. In both of these Minnelli sequences, we have highly emotional protagonists driving in obvious studio mock-ups of automobiles, the vehicles spinning out of control in relation to the emotional states of these protagonists. In *The Bad and the Beautiful*, the sequence is economically handled, filmed in a single take (with one brief insert shot), the camera slowly tracking into Georgia, first toward her face and then around to her back and then back to her face as she becomes increasingly hysterical and rain suddenly begins to pour against the windshield, as though the rain has been summoned in

Figure 3.12. *Contempt*: The fatal car crash.

response to her tears; the steering wheel then implausibly spins out of control as the car nevertheless continues to move in a linear path and she throws her entire body weight against the frame of the inside of the car, its physical dimensions unable to control the sheer enormity of her emotions.

In *Two Weeks*, Minnelli not only repeats but attempts to top that earlier sequence, creating something that, purely on a formal level, is much more impressive. All of the stylistic and emotional content of *The Bad and the Beautiful* is heightened in *Two Weeks*, doubled in intensity. Instead of one hysterical character in the car, we have two and they both maintain a constant stream of dialogue in contrast to Georgia's weeping and screaming, which functions in more traditional melodramatic terms as a "text of muteness," an emotion so intense that it cannot be articulated into language.[83] The artificiality is more extreme in *Two Weeks* with a blatant use of a rear-projection screen for the car ride (the earlier sequence made use of an abstract flashing of lights and the splashing of rain against the windshield to signify the outside world) and far more camera angles, cutting to both inside and outside, front and back of the car, which this time is a convertible instead of the earlier enclosed vehicle. Not the slightest attempt is made to offer this moment up as one that exists within a realist framework. Whereas not precisely a dream se-

Figure 3.13. *The Bad and the Beautiful*: Georgia's tumultuous car ride.

quence, it visually has the feel and appearance of a nightmare in a manner similar to the set pieces in all of the Minnelli melodramas. Minnelli's use of rear projection here leaves no room for ambiguity of intentions. The experience of the sequence is determined by our noting and responding to the artificiality of means here. Like a ride in an amusement park, Minnelli's stylistic strategies are designed to be both artificial and thrilling. Whereas the camera movements for Georgia's car ride were relatively discreet, here they are quite flamboyant: at the climax of the sequence, the car begins spinning in a 180-degree arc as the camera begins to move in the opposite direction, first by 90 degrees and then, without a cut, reverses its direction and executes a full 180-degree movement back around the spinning car. (Frame enlargements cannot begin to do the sequence justice.) Imagining that anyone sufficiently appreciative of Minnelli's melodramas could not be impressed by this sequence is difficult. But Naremore does not think that it comes anywhere close to the power of the car ride in *The Bad and the Beautiful*[84] and Harvey regards it as "just longer and noisier" than the previous one.[85] Looked at within this perspective, we might see the sequence as a decadent replay of the first one. And this would be essentially correct. Without losing sight of this essential "corruption," however, the sequence needs to be understood within these terms rather than used only as the sign of a thoroughgoing failure and paucity of imagination.

The car ride in *The Bad and the Beautiful* is entirely related to Georgia's psychological state in the aftermath of Jonathan's betrayal when she finds him with another woman. Although stylized, it has a cogency and clarity to it. Although melodramatic, it is also economically handled. The character may be out of control, but the film is not. When Georgia pulls off her fur piece in *The Bad and the Beautiful* and throws her body

Figure 3.14. Jack and Carlotta's even more tumultuous car ride in *Two Weeks in Another Town*.

around the inside of the car, it is as though this moving vehicle cannot contain all of her emotions: The movements of the car do not observe any kind of logical direction but simply follow the path of Georgia's psychological state. In *Two Weeks*, the ride serves a different function. As in *The Bad and the Beautiful*, what immediately precipitates the ride is a sexual betrayal: Jack discovers Carlotta making love to another man. This could hardly be the same kind of shock to him that Georgia's discovery of Jonathan's betrayal is to her because Carlotta's infidelity is already well known to Jack. Nevertheless, he spins out of control, punching the man and slapping Carlotta before he runs out of the house and jumps into a car, Carlotta chasing after him. The trauma is not the witnessing of the act of infidelity itself but the memory that this witnessing unleashes in Jack. Both the discovery of Carlotta making love to a man and the car ride itself are repeated acts, deeply traumatic events that evoke traumas of a moment earlier in Jack's life: In the cafe sequence with Veronica he explains that years earlier, after their divorce, he had stopped by their house in the Hollywood Hills in response to her open invitation to have sex with her at any time. But as he walks into their former bedroom, he finds her already engaged in some kind of sexual act. During his marriage to Carlotta in Hollywood, he almost crashed his car into a wall after seeing her in their bed with someone else and has been haunted both by the memory of that image and a question he considers to be fundamental to his understanding of his own psychic state: Was he simply drunk and out of control on that earlier evening or was he consciously attempting suicide? This issue of memory, of being haunted by past events, is something that dominates the conception of *Two Weeks* and gives the film its somewhat different atmosphere and sense of movement in comparison with the sequence from *The Bad and the Beautiful*, which dramatizes a response to an immediate, present-tense event.

The car ride in *Two Weeks* is largely intended to serve a therapeutic function, a traditional form of catharsis in which, as at the end of *Marnie*, a traumatic event is remembered and reenacted. But the sequence is constructed in such a way that focusing on its ostensible therapeutic function is difficult. When Jack stops the car and does not hit the wall, saying, "Well, now we know" (that is, "I did not intend to kill myself during that other car ride."), more than once when I have seen this film with an audience spectators around me in the theater mutter, "Know what?" So much of the backstory material that seems to be generating this sequence is obscure so that its traditional effectiveness as a Minnelli set piece gets lost: It takes a certain amount of work on the part of the spectator to understand fully the intensity of Andrus's ordeal because it requires a lot of backtracking over psychological and narrative material that the film has been obscure about (and that possibly was clearer in the original cut of the film). Because the sexual betrayal here of which Carlotta is guilty is not conventional, grasping the full extent of Jack's response to the witnessing of her sexual activity is difficult except to read it in terms of the two words he disparagingly uses earlier in the film: *sublimation* and *transference*. Are we meant to read Jack's horror over seeing Carlotta in their former bedroom as yet another perverse and extreme variation on the primal scene? Carlotta here becomes not simply a devouring, sexual mother but (as Jeffrey Cordova defines Mephistopheles) Evil Personified. In this regard, Jack must exorcise Carlotta, hence the importance of her presence in the car and of her being the final recipient of the film's string of violent acts. The car ride itself even becomes a type of symbolic rape of Carlotta and the tears and emotional breakdown she undergoes seem designed to humanize her.

In the final shot of *The Bad and the Beautiful*, we are in Hollywood with Fred Amiel, Georgia Lorrison, and James Lee Bartlow gathered around a telephone listening in on Shields (whose face we do not see and voice we do not hear) in Paris, as he tells his former studio boss, Harry Pebbel, his idea for a comeback film. The three of them listen with gathering interest, huddled within the frame as Georgia passes the phone back and forth from her right ear to her left as the two men on either side of her try to catch bits of the conversation. As the music swells, the image fades to black without showing whether they have decided to accept Jonathan's offer. As Naremore has argued, whether they accept this offer fundamentally does not matter. This final shot is about something else. The unseen Jonathan functions here as "an emblem of the movies" with his three former colleagues standing in for the reactions of the film spectator: "their rapt, curious expressions, framed by a dramatic spotlight and set off from the surrounding darkness, indicate how much they will always been drawn to the siren call of entertainment, and to the lure of the imaginary signifier."[86] This siren call becomes the explicit message of the final image of *The Band Wagon* as the entire company, looking directly into the camera, extols the virtues of entertainment to the film spectator as they sing the anthem "That's Entertainment."

The final sequence of *Two Weeks*, however, aims for neither the metaphoric power of *The Bad and the Beautiful* nor an image that connotes the joys of the aesthetic collective in the manner of *The Band Wagon*. We see Jack dashing through the airport, the camera tracking alongside of him as he checks in, runs through the terminal, and gets on the plane, all the time talking to Davie and explaining his discovery of a newfound freedom and a decision to begin again. "I came here to find the past," he says, "I did. And to hell with it," in this regard making the resolution of the film the opposite of *Marnie* in terms of the therapeutic theme. His rapid movements, direct and purposeful, appear to restore "normal" movement to Andrus and the film after the petrification of the orgy and the hysteria of the car ride. The final shot of the film is of Andrus boarding a plane, the door closing behind him as the stairway pulls away. In a sense, this answers the opening shot of the film, giving Andrus a precise direction (literally and symbolically), which he did not have as the film opened. But unlike *The Bad and the Beautiful* and *The Band Wagon*, the film is unable to offer a suitable metaphoric final image with which to resolve itself. Elsaesser writes that the ambiguous logic of the final sequence is based on Jack's "freedom" and return to Hollywood as also being another kind of escape from "reality," and that consequently the ending of the film is open: "What weighs, however, more heavily is the 'death' of the director in the film—Minnelli's alter ego—whose once creative vision has turned into a morbid and self-destructive introspection, to which he finally succumbs."[87] The death of the director in the film, then, is the death of a particular kind of director—the studio craftsman, the metteur en scène—and of the kind of cinema he represented.

Figure 3.15

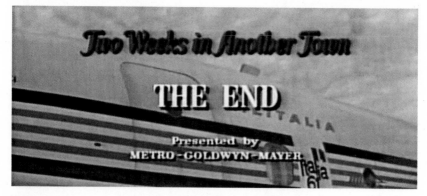

Figure 3.16
Opening and closing images of *Two Weeks in Another Town*.

Although Minnelli's position as a filmmaker was always divided between the craftsman and the serious artist who transcended the studio system to create works that had their own distinctive style, what *Two Weeks in Another Town* suggests is that even this paradoxical relation may no longer be valid because it is the result of a network of circumstances that are no longer in existence.

However, the film does not confirm if Kruger is literally dead. In fact, no one in this melodrama of corruption and conspiracy dies but, like the film itself, mainly seems to be suspended somewhere between life and death, decadence and renewal, movement and stasis. Reading the film from within its own Oedipal perspective, the death of the director must take place because Jack finally moves beyond Kruger as a father figure, ready to "grow up" and face the world on his own. We do not find out (nor presumably are we even supposed to care) whether Kruger successfully finished working on his film. In describing the end of Goethe's *Faust*, Harold Bloom writes that Faust learns to reject magic, "resolving to stand up against nature by himself, rejecting every possibility of transcendence" and thereby "begins to become Freudian man, embracing the reality principle."[88] What Faust does not realize is that he is dying and that Mephistopheles has arranged for the digging of Faust's grave. At the end of *Two Weeks*, Jack seems to want to move beyond both Faustian and Freudian man. He rejects magic and learns to stand up against nature, but he does not completely embrace the reality principle either. As Jack is racing through the airport, Davie tells Jack that Veronica is waiting for him on the runway. This turns out to be a tease for the audience because Jack's passionate kiss for her is a goodbye kiss. She does not get on the plane but stays in Rome with Davie. The airplane door that closes firmly behind Jack, although a gesture of finality, also represents the possibility of renewal because Jack is being sealed within a vehicle of transport, of movement, and of flight. Jack "grows up" by the end of the film, but he still avoids the "mature" Oedipal process of settling down into marriage. Within the context of Minnelli's cinema, however, this may also be interpreted as a positive gesture because marriage in this world of aesthetes serves a mainly repressive function, a world of "lawful wedded nightmares," unless it can be tied back into the fluid world of theatricality and performance, a world in which you learn to draw a moustache on a portrait of your father and laugh.

In both the specific form it embodies and in the history of its production and reception, *Two Weeks in Another Town* is surrounded by a myth of finality, of the destruction and end of Hollywood cinema, as well as Vincente Minnelli's career, at least as a serious film artist. And yet precisely by turning the tentativeness, the uncertainty about classical cinema into a spectacle in its own right, Minnelli is able to make a significant passage into this new kind of art cinema, which poses such an apparent challenge to him. If *Two Weeks in Another Town* is a document of the failure of classical cinema at a particular moment of crisis it is also, precisely for the same reason, a testament to that cinema's power and its ability to perpetually renew itself.

Conclusion

Or The Death of Cinema Is No Solution

> It is foolish to talk about the death of the cinema because cinema is
> still at the beginning of its investigations.
>
> —Gilles Deleuze, *Cinema 2: The Time-Image*

In March 1976, Hitchcock's final film, *Family Plot*, opened to mixed
reviews and failed to find a large popular audience. In August
of the same year, Lang died in Hollywood at age eighty-six. Two
months later, Minnelli's last film, *A Matter of Time*, opened (as so many
of Minnelli's films did) at Radio City Music Hall. It was a critical and
financial disaster, the worst of his career. By the time of Lang's death, and
by the time that Hitchcock and Minnelli had made their final films, all
three directors had passed from their first major period of their work
being appropriated and cited (principally through the French New Wave,
at least in the case of the first two filmmakers) to a second period of this
process, occurring principally through the generation of New German
Cinema and of New Hollywood, filmmakers born during and immediately after World War II. The relationship of these post–New Wave
cinemas to the work of Lang, Hitchcock, and Minnelli has been sporadi-
cally dealt with throughout earlier sections of this book so my concluding
comments in this regard will be brief.

After *The Thousand Eyes of Dr. Mabuse*, Lang devoted sustained attention to only one other project, *Death of a Career Girl*, a film to star
Jeanne Moreau and that, like *The Thousand Eyes*, would have involved a

significant citation and reworking of elements from Lang's body of work, including another variation on the "thousand eyes" idea of surveillance.[1] Hitchcock and Minnelli continued to work throughout the 1960s and early to mid-1970s although both showed various signs of slowing down, related not only to age and physical health, but also to changes in the nature of film production of which neither director was able to completely and comfortably adapt. At the time of their release, none of their later films (for Hitchcock, *Torn Curtain* in 1966, *Topaz* in 1969, *Frenzy* in 1972, and *Family Plot*; for Minnelli, *The Courtship of Eddie's Father* in 1963, *Goodbye Charlie* in 1964, *The Sandpiper* in 1965, *On a Clear Day You Can See Forever* in 1970, and *A Matter of Time*) received the kind of auteurist and cinephilia-informed devotion of *Marnie* and *Two Weeks in Another Town*, although *Frenzy*, a financial and mainstream critical success, came closest. And although the academic industry that has arisen in relation to Hitchcock studies in the years since his death has managed to produce some significant work on the post-*Marnie* films, no major revisionism of this sort has happened to the later Minnellis even though at least one of these films, *The Courtship of Eddie's Father*, is a major work and none of the later Minnelli films are without interest.

When Lang died, Wim Wenders published an obituary that opened by quoting the "Death is no solution" line Lang famously utters in *Contempt* and that Wenders also used as his title for the obituary: "Death Is No Solution: The German Film Director Fritz Lang." Earlier that year, Wenders released *Kings of the Road* (1976) with its now-emblematic opening sequence of Bruno Winter, a repairer of motion picture projectors, talking to an aging projectionist (and former member of the Nazi party) who speaks to Winter of having once shown *Die Nibelungen*. Lang's mythological status as an auteur, which Godard's film had served as a primary source of confirmation thirteen years earlier is, in effect, passed on to another, slightly younger group of cinephiles and filmmakers born a decade after Godard's generation. Wenders's obituary opens with his desperate and unsuccessful attempt to search for a print in Germany not of any film that Lang himself directed, but a print of *Contempt*, simply to hear Lang speak the "death is no solution" line. But *Contempt* itself has now become elusive and seems to be fading into history as evocatively as *Die Nibelungen*, whereas the auteur of *Die Nibelungen*, ghostlike even before his actual moment of death months later, slips into the work of one of the most important figures of the New German Cinema.

At nearly three hours, *Kings of the Road* is itself an epic, although not conceived on the grandiose and popular scale of *Die Nibelungen* or any of Lang's other Weimar classics. The problem and indeed the dream of speaking to a popular audience, but on the filmmakers' own terms, will be a major concern to several of the New German filmmakers, perhaps none more so than Fassbinder, for whom *The Marriage of Maria Braun* will become his one major achievement in this regard. The achievement itself, however, is an isolated one and the connection between a formally innovative (and especially crucial for Fassbinder, socially critical) cinema remains elusive. The cinema of Lang (central to Wenders and many other New German filmmakers although apparently of little concern to Fassbinder) remains, if not utterly singular, at least an extraordinary example of the possibilities of linking genuinely innovative form to what may be now be seen as (perhaps in retrospect) an ambitious cultural project stretching from Weimar Germany to 1930s, 1940s and 1950s America, to Adenauer Germany.

At the end of *Kings of the Road*, another projection room sequence occurs in which Lang and *Contempt* are cited. A photo of Bardot from the film is pinned to the wall as is a photo of the aging Lang wearing his eye patch. The daughter of a former motion picture theater owner tells Winter that she refuses to show films that leave people stunned and rigid with stupidity, films that destroy any feeling for themselves and the world. Better no cinema at all than the way cinema is now: "Films, my father said, are the art of seeing." *Kings of the Road* is a primary example of a certain type of cinephilic attitude, no doubt nurtured by the economic and cultural problems of being a postwar German filmmaker, but that also exist within a history of melancholia about the future of cinema, which *Contempt* officially initiates: How does one continue to make films

Figure C.1. *Kings of the Road*: "Films, my father said, are the art of seeing." A portrait of Lang hangs on the wall behind her.

when the act of making films is increasingly an act of filming over the already filmed? This film-as-palimpsest idea is cited indirectly in *Kings of the Road* when the film's other male protagonist, Robert Lander, refers to an ink that allowed one to erase old writing while also allowing one to write something new at the same time. Somewhat disingenuously, Wenders claims that the citations of Lang in the film were not used intentionally: "In this film about the consciousness of the cinema in Germany, the father who left us, the father we let go, imposed his point of view, slipped in of his own accord."[2] Lander holds up a film magazine with a still on the back from *Contempt* showing Lang on the set of the film, surrounded by Jack Palance and Michel Piccoli, although after examining the photo for a moment Lander takes his hand and places it over Palance and Piccoli, isolating Lang from the group.

During the same period in which Hitchcock was making his last film, Brian De Palma released two of his most recent attempts (following *Sisters* in 1973) to explicitly draw upon Hitchcock's work. For De Palma, Hitchcock had become an exemplary filmmaker for his pursuit of "pure cinema" and in 1976 De Palma released the horror film *Carrie* (set in "Bates High School") and *Obsession*, a re-reworking of *Vertigo*, complete with a plush Bernard Herrmann score. This Hitchcock-inspired project is one that De Palma will sustain over the next two decades (and has still not completely abandoned, although in their concern with technology and large social methods of seeing and constructing images, his films increasingly seem to owe as much to Lang as they do to Hitchcock). But this Hitchcock period was preceded in De Palma's career by a period in the late 1960s when Godard had served as a similar point of contact, an interesting reversal of modernist hierarchies in which the filmmaker typically thought of as the more avant-garde of the two becomes the first stage rather than second or later stage in the evolutionary process of an artist.[3] If for the French New Wave classical cinema (particularly of Hollywood) formed a type of mourning text through which a modernist cinema emerged, for the New Hollywood of De Palma's generation, the style and structure of classical Hollywood was revived and relegitimated, sometimes uncritically but also quite often informed by the ambivalence largely brought about by various modernist developments in cinema during the 1960s. De Palma's public attitude toward Hitchcock was itself marked by an ambivalent "anxiety of influence." While embracing Hitchcock as the filmmaker who, as a veritable grammarian of cinema "distilled the essence of film," De Palma's public dismissal of late Hitchcock has a sting of youthful cruelty to it that someone such as Wenders carefully avoids in his references to Lang. Claims De Palma, "Anyone who says that Hitchcock's last film

[*Family Plot*] was a masterpiece is a fool. The man has clearly lost his sense of timing, of cinema. He's 75! You can't be a genius forever."[4] A recurring element of the most influential critical discourses surrounding De Palma in the 1970s and 1980s was that he had surpassed Hitchcock, of which Pauline Kael's review of De Palma's *The Fury* (1978) certainly stands as a classic example: "No Hitchcock thriller was ever so intense, went so far, or had so many 'classic' sequences."[5]

Scorsese began shooting his 1940s musical *New York, New York* in 1976, and it was released the following summer. Minnelli himself was photographed visiting the set of the film, flanked by his daughter, Liza Minnelli, and Scorsese, as though Minnelli was implicitly putting his blessing on this new Hollywood. Like most of Minnelli's own musicals, Scorsese photographed *New York, New York* entirely on Hollywood soundstages, and the film is both an extended homage to and an act of revisionism of the Hollywood musical and the cinema of figures such as Minnelli.[6] What is "repressed" in Minnelli's work, specifically realism, becomes the source of a deep structural contrast in Scorsese between the artifice of the mise-en-scène and the "realistic" psychodrama being played out by the protagonists. The nature of this project is in itself an expensive and grandiose extension of Godard's "neorealist" musical *A Woman Is a Woman* although both the tone and the nature of Godard's realism are quite different from Scorsese's—far less emotionally anguished and essentially comic in nature in the Godard. It is the ironic and playful Lubitsch, his name directly cited in the credits (not Minnelli) who becomes a principal guiding spirit of Godard's film.[7]

In the midst of all this, and emerging as something of an afterthought, we have *Family Plot* and *A Matter of Time*. At first glance, and particularly in comparison with the self-confidence of the work of the younger directors emerging during this period who so regularly cite Hitchcock and Minnelli as important figures, both films might seem tepid, awkward, and anachronistic. *Family Plot* shows little of the concern with the "pure cinema" that so fascinated De Palma. The film is dialogue heavy, much of it expository (even if also filled with typical Hitchcockian word play), and the film largely avoids the major suspense set pieces with which Hitchcock's name is so identified. The one major action-based suspense sequence of Blanche and George attempting to escape alive from a car whose brakes have been tampered with is handled in a comic fashion, diffusing conventional suspense. The film often plays like an extended and updated version of an episode of *Alfred Hitchcock Presents*, complete with flat, 1970s television-style lighting. But these apparent formal and technical shortcomings are nothing in comparison with the wreck that is *A Matter of Time*.

A Matter of Time was made in Italy in production and postproduction circumstances that mirrored the ones depicted in *Two Weeks in Another Town*. (And as with *Two Weeks*, the film is largely set in a hotel.) The "international peddler" Tucino in *Two Weeks* materializes in reality for Minnelli as Samuel Z. Arkoff, head of American International studios (known mainly for its low-budget exploitation films of the 1950s and 1960s) and the improbable distributor of the film. The humiliation of the failure of *A Matter of Time* for Minnelli was probably compounded rather than lessened by the fact that Arkoff took the final cut out of his hands very early in the postproduction process before Minnelli was even able to supervise the dubbing and scoring (both of which are atrocious in the released version), and the film was greatly reduced in length to ninety-seven minutes from its original conception with footage another director shot added as a prologue and an epilogue, along with stock travelogue footage of Rome periodically inserted at various moments. No MGM gloss is left here, no genre structures anchor the film, no witty screenplay exists, and apart from Ingrid Bergman and Charles Boyer, no good performances are in the film either. All that is here are the ruined remains of Minnelli's cinema, the themes that once gave it its urgency, and the occasional evidence of the visual flair and style which gave it its distinction. To respond to *A Matter of Time* favorably at all performing a kind of dual operation is necessary, observing the film that is being projected while simultaneously imagining another one, not Minnelli's original cut (so far no research has been done to show what that might have been) but a version of it which works. What the film needs, then (aside from a dedicated film restorer), is an auteurist cinephile, someone who can bring this "dead" object to life. If cinephilia has been so often fixated on the fragmentary, the incomplete, fixated on the ruins of cinema, *A Matter of Time* must surely stand as one of its ultimate examples and great challenges.[8]

Although in his later years and in the decades after his death virtually all of Hitchcock's work received detailed academic attention (as well as significant restoration and ongoing popular acclaim), neither Lang nor Minnelli has received anything comparable, although by now most of Lang's Weimar films have been restored and most of Minnelli's films are readily available and in excellent viewing condition. Although the Hitchcock centenary in 1999 was a massive, yearlong academic and cultural event cutting across all media, the Lang centenary nine years earlier was largely ignored. In the years since the Lang centenary, some important academic work has been done on Lang, although in sheer volume it pales in comparison with the literature on Hitchcock. As I write these words, we are in the final months of the Minnelli centenary, which is being received with the same indifference as the Lang, although for different reasons. The indifference with which Minnelli's work continues to be greeted today is most likely bound up with a twofold problem: On the one hand, we have its seemingly transparent nature, a world of entertainment with its self-evident pleasures; on the other, there is the work's "heaviness," its ambivalent and often bitter tone. Doubtless for many viewers, the films not only seem insufficiently "serious," but also insufficiently lighthearted. In his later years, Minnelli received little in the way of career honors. Three years after his death in 1986, the Museum of Modern Art produced a retrospective (which later toured the United States) and a lavish book was published in conjunction with it, Stephen Harvey's *Directed by Vincente Minnelli*. But Harvey's critical methods (to say nothing of his frequently irritating and conventional opinions) merely confirmed existing prejudices.

However, in drawing this book to a close, I would like to imagine for a moment that Lang was able to make *Death of a Career Girl* and that it stands as his final work, allowing us to place it alongside of *Family Plot* and *A Matter of Time*. At the center of all three films is a woman. In the Lang, that woman is played by a major 1960s art house star, Moreau, as we observe her character undergo a series of extreme adventures from 1943 to 1966: her involvement in the French resistance (in which she is raped by twenty drunken members of this group); has a child out of wedlock and attempts to murder the child but instead leaves it outside of a convent door; becomes the mistress of a wealthy man; marries a rich industrialist (whom she later drives to suicide); and becomes an extremely powerful businesswoman and unwittingly sleeps with her own by-now adult son. Her eventual knowledge of this incestuous act causes her to contemplate slitting her wrists in the bathtub with a razor blade before her focus on this is diverted when she is called to a meeting with her business associates. One can easily see the somber face of Moreau, in the aftermath of films such as *Eva* (1962) and *The Bride Wore Black* (1968), going through these episodes. But the synopsis, in spite of its postwar setting, suggests something of Weimar melodrama, closer to Pabst, perhaps, than Lang—even the title suggests a variation on Pabst's *Diary of a Lost Girl* (1929). Typical of much of Lang, the scenario creates the impression of an environment everywhere permeated by death. Every step of the heroine's ascent up the social and economic ladder is inextricably related to a death drive but in which her actual moment of death is averted: Once again, "death is no solution."

At the center of Hitchcock's last film we find, once again, a blonde, the mystic Blanche Tyler. As the film opens Blanche is in a trance, apparently possessed by someone dead while chanting, "Too many memo-ries, too much sorrow, too much pain." But the trance is a phony one in this film about actors, impersonation, and role playing, a film filled with amateur detectives and fake mystics—standard Hitchcock material. How-ever, the actress playing Blanche is neither a "cool" Hitchcock blonde along the lines of Grace Kelly or Tippi Hedren nor is she an actress associated with European art cinema, such as Moreau. Instead, she is a woman whose roots are largely in improvisational theater and musical comedy, Barbara Harris.[9] Although Karen Black, an actress known for her work in the New Hollywood, had top billing, Harris received the bulk of Hitchcock's attention. (Black is a blonde at the beginning of the film thanks to a wig which she later, in a Surrealist gesture, stuffs into the vegetable container of her refrigerator.) Hitchcock apparently was so taken with Harris's performance that he frequently readjusted his storyboards and improvised on the set to accommodate the kind of spontaneous work that she (as well as Bruce Dern) was doing, leading Bill Krohn to later write that "*Family Plot* may be the only film in history to be made 'against' its storyboards."[10]

The entire process of making *Family Plot*, from adapting its source novel, *The Rainbird Pattern*, to shooting the film, involved a continuous lightening of tone, a film in which (unlike his great comic film of 1955, *The Trouble with Harry*, with the title character's dead body at its center) no major character dies. If Hitchcock has "lost his timing" at the end of his career, we might also argue that he has moved beyond many of the obsessions that once structured his cinema. Although *Marnie* has a fetish-istic purse that Hitchcock's camera cannot seem to tear its eyes away from, in *Family Plot* our blonde heroine has an ordinary knapsack, and although it eventually becomes spotted with blood, those spots never assume the massive "stain on the landscape" idea of earlier Hitchcock films. Having this inventive musical comedy performer at the center of his final film allows Hitchcock to take pleasure in someone whose appeal lies precisely in her improvisational and corporeal nature, devouring ham-burgers, someone who resists becoming "fetishistic and frozen."

Family Plot, a film Hitchcock made when he was in less-than-perfect health and only four years away from death, a film that is not beautiful in any conventional sense, becomes extremely moving not only because it is, as Krohn puts it, "a light-hearted last testament,"[11] but also because it is a film that looks death in the face for two hours and then chooses to laugh about it. Hitchcock's final cameo appearance is one in which his body is shown only in silhouette, behind a door. Typically, however, it is not a tightly closed door, containing impenetrable mysteries on the other side of it, but a door with a smoked glass window in which Hitchcock's famous silhouette is clearly visible as he gestures to a woman. The sign painted on the door reads: Registrar of Births and Deaths.

Family Plot, then, is a film that not so much refuses death as temporarily puts it at bay but without the relentless somberness of *Death of a Career Girl*. Hitchcock's more modest career girl, rather than contemplating suicide and then opting to become a member of the walking dead, playfully winks into the camera in the film's final shot. Blanche appears to gain genuine psychic powers at the end of the film and locates a missing diamond hidden in a chandelier. Her wink into the camera may be read ironically and within the logic of the narrative itself, a signal to the spectator that she is not really psychic and that some logical explanation exists for her sudden insight. But this direct address to the spectator also functions outside of the film's diegetic world, assuming the status of an authorial flourish, Blanche as a stand-in for Hitchcock, winking at the audience. In light of the fact that this eventually became Hitchcock's final film, not viewing this shot as his farewell gesture to the spectator, whose inclusion in the formal organization of his films had always been so central, is difficult. However, we are also reminded here of Godard's statement, cited in chapter 2, that Hitchcock believes in destiny (that word so often used to describe Lang's work), but with a smile on his lips—and here, a wink.

A Matter of Time also has a musical comedy performer at its center, a performer who was, in fact, Universal's first choice for the lead in *Family Plot*, Liza Minnelli.[12] Of course casting a musical comedy performer would scarcely be an anomaly in a Vincente Minnelli film. What

Figure C.2. *Family Plot* (1976): Hitchcock's last cameo appearance.

is perhaps more interesting here is who plays opposite her, Ingrid Bergman, a star widely associated not only with Hitchcock, but also with Rossellini, a star whose mythology is bound up not only with Hollywood, but also with a rejection of it, via Rossellini and Italian neorealism. For *A Matter of Time* Bergman returns to Italy to make a film set in Rome in 1949, the same year she worked with Rossellini for the first time (in *Stromboli*), but here working for a director whose approach is almost completely bound up with the Hollywood studio system. Among the supporting cast is Anna Proclemer, who played the prostitute in Rossellini's *Voyage in Italy* (1953), although Arkoff removed her from the final cut; and one of Bergman's daughters from her marriage to Rossellini (and eventually to become her most famous child), Isabella Rossellini, turns up playing a nun in a scene near the end of the film, looking rather like her mother in one of Bergman's most notable Hollywood roles, Leo McCarey's *The Bells of St. Mary's* (1945). This neorealist moment in film history becomes part of the subject matter of the film as the chambermaid Nina (Minnelli), a young woman with no apparent acting ability or ambitions along those lines, is discovered by a director (played by Gabriele Ferzetti, best known for his leading role in *L'avventura*) and put into a film. Although this casting gesture has a neorealist quality to it, Nina ends up becoming some kind of musical film star as *A Matter of Time* gives way to a Cinderella-like structure and happy ending. Although this resolution was apparently not part of Minnelli's original conception for *A Matter of Time*,[13] it does not entirely violate the film's tone or style that, in spite of its neorealist citations, remains firmly grounded in an aesthetics of artifice, closer to Josef von Sternberg's *Anatahan* (1953) than to *Voyage in Italy*.[14]

The subject of aging and death is central to this final film of Minnelli's. Not seeing Bergman's Contessa, a woman who is out of step with the contemporary world and somewhat detached from reality in general, as an extension of Minnelli himself in 1976, is difficult. This may be an unfair and inaccurate description of Minnelli at this time, but it certainly surrounded the production and reception of the film. As with *Family Plot*, however, I think we may also see that Minnelli is not falling back on old methods here but instead is taking his cinema in some new directions, directions that may be difficult for many spectators to perceive due to the problematic production and postproduction circumstances of the film. Central to *A Matter of Time*, as with so much of Minnelli, we find this desire for characters to surround themselves with beautiful objects, to be absorbed by the decor of their own lives. The Contessa is, along with the version of Van Gogh we see in *Lust for Life*, arguably the most extreme example in all of Minnelli's cinema of this type of character in that she pushes this desire to the point of madness and, eventually, her own death. Unlike Van Gogh, she does not experience transcendence through the practice of her own art but by inspiring other male artists, by serving as their muse until age and mental instability eventually deny her even this function.

Where the film takes the implications of Minnelli's cinema in some new directions is in the relationship between the Contessa and Nina, particularly the sequences in which the Contessa shares her memories of her glorious past with the chambermaid, handled in the film through flashbacks. But the Contessa's memories are so seductive and powerful for Nina that Nina gradually begins to imagine herself inhabiting the Contessa's past, as simple flashbacks give way to fantasy/dream spaces in which Nina sees herself enacting the role of the Contessa. (Arkoff reportedly did not understand the structure of the film and removed much of this footage but enough survives to make some tentative arguments here.) The structure itself emerges out of Minnelli's previous film, *On a Clear Day You Can See Forever*. In that film, Daisy Gamble's memories of her past life as Melinda Tentrees in eighteenth-century England are produced under a hypnotic state by her psychiatrist, Dr. Chabot, causing Chabot to fall in love not with Daisy but with Melinda. Chabot increasingly seems to take possession of Daisy's own past, summoning up Melinda through Daisy, although only in one fleeting moment (or, to be precise, through two brief subjective shots) is he able to enter into this space from the past. In this manner, *On a Clear Day* more purely fits into the notion of Minnelli's cinema being dominated by the "passage from one world to another, entry into another world, breaking in and exploring."[15]

Although in Minnelli's previous work this plurality of worlds was often predicated on power struggles taking place within these dream spaces, in *A Matter of Time* we find the characters freed from these struggles. The Contessa happily and willingly passes on her visions to Nina and the space of the Contessa's imagination, the film implies, then lives on in Nina who nevertheless inhabits this space in her own particular way after the death of the Contessa. If *Family Plot* is a film that implicitly winks at death, *A Matter of Time* suggests that the finality of death can be resisted through the sheer force of the imagination, through dream states that live beyond the physical life of the individual. "No one dies unless we wish them to," the Contessa declares. In this regard, *A Matter of Time* may also be seen as a film about cinema itself, a form that (at least in its classical state) gives rise to spectatorial fantasies of identification and projection onto other (virtual) worlds; that photographically preserves movements in time (the title of the film itself suggests a kind of Deleuzian/Bergsonian idea), projected movements that simultaneously evoke a presence more magically lifelike than life itself while also suggesting an embalming property that evokes death; and that documents the process of aging and physical decay, filming "death at work" in Jean Cocteau's famous phrase.

Figure C.3. *A Matter of Time* (1976): "No one dies unless we wish them to."
Photo courtesy of Photofest, New York, N.Y.

A Matter of Time was not only Minnelli's final film, it was also Boyer's and it was Bergman's penultimate theatrical one. But it is also a film that resists the very idea of the end and instead puts its faith in the notion of not only time, but also implicitly cinema itself existing as perpetual and evolving continuums, passed from one generation to another. It may very well have been the awareness, coming at the end of his career, that his body of work would "live on" through succeeding generations of filmmakers that allowed Minnelli to conceive of his final film in this way.

This study has attempted to show that the analysis of figures such as Hitchcock, Lang, and Minnelli is not simply one that involves the celebration of auteurs. It also involves the study of forms, of discourses, and of histories that helped to define that perpetually shifting and ambiguous term classical cinema. But as I hope is abundantly clear throughout this text, I also love these films and the work of these filmmakers, and a primary motivation here was to convey that enthusiasm, to extol, to proclaim, to hector, and to force the reader to see something that may have been overlooked or misunderstood, to use a certain basic impulse behind cinephilia for the study of something I hope also has broader historical implications. I conclude, then, on an optimistic note not only of evoking the perpetual and evolving impulse of cinema, but also of the perpetual and evolving impulse of cinephilia.

Notes

Introduction: Writing the History of Classical Cinema

1. See, for example, Raymond Bellour: "For half a century, [classical cinema] was, in its American form especially, the only 'innocent' art, identified as if by nature with the societies whose image it constructed, so speak, at a distance. . . ." Bellour, "(Not) Just an Other Filmmaker," *Jean-Luc Godard: Son + Image*, ed. Raymond Bellour and Mary Lea Bandy, trans. Georgia Gurrieri (New York: Museum of Modern Art, 1992), p. 217.

2. Noël Burch, "Fritz Lang: The German Period," *Cinema: A Critical Dictionary*, ed. Richard Roud (London: Secker and Warburg, 1980), p. 584.

3. Jacques Aumont, "The Fall of the Gods: Jean-Luc Godard's *Le Mépris*," in *French Film: Texts and Contexts*, ed. Susan Hayward and Ginette Vincendeau (London: Routledge, 1990), p. 219.

4. Aumont writes, "What is basically at issue here is Godard's conception of the cinema, which attempts to combine and to embrace both the classical heritage (the conception of the open, transparent window) and something which can now clearly be seen to be modernity (distancing, the play on shifters)," p. 223.

5. Andrew Sarris, "Waiting for Godard," in *Jean-Luc Godard: A Critical Anthology*, ed. Toby Mussman (New York: Dutton, 1968), p. 132.

6. Serge Daney and Jean-Pierre Oudart, "Work, Reading, Pleasure," *Cahiers du Cinéma: 1969–1973: The Politics of Representation*, ed. Nick Browne, trans. Diana Matias (Cambridge, Mass.: Harvard University Press, 1990), p. 122.

7. Geoffrey Nowell-Smith, *L'avventura* (London: BFI Publishing, 1997), p. 11.

8. Manny Farber, *Negative Space* (New York: Da Capo Press, 1998), p. 143. Originally published in *Film Culture*, Winter 1962–1963, as "White Elephant Art vs. Termite Art."

9. In the late 1960s, Lang stated, "My way of shooting is through disciplined selection. I'm therefore absolutely opposed in principle to what the *nouvelle vague* does. I think it is the death of art, which is primarily selection. . . . Perhaps the younger people today are creating genuine new forms; I really don't know."

Charles Higham and Joel Greenberg, *The Celluloid Muse: Hollywood Directors Speak* (Chicago: Henry Regnery Company, 1969), p. 127.

10. Donald Kuspit, *The Dialectic of Decadence: Between Advance and Decline in Art* (New York: Allworth Press, 2000), p. 28.

11. Charles Rosen, *The Classical Style: Haydn, Mozart, Beethoven* (New York: Norton, 1973), p. 19.

12. David Bordwell, Janet Staiger, and Kristin Thompson, *The Classical Hollywood Cinema: Film Style and Mode of Production to 1960* (New York: Columbia University Press, 1985), p. 4. The chapter of the book from which this quote was taken, "An Excessively Obvious Cinema," is signed entirely by Bordwell.

13. Bordwell et al., *Classical Hollywood Cinema*, p. 81.

14. Bordwell et al., *Classical Hollywood Cinema*, p. 81.

15. Bordwell et al., *Classical Hollywood Cinema*, p. 82. Bordwell's example here is Lang's *You Only Live Once* (1937).

16. Bordwell et al., *Classical Hollywood Cinema*, p. 81.

17. Bordwell et al., *Classical Hollywood Cinema*, p. 381.

18. Bordwell et al., *Classical Hollywood Cinema*, p. 384. This section of the book, chapter 31, "Alternative Modes of Film Practice," is signed entirely by Bordwell.

19. See, for example, chapter 7, "The Bounds of Difference," in which Bordwell writes, "Nothing in any Hollywood auteur film rivals the idiosyncratic systems of space or time operating in the work of Dreyer, Bresson, Mizoguchi, Straub/Huillet, Ozu, Resnais, or Godard. In such works, narration is pervasive, constantly foregrounded, because these modernist works create unique *internal* stylistic norms," p. 81.

20. Miriam Bratu Hansen, "The Mass Production of the Senses: Classical Cinema as Vernacular Modernism," in *Reinventing Film Studies*, ed. Christine Gledhill and Linda Williams (London: Arnold, 2000), p. 337.

21. Hansen, p. 343.

22. Hansen, p. 339.

23. Hansen, p. 337. Other essays that question the validity of *The Classical Hollywood Cinema* include Rick Altman's "Film Theory Today" and Bill Nichols's "Form Wars: The Political Unconscious of Formalist Theory," both in *Classical Hollywood Narrative: The Paradigm Wars*, ed. Jane Gaines and Bill Nichols (Durham: Duke University Press, 1992). The most violent attack on *The Classical Hollywood Cinema* is Andrew Britton's "The Philosophy of the Pigeonhole: Wisconsin Formalism and 'The Classical Style,'" in *CineAction!* 15 (Winter 1988–1989).

24. Hansen, p. 337.

25. Eric Rohmer, *The Taste for Beauty*, trans. Carol Volk (Cambridge, England: Cambridge University Press, 1989), p. 41. Originally published as "The Classical Age of Film," *Combat*, June 15, 1949.

26. James Naremore, *The Films of Vincente Minnelli* (Cambridge, England: Cambridge University Press, 1993), p. 17.

27. Peter Brooks, *The Melodramatic Imagination: Balzac, Henry James, and the Mode of Excess* (New York: Columbia University Press, 1985), p. 20.

28. Irving Howe, "The Idea of the Modern," in *The Idea of the Modern in Literature and the Arts*, ed. Irving Howe (New York: Horizon Press, 1967), p. 13.

29. See Richard Sheppard's distinction between premodern explorations of the crisis of language in poetry in which the crisis results in "a clearing away of lumber prior to a fresh burst of creativity" with the modernist crisis. Here, we see "a real pessimism about the possibility of revivifying language." In "The Crisis of Language," in *Modernism: A Guide to European Literature 1890–1930*, ed. Malcolm Bradbury and James McFarlane (London: Penguin Books, 1991), p. 324.

30. Gilles Deleuze, *Cinema 1: The Movement-Image*, trans. Hugh Tomlinson and Barbara Habberjam (Minneapolis: University of Minnesota Press, 1986), p. 23. Originally published in 1983 as *Cinéma 1. L'Image-Mouvement*, Paris, Les Editions de Minuit.

31. Gilles Deleuze, *Cinema 2: The Time-Image*, trans. Hugh Tomlinson and Robert Galeta (Minneapolis: University of Minnesota Press, 1991), p. 40. Originally published in 1985 as *Cinéma 2, L'Image temps*, Paris, Les Editions de Minuit.

32. Deleuze, *Cinema 2*, p. xi.

33. Deleuze, *Cinema 2*, p. xiii.

34. Deleuze, *Cinema 2*, p. 138.

35. Deleuze, *Cinema 2*, p. 63.

36. Deleuze, *Cinema 1*, p. 204.

37. David Bordwell, *On the History of Film Style* (Cambridge, Mass.: Harvard University Press, 1997), pp. 116–117.

38. In a 1983 *Cahiers du Cinéma* interview with Pascal Bonitzer and Jean Narboni, Deleuze explicitly states, "I don't . . . claim to have discovered anyone, and all the auteurs I cite are well-known people I really admire." *Negotiations*, trans. Martin Joughin (New York: Columbia University Press, 1995), p. 50. Originally published in French as *Pourparlers*, Paris, Les Editions de Minuit, 1990.

39. Marie-Claire Ropars-Wuilleumier, "The Cinema, Reader of Gilles Deleuze," trans. Dana Polan, in *Gilles Deleuze and the Theater of Philosophy*, ed. Constantin V. Boundas and Dorothea Olkowski (New York: Routledge, 1994), p. 259. Originally appeared in *Camera Obscura* 18 (September 1989).

40. Annette Michelson, "Gnosis and Iconoclasm: A Case Study of Cinephilia," *October* 83 (Winter 1998): 3. Michelson's essay concerns itself with cinephilia as experienced by the American avant-garde. Marc Vernet has divided cinephilia into two categories: The first is based on "the desire to know everything about films, to develop an encyclopedic knowledge about them, a desire which privileges secondary information," whereas the second "has to do with the cultural eclecticism offered by noncommercial screenings rather than movies playing in ordinary theaters." Marc Vernet, "Fetish in the Theory and History of Cinema," trans. Hamilcar Otopengo, in *Endless Night: Cinema and Psychoanalysis, Parallel Histories*, ed. Janet Bergstrom (Berkeley: University of California Press, 1999), pp. 92–93.

41. For the concerns of this study see, in particular, Jonathan Rosenbaum's 1997 exchange of letters among a group of contemporary film critics (Rosenbaum, Adrian Martin, Kent Jones, Alex Horwath, Nicole Brenez, and Raymond Bellour)

to evaluate the current position of cinephilia in relation to the cinephilia of the French New Wave critics and filmmakers. "Movie Mutations: Letters from (and to) Some Children of 1960," *Film Quarterly* 52 (Fall 1998). An unedited version of this exchange is the opening chapter of an anthology ed. Rosenbaum and Martin, *Movie Mutations: The Changing Face of World Cinephilia* (London: BFI Publishing, 2003), pp. 1–34.

42. Paul Willemen, *Looks and Frictions: Essays in Cultural Studies and Film Theory* (Bloomington: Indiana University Press, 1994), p. 239. Christian Metz also discusses cinephilia in relation to fetishism and the notion of the "good object" in *The Imaginary Signifier*, trans. Celia Britton, Annwyl Williams, Ben Brewster, and Alfred Guzzetti (Bloomington: Indiana University Press, 1982), pp. 10–11, 74–76.

43. Willemen, p. 227.

44. T. L. French [Bill Krohn], "Les Cahiers du Cinéma 1968–1977: Interview with Serge Daney," *The Thousand Eyes* 2 (1977): 20.

45. Willemen, p. 256.

46. French [Krohn], p. 29.

47. Rosenbaum and Martin, p. 29.

48. Willemen, p. 232.

49. Thomas Elsaesser, "Vincente Minnelli," in *Genre: The Musical*, ed. Rick Altman (London: Routledge and Kegan Paul, 1981), p. 10. Originally appeared in *Brighton Film Review* no. 15, December 1969 and no. 18, March 1970.

50. Elsaesser, "Vincente Minnelli," p. 11.

51. Hansen, pp. 337–338.

52. Although Bogdanovich historically belongs to the Film School Generation, he was not someone who went to film school but rather began as an auteurist film critic and stage director.

53. Here I offer a *Cahiers* influenced reading of American cinema. The more or less contemporaneous writings of the other major French film magazine, *Positif*, do not exert an influence in this book. This has little to do with the value of the criticism in that magazine. (Their writings on Minnelli, for example, are at least as strong and interesting as *Cahiers*'s.) But I did not begin reading *Positif* until more recently and as this book is, among other things, a kind of academic working through of a youthful cinephilia, *Positif* simply did not exist as part of this personal history for me.

54. French [Krohn], p. 20.

55. Daney and Oudart, "Work, Reading, Pleasure," p. 133.

56. As Renoir stated in a 1954 interview with Rivette and Truffaut, "The actors are also the directors of the film." Jean Renoir, *Renoir on Renoir*, trans. Carol Volk (Cambridge, Mass.: Cambridge University Press, 1989), p. 4. Interview originally published in *Cahiers du Cinéma*, nos. 34 and 35, April and May 1954.

57. Jean Douchet, *French New Wave*, in collaboration with Cédric Anger, trans. Robert Bonnono (New York: Distributed Art Publishers, 1999), p. 138.

58. Mary Ann Doane, "The Object of Theory," in *Rites of Realism: Essays on Corporeal Cinema*, ed. Ivone Margulies (Durham, N.C.: Duke University Press, 2002), pp. 80–89.

59. Serge Daney, "Godard Makes [Hi]stories," in *Jean-Luc Godard: Son + Image, 1974–1991*, eds. Raymond Bellour and Mary Lea Bandy (New York: Museum of Modern Art, 1992), p. 160.

60. Craig Owens, "The Allegorical Impulse: Toward a Theory of Postmodernism," in *Art After Modernism: Rethinking Representation*, ed. and intro. Brian Wallis (New York: New Museum of Contemporary Art/Boston: Godine, 1984), p. 203. Originally published in *October* 12, Spring 1980 and *October* 13, Summer 1980.

61. Owens, p. 206.

62. Owens, p. 215.

63. French [Krohn], p. 29.

64. Owens, p. 212.

65. Vivian Sobchack, *The Address of the Eye: A Phenomenology of Film Experience* (Princeton, N.J.: Princeton University Press, 1992), p. 15.

66. Serge Daney, *La rampe: Cahier critique 1970–1982* (Paris: Éditions Gallimard, 1996), pp. 207–208.

67. Gilles Deleuze, "Letter to Serge Daney," in *Negotiations*, trans. Martin Joughin (New York: Columbia University Press), p. 68. Originally published as the preface to Daney's *Cine-Journal*. "The great problem which obsesses classical cinema," Bonitzer writes, "is, as we know, 'how to get from one shot to the next'; how to get to the next shot without stumbling or tripping up. . . . What must be preserved at all costs is the unity, the homogeneity, the continuity of this ideological scene. . . . "Off-screen Space," in *Cahiers du Cinéma*, ed. Nick Browne (Cambridge, Mass.: Harvard University Press, 1990), p. 297. Originally published in *Cahiers du Cinéma* 234–235 (December 1971/January–February 1973).

68. See Thierry Kuntzel's analysis of *The Most Dangerous Game* (1932) as a "classical" film text, which strongly draws on the metaphor of the secret beyond the door. "The Film Work, 2," trans. Nancy Houston, *Camera Obscura* 5 (Spring 1980): 7–68.

69. Daney and Oudart, "Work, Reading, Pleasure," p. 131.

70. Luis Buñuel, *An Unspeakable Betrayal: Selected Writings of Luis Buñuel*, trans. Garrett White (Berkeley: University of California Press, 2000), p. 114. Originally published in *Gaceta literaria*, no. 35, June 1, 1928.

71. For example, in discussing the gothic melodrama *Rebecca* with Hitchcock, Truffaut refers to the "fablelike quality" of the film, suggested by the "emphasis on keys to the house, by a closet that no one has the right to open, or by a room that is sealed off." *Hitchcock*, in collaboration with Helen G. Scott (New York: Simon and Schuster, 1984), p. 131.

73. Gaston Bachelard, *The Poetics of Space*, trans. Maria Jolas (Boston: Beacon Press, 1994), p. 222. Originally published in French as *La poétique de l'espace*, Paris, Presses Universitaires de France, 1958). Translation first published by Orion Press, 1964.

73. Christian Metz, *The Imaginary Signifier*, trans. Celia Britton, Annwyl Williams, Ben Brewster, and Alfred Guzzetti (Bloomington: Indiana University Press, 1982), p. 77. Originally published in 1977 by Paris, Union Générale d'Éditions.

74. Metz, p. 77.

75. Georg Simmel, "Bridge and Door," in *Simmel on Culture*, ed. David Frisby and Mark Featherstone, trans. Mark Ritter (London: Sage Publications, 1997), p. 173.

76. Simmel, p. 174.

Chapter 1. Dr. Mabuse, The Cliché: *The Thousand Eyes of Dr. Mabuse*

1. A claim Raymond Bellour put forth in "On Fritz Lang," in *Fritz Lang: The Image and the Look*, ed. Stephen Jenkins, trans. Tom Milne (London: BFI Publishing, 1981), p. 27. The word *paradox* recurs in the literature on Lang. For example, in the side-by-side essays by Noël Burch and Robin Wood on Lang in Richard Roud's anthology on film directors, both writers see paradox as fundamental to Lang's cinema, albeit in different terms. Burch refers to Lang's work and the body of writing surrounding it as presenting "a double paradox," Roud, p. 583. Wood writes of how Lang's films present the spectator with "continuous paradox" for the manner in which the characters are presented as both doomed and responsible. Roud, p. 607.

2. See David Kalat's history of the Mabuse phenomenon, stretching from Norbert Jacques's original novel up through Claude Chabrol's 1990 Mabuse reworking, *Club Extinction*, in *The Strange Case of Dr. Mabuse: A Study of the Twelve Films and Five Novels* (Jefferson, N.C.: McFarland, 2001).

3. Patrick McGilligan, *Fritz Lang: The Nature of the Beast* (New York: St. Martin's Press, 1997), p. 441.

4. According to Kluge, Lang was interested but the older director's health, combined with the hostility of one of the officials connected with the project toward Lang, resulted in this situation never coming to pass. In "The Early Days of the Ulm Institute for Film Design," in *West German Filmmakers on Film: Visions and Voices*, ed. Eric Rentschler (New York: Holmes and Meier, 1988), p. 111. Lang later felt Kluge betrayed him as the result of a 1966 interview the younger director gave. In this interview, Kluge claimed that Lang, due to excessive interference from the film's producer, stopped directing *The Tiger of Eschnapur* after the third day of production and merely supervised the shoot instead. In *Fritz Lang: His Life and Work: Photographs and Documents*, ed. Rolf Aurich, Wolfgang Jacobsen, and Cornelius Schnauber (Berlin: Jovis, 2001), pp. 407–408.

5. Jonathan Crary, "Dr. Mabuse and Mr. Edison," in *Art and Film Since 1945: Hall of Mirrors*, ed. Russell Ferguson (Los Angeles: Museum of Contemporary Art/New York: Monacelli Press, 1996), p. 271.

6. In defending the Indian diptych, Straub has argued that they are "the only films that are superproductions without being superproducts, which are made with all the money that he had at his disposal without creating a smokescreen. And which nevertheless are not made *against* money; because now, that's easier to do. Godard, in his evolution, had discovered that it is necessary to make oppositional films. But for a man of Fritz Lang's generation, this wasn't possible, an

idea like that." Cited by Barton Byg, *Landscapes of Resistance: The German Films of Danièle Huillet and Jean-Marie Straub* (Berkeley: University of California Press, 1995), pp. 41–42. Quote taken from "Straub and Huillet on Filmmakers They Like and Related Matters," Film at the Public program for Straub/Huillet series, ed. Jonathan Rosenbaum, November 1982, p. 5.

7. According to Kalat, a later non-Lang Mabuse film Brauner produced, *The Death Ray of Dr. Mabuse* (Hugo Fregonese, 1964), tried to cash in on the international fascination with the Bond films, particularly drawing on Ian Fleming's *Thunderball* a year before the novel was filmed. Pp. 207–210.

8. Eric Rentschler, "Germany: Nazism and After," in *Oxford History of World Cinema*, ed. Geoffrey Nowell-Smith (Oxford, UK: Oxford University Press, 1996), p. 382.

9. Roger Greenspun, "*The Thousand Eyes of Dr. Mabuse*," *Film Comment* (March 1973): 54.

10. Crary has argued that Mabuse needs to be understood less as a character than as "the name of a system" undergoing constant metamorphoses, both within and across the three Mabuse films. P. 274.

11. McGilligan writes of Lang's behavior on the set of *Metropolis*: "Lang believed in his own superhuman willpower, and tried to use that Mabusian belief to hypnotize everybody, pushing them to their limits." *Fritz Lang*, p. 117. Geoffrey O'Brien likewise succumbs to this mythological reading of Lang, picking up cues directly from Lang himself and crossed with elements from *Testament of Dr. Mabuse*, "When he worked he felt 'almost as though I were sleepwalking.' He would read the script and then close his eyes, sink into a sort of trance, and allow images to well up. In this way he 'saw' the film with his inner eye, as if its finished form already existed within him. And so he became himself a Fritz Lang movie: a film director, reading a lurid, melodramatic scenario, falls into a hypnotic state in which he receives commands from an unknown source; on waking he proceeds to carry them out with compulsive precision." *The Phantom Empire* (New York: Norton, 1993), pp. 122–123. Elsaessser points out that not until after World War II did Mabuse begin to be read in such metaphoric terms, especially through the influence of Siegfried Kracauer's *From Caligari to Hitler*. In Elsaesser, *Weimar Cinema and After: Germany's Historical Imaginary* (London: Routledge, 2000), p. 157.

12. Cited by Lotte Eisner in *Fritz Lang* (London: Secker and Warburg, 1976), pp. 57–58.

13. Crary, p. 273.

14. In writing of the Mabuse films in passing, Phil Hardy argues that they express "Victorian notions of conspiracy." For Hardy, this comes about through the creation of "separate under and overworlds and the point where the two come into collision is often the attempted seduction of an innocent." From "Crime Movies," in *The Oxford History of World Cinema*, p. 304.

15. Eisner, *Fritz Lang*, p. 390. Tom Gunning refers to the film's "cops and robbers story" as being possibly inadequate in dealing with the issue of Nazi legacy that the film indirectly addresses. *The Films of Fritz Lang: Allegories of Vision and Modernity* (London: BFI Publishing, 2000), p. 473.

16. Eisner, *Fritz Lang*, p. 390.

17. Jean Douchet, *L'Art d'aimer* (Paris: Petite bibliothèque des Cahiers du cinéma, 2003), pp. 88–89. Originally published as "L'Étrange Obsession," *Cahiers du Cinéma*, August 1961.

18. Jonathan Rosenbaum, *Rivette: Texts and Interviews*, ed. Jonathan Rosenbaum (London: BFI Publishers, 1977), p. 3. When Rivette's film opened in the United States, Jonas Mekas wrote, "If one knows how, one can read from this film more about the mind and heart of Europe 1962 than from any other movie or any book." *Movie Journal: The Rise of the New American Cinema 1959–1971* (New York: Collier Books, 1973), p. 74. Originally published in *Village Voice*, November 25, 1962.

19. In referring to the structure of *Paris nous appartient*, Rivette has drawn attention to "the labyrinth that the décors create among themselves, the idea that one brings away from the film, of a sort of series of settings with relationships between them—some cut off, others communicating, others that are optional itineraries—and people moving about like mice inside these labyrinths, ending up in culs-de-sac or caught nose to nose. Then at the end it all disappears and there's nothing left but this lake and some birds flying away. . . ." Rivette, "Time Overflowing," in *Rivette: Texts and Interviews*, p. 28.

20. Jean-André Fieschi, "Jacques Rivette," in Roud, p. 875. Fieschi also writes of the film: "There is no center to this drifting (no climax either, no thesis), which seems solely the pursuit of a delusion, its faint adumbration." Similarly, he writes of Rivette's *Out One: Noli me Tangere* (1971) that we find "conspiracy as a metaphor for all mise-en-scène, but with no Mabuse in evidence." P. 876.

21. Stan Brakhage, for example, refers to Lang's Hollywood work as "an endless stream of films which need not concern us . . . anymore than they only temporarily concerned him." In *Film Biographies* (Berkeley, Calif.: Turtle Island, 1977), p. 237.

22. Volker Schlöndorff, "The Stranger," in *Out of the Dark: Crime, Mystery and Suspense in the German Cinema, 1915–1990*, ed. Willi Johanns (Munich: Goethe-Institut, 1992), p. 47.

23. Eisner, *Fritz Lang*, p. 390.

24. Gunning, p. 461.

25. Elsaesser, *Weimar Cinema and After*, p. 155.

26. Daney, "Work, Reading, Pleasure," p. 123. Owens writes that "the paradigm for the allegorical work is . . . the palimpsest." Pp. 204–205.

27. Elsaesser has specifically drawn attention to this triad and writes that it is one in which "contending claims on perception and reason the radical sceptic in Lang never ceases to play off against each other." *Weimar Cinema and After*, pp. 149–150. Of *Dr. Mabuse, the Gambler*, Elsaesser also writes, the "film fosters an attitude of fascination and scepticism at the same time." P. 161.

28. Jacques Derrida, *Memoirs of the Blind*, trans. Pascale-Anne Brault and Michael Naas (Chicago: University of Chicago Press, 1993), p. 1. Originally published as *Mémoires d'aveugle: L'autoportrait*, Paris, Editions de la Reunion des musees nationaux, 1990.

29. Cited (and presumably translated) by Elsaesser in *Weimar Cinema and After*, p. 160. Appeared originally as "Keine Monument," in *Fritz Lang* (Munich: Hanser, 1976).

30. In referring to this film (and the Indian diptych that preceded it), Bellour detects a quality that is "at once remarkably veiled and disconcertingly open. Seemingly naïve, almost puerile . . . theoretical in the extreme [they] discard the reassuring alibi of the American tradition while simultaneously transposing the tradition's basic artificiality to a Germany where nothing has survived: they repudiate the positive aspects of the myths underlying Lang's German period, reducing them to their own level within a dual adventure, individual and collective, involving the cinema and historical awareness." Pp. 28–29.

31. McGilligan, *Fritz Lang*, p. 437.

32. Hence the disagreement between Brauner and Lang over precisely identifying this Mabuse's origins. Brauner had wanted the character to be Mabuse's son, repeating and extending his father's deeds in the postwar era (and this was how Mabuse was identified in the promotional material for the film). But Lang refused this kind of biological connection. All Lang was interested in was a character who was a copy of the original. See Kalat, p. 124. One may see this as a culminating gesture of abstraction on Lang's (and Thea von Harbou's) part in the creation of Mabuse begun with *Dr. Mabuse, the Gambler*, where they dropped a clear motivation for Mabuse's activities that had been in Norbert Jacques's novel: Mabuse wants to establish his own country in a Brazilian jungle. See Kalat, p. 41.

33. Carlo Ginzburg, *Clues, Myths, and the Historical Method*, trans. John and Anne C. Tedeschi (Baltimore: Johns Hopkins University Press, 1989), p. 119.

34. Peter Brooks has written of the "anxiety and fascination of the hidden, masked, unidentified individual" that persists across history and finds a particularly rich manifestation in the detective story as it began to develop in the nineteenth century. The detective story "testifies to this concern to detect, track down, and identify those occult bodies that have purposely sought to avoid social scrutiny." *Body Work: Objects of Desire in Modern Narrative* (Cambridge, Mass.: Harvard University Press, 1993), p. 26. The same year in which *Dr. Mabuse, the Gambler* was released, Jorge Luis Borges published an essay titled "The Nothingness of Personality," with its repeated declaration, "There is no whole self," a declaration that in itself is a central definition of the individual in relation to the modern world. *Jorge Luis Borges: Selected Non-Fictions*, ed. Eliot Weinberger, trans. Esther Allen (Harmondsworth, UK: Penguin Books, 1999), pp. 4–9.

35. Deleuze, *Cinema 2*, p 264.

36. Citing Daney, Deleuze writes, "what has brought the whole cinema of the movement-image into question are 'the great political *mises-en-scène*, state propaganda turned *tableau vivants*, the first handling of masses of humans,' and their backdrop, the camps." *Cinema 2*, p. 164.

37. Rentschler, p. 378.

38. Rentschler, p. 379. Also, if much of the boldness of Lang's montage strategies from his first German period only occasionally surfaces during his Hollywood years, we must also stress that this "repression" of montage is one that is specific not only to Lang. Eisenstein and other Soviet montage filmmakers under Stalin, for example, found themselves working in an environment in which the bold montage strategies of their silent and early sound work were repressed, and they were encouraged instead to edit closer to the continuity style of Hollywood. For both the Soviet cinema under Stalin and the Nazi government under

Hitler, classical Hollywood was increasingly becoming the standard bearer, a model for a form of cinema addressing a popular audience of which neither the Weimar art films nor the Soviet montage classics of the 1920s were fully capable.

39. Siegfried Kracauer, *From Caligari to Hitler* (Princeton, N.J.: Princeton University Press, 1947), p. 84.

40. McGilligan writes, "[Lang] often complained that the history of German film had been falsified by Kracauer—'consciously or unconsciously, I'm not quite clear on that.' Indirectly, he meant that the history of his own life had been distorted. Was it not a bitter experience to have been one of the geniuses of the cinema, then to be ignored in the United States and reviled in Germany?" *Fritz Lang*, p. 457.

41. As Elsaesser points out, Kracauer's book became the definitive text for shaping postwar attitudes about Weimar cinema in the United States. But Eisner's art historical approach in *The Haunted Screen* was widely influential in France, where Kracauer's book was largely ignored. *Weimar Cinema and After*, p. 422.

42. Lang reportedly asked Brauner, "Where do you get the actors? As figures in heroic legend how do they move, how do they speak? What sort of things do they say?" In John Russell Taylor, "The Nine Lives of Doctor Mabuse," *Sight and Sound* (Winter 1961–1962): 43–44.

43. Ironically, however, Eisner reads Lang making *The Tiger of Eschnapur* and *The Indian Tomb* as a gesture toward "creating fairytale splendour for a Germany that was not rich." P. 384. This is very similar to Jean-Marie Straub's take on the films cited earlier.

44. Theodor Adorno, *Minima Moralia*, trans. E. F. N. Jephcott (London: Verso, 1978), p. 241. Originally published by Suhrkamp Verlag, Frankfurt am Main, 1951. The nature of Adorno's attitude toward the occult in relation to German culture can be traced back at least as far Georg Simmel's 1892 essay, "A Few Words on Spiritualism." Simmel asks whether "we will have the strength to transfer our ideals to the social interests that constitute the lodestar of the future—or whether we will stick to the empty husks of the past and attempt to fill them with absurdities like spiritualism." In *Simmel on Culture*, p. 294.

45. Fifty years after *Dr. Mabuse, the Gambler*, another German filmmaker, Werner Herzog, appropriates the role of the film director as hypnotic figure in a way that is both more extreme and more benign than Lang. In *Heart of Glass*, Herzog literally hypnotized some of his cast members to extract a certain kind of glacial, stylized performance from them. For Herzog, however, because the actors submitted willingly to the process and because Herzog believes that no one under hypnosis will do what they would not do consciously, he does not view his experiment as one of a power-crazed film director exerting control. In this regard, Herzog seems to be rewriting the possibilities of hypnosis in cinema, modifying and finding new, potentially positive capabilities in what was once a largely negative and quasi-fascistic aspect of German cinema and German cultural history. His later film *Invincible* (2001) treats the subject explicitly and historically.

46. Deleuze argues that the opening parallel editing sequence of *Dr. Mabuse, the Gambler* represents a model the classical action-image will "remain marked by." Here, Lang presents us with "an organised action, segmented in space and

in time, with the synchronised watches whose ticking punctuates the murder in the train, the car which carries off the stolen document, the telephone which warns Mabuse." *Cinema 1*, p. 69. Detailed analyses of this sequence may be found in both Burch and Gunning.

47. The most recent translation of these intertitles, on the Kino DVD of the film, reads, "Almighty God, what power is at play here?" This is followed by Haghi's simple declaration: "I."

48. Gunning writes of *The Thousand Eyes*, "The essential question of Lang's master criminal films: 'Who is behind all this?' is no longer explicitly articulated, let alone answered." P. 462.

49. As Gunning writes, "Lang not only frames a world, but creates a space of significance which contains and poses emblems and riddles, allegories and demonstrations." P. 310.

50. Bellour writes of the recurrence in Lang of "doors opening and closing, constantly modifying space depending on whether they reveal more hidden depths or not," a recurrence that becomes "almost a thematic element." "On Fritz Lang," p. 32. "The passage from one shot to another," writes Oudart, "and one place to another (through a door) is, for Lang, much more than a means of credibility— it is a means of signifying the existence of the character." In Daney and Oudart, "Work, Reading, Pleasure," pp. 132–133.

51. Daney has written that Lang belongs to a generation of filmmakers who are "masters of a chain where nothing allows the end to be envisaged, masters of a frenetic transitivity which condemns them to say nothing real, never to come to a stop, were they not flagged down by the actual, material end of the film. . . ." Daney and Oudart, "Work, Reading, Pleasure," p. 121.

52. According to Kristin Thompson, the continuity style had been almost completely established in the United States by 1917. See *Classical Hollywood Cinema* , p. 157, as well as Thompson in chapter 18, "The Stability of the Classical Approach after 1917," pp. 231–240.

53. Elsaesser notes that Lang "as early as *Die Spinnen* [*Spiders*, 1919] demonstrated an effortless facility with Hollywood continuity editing, and he never dispensed with basic principles of scene dissection." *Weimar Cinema and After*, p. 160.

54. Elsaesser has written in relation to *Dr. Mabuse, the Gambler*, "The film establishes a causal chain that is driven less by character psychology than by editing patterns, a peculiarity not only of Lang's *mise-en-scène*, but typical of Weimar cinema's distinct approach to the legacy of Griffith. . . ." *Weimar Cinema and After*, p. 175.

55. The practice of both of them within American cinema, and D. W. Griffith's work in particular prior to the end of World War I, was widely influential in this regard. The melodramatic nature of many of the scenarios of Griffith's films, their reliance on themes of persecuted innocence, of sympathetic protagonists trapped within confined spaces by menacing villains as a last-minute rescue is launched—all of this relied heavily on crosscutting for suspense. But in films such as *A Corner in Wheat* (1909) and, especially, *Intolerance* (1916), Griffith makes use of parallel editing to make specific thematic and metaphoric parallels between

narrative actions (although without completely abandoning the possibilities of using this same technique for suspense, as in the climax to *Intolerance*).

56. Deleuze, *Cinema 1*, p. 54.

57. Deleuze, *Cinema 1*, p. 30. Perhaps the central text for analyzing the strengths and limitations of the American practice of parallel editing and its dualistic manner of thinking is Eisenstein's essay, "Dickens, Griffith and the Film Today," in *Film Form*, ed. and trans. Jay Leyda (New York: Harcourt Brace Jovanovich, 1949).

58. Deleuze, *Cinema 1*, p. 30.

59. Deleuze, *Cinema 1*, p. 148.

60. As Anton Kaes points out, when *M* opened in New York in 1933 the film appeared to certain critics to be the antithesis of the American gangster film: "It did not share the gangster film's dream of upward mobility, its moral certitude and love of violent action. 'It is a picture,' the film critic of the *New Republic* remarked, 'which I do not think could under any circumstances been made in Hollywood. . . .'" Anton Kaes, *M* (London: BFI Publishing, 2000), p. 79.

61. Deleuze, *Cinema 1*, p. 152.

62. Also important to note is the 1953 publication of Karel Reisz's widely influential *The Technique of Film Editing*, which attempts to historicize and canonize this art and craft. Only one Lang film, *You Only Live Once*, is discussed in this book and only briefly, perhaps an indication of how little recognized Lang's work was at that time within the history of montage.

63. Bazin lays out this historical argument most clearly in "The Evolution of the Language of Cinema," from *What Is Cinema? Volume 1*, selected and trans. Hugh Gray (Berkeley: University of California Press, 1967), pp. 23–40. See also Rivette's description of the "Renoir-Rossellini-Bazin trilogy" as a reaction against the "generalised 'perversion' of Eisensteinian practice" via Pudovkin and Hollywood. In Jean Narboni, Sylvie Pierre, and Jacques Rivette, "Montage," in *Rivette: Texts and Interviews*, pp. 81–82. Originally appeared in *Cahiers du Cinéma*, no. 210, March 1969.

64. Although imagining a filmmaker who had less in common with the Italian neorealists than Lang would be difficult, Lang was apparently an admirer of Rossellini's *Rome, Open City* (1945), hosting a VIP screening of it in Hollywood in 1946. See McGilligan, *Fritz Lang*, p. 348.

65. Bazin, "An Aesthetic of Reality," in *What Is Cinema? Volume 2*, selected and ed. Hugh Gray (Berkeley: University of California Press, 1971), p. 35.

66. Bazin, "The Evolution of the Language of Cinema," p. 32. Actually, Bazin misdescribes this moment from *Fury* as a cut from "a series of shots of women dancing" to the chickens.

67. The abstract nature of Lang's cinema probably prevented Bazin from "bending" this body of work to a realist aesthetic, which Bazin attempted with Stroheim and Murnau.

68. Rosenbaum has drawn attention to the complicated relationship between Bazin and Rivette in this regard. Rivette's review of Rossellini's *Voyage in Italy* (1953) would seem to be directly Bazinian in its approach. But Rivette's review of *Beyond a Reasonable Doubt*, a film Bazin dismissed, is clearly indicative of

Rivette's fascination with "a totally closed world." Rosenbaum detects a split within *Paris nous appartient* itself between its realistic and phenomenological side (the Bazin influence) on the one hand, and its closed, abstract side (the Lang influence) on the other. Introduction to *Rivette: Texts and Interviews*, p. 3.

69. Jean Domarchi, Jacques Doniol-Valcroze, Jean-Luc Godard, Jacques Rivette, and Eric Rohmer, "Hiroshima, Notre Amour," in *Cahiers du Cinéma; The 1950s: Neo-Realism, Hollywood, New Wave*, ed. Jim Hillier (Cambridge, Mass.: Harvard University Press, 1985), p. 60. Hillier notes that this discussion is "markedly and crucially transitional" for the group as it begins to question its investment in classical narrative. But it was not so much classical narrative that concerned the group (Italian neorealism was hardly a model of classical narrative) as much as a cinema that privileged mise-en-scène over montage.

70. In 1968 Rivette isolated four major moments in the history of montage: "the invention of montage (Griffith and Eisenstein), its deviation (Pudovkin Hollywood, elaboration of the techniques of propaganda cinema), the rejection of propaganda (a rejection loosely or closely allied to long takes, direct sound, amateur or auxiliary actors, nonlinear narrative, heterogeneity of genres, elements or techniques, and so forth) and finally, what we have been observing over the last ten years, in other words the attempt "to reinject into contemporary methods the spirit and *theory* of the first period, though without rejecting the contribution made by the third, but rather trying to cultivate one through the other, to dialectise them and, in a sense, to *edit* them." "Montage," p. 82.

71. Deleuze, *Cinema 2*, p. 214. Welles at the end of his Hollywood career and then onto his European films had already anticipated this approach in *The Lady from Shanghai*, *Othello* (1952), and *Mr. Arkadin*. These films, while still maintaining a link with the deep focus and (occasional) long take style alternating with the (more or less) classically constructed montage sequences of his earlier work, much more aggressively flaunt their discontinuous nature.

73. Marie-Claire Ropars-Wuilleumier has written of the "splintered style" of *Hiroshima, mon amour,* "which seems contaminated by the editing of the film: an accumulation of brief notes, corrections, additions and shifts, as if the enunciator was grabbing at straws in the wind." "How History Begets Meaning: Alain Resnais' *Hiroshima mon amour* (1959)," trans. Susan Hayward, in *French Film: Texts and Contexts*, p. 183, n. 1.

73. Burch has claimed that the Lang stretching from *Dr. Mabuse, the Gambler* to *The Testament of Dr. Mabuse* ten years later is one of the great masters of the early period of film history, comparable to Eisenstein and Dreyer for the manner in which he explored the possibilities of a montage conception largely in opposition to the traditional American continuity style. After *The Testament of Dr. Mabuse*, however, we find "a silence lasting some thirty years." This metaphoric silence is Lang's Hollywood career (as well as, presumably, the work produced during his brief return to Germany), in which Lang "accepted all the (essentially regressive) inferences which the American sound film had drawn in particular from his best work in Germany." Burch, p. 599. Burch is writing in the 1970s in the aftermath of approximately two decades of auteurist writings on Lang that frequently argued either for the superiority of Lang's Hollywood work over that

of his first German period, or instead saw the films as forming one seamless vision. Burch's dismissal of all of Lang's American work (as well as the later German films) cannot be divorced from its deliberate attempt at provocation in the aftermath of this auteurist approach. His arguments about Lang form part of a much larger agenda of Burch's that insists on the primacy of modernist strategies of filmmaking that are strongly opposed to those of mainstream cinema, including most of the Hollywood films and filmmakers the auteurists had elevated to the pantheon of cinema. Whereas Burch's position toward Lang is extreme and apparently inflexible, it is as strongly bound up with the historical moment in which he is writing as is that of the *Cahiers* critics in the preceding two decades. For an account of this period, see Bordwell, *On the History of Film Style*, chapter 4, "The Return of Modernism: Noël Burch and the Oppositional Program," pp. 83–115.

74. In drawing a distinction between the classical intellectual cinema (such as Eisenstein's) and the modern (such as Resnais's), Deleuze argues, "The 'classical' conception developed along two axes; on the one hand integration and differentiation, on the other association, through contiguity and similarity." *Cinema 2*, p. 210. In the modern, however, there is "no longer association through metaphor and metonymy, but relinkage on the literal image; there is no longer linkage of associated images, but only relinkages of independent images. Instead of one image after the other, there is one image *plus* another, and each shot is deframed in relation to the framing of the following shot." *Cinema 2*, p. 214.

75. Kalat, for example, complains that the opening of *Dr. Mabuse, the Gambler* "is perhaps too well-made for its own good; the rest of the gargantuan picture cannot quite live up to the promise set by the first 20 minutes." P. 37.

76. In the most strongly argued piece about Lang's cinema in relation to the issue of death, Jean-Louis Comolli and Francois Géré write, "If the fiction [of Lang's cinema] makes death circulate among the characters, the fictional scheme which governs the spectator's place makes it a journey of *mortification*." Although Comolli and Géré are writing on *Hangmen Also Die*, their argument could apply to several Lang films, including *The Thousand Eyes*. Jean-Louis Comolli and Francois Géré, "Two Fictions Concerning Hate," in *Fritz Lang: The Image and the Look*, trans. Tom Milne, p. 146. Originally published in *Cahiers du Cinéma*, no. 286, October 1969.

77. Elsaesser has written on Lang's general methods during the Weimar period: "The impression of violence comes from the nakedness with which the framing and editing exposes the act of representation as an interference, an incision almost of a surgical operation, and Lang's cinema reminds us of the violence done to things made visible when representing them." P. 163. Douchet makes a similar argument in "L'Étrange Obsession" about the opening montage of *The Thousand Eyes*, p. 50.

78. No doubt the central function death assumes here is partly the result of Lang's contact with an extensive German fascination with figures of death. See Eisner, for example, when she writes in a controversial passage in relation to Lang's *Der müde Tod*, "The difference between the Germans and other races, said Clemenceau, is that the Germans have a taste for death, whereas other nations

have a taste for life. But the truth of the matter is perhaps—as Hölderlin implies in *Hyperion*—that the German is obsessed by the phantom of destruction and, in his intense fear of death, exhausts himself in seeking means of escaping destiny." *The Haunted Screen*, rev. ed. (Berkeley: University of California Press, 1969), p. 89. English translation originally published by Thames and Hudson, London, 1969. First published in France in 1952 as *L'Ecran Démoniaque*, revised and reissued 1965, Paris, Le Terrain Vague.

79. Both Tom Gunning and Catherine Russell have discussed Lang's work in relation to the allegorical figuration of death. Working out of Walter Benjamin's writings on German *Trauerspiel*, both note how death for Lang serves not as the site of a morbid fascination but as the very boundary in art of the expressive and inexpressive, and of the classical and the modern. For Russell, the loss the representation of death points toward is experienced not simply through the death of the protagonist, but is also a loss "articulated on the level of the image and the very language of representation, an allegory produced through an interpretive reading of the texts in question." *Narrative Mortality* (Minneapolis: University of Minnesota Press, 1995), p. 3. The Lang film Russell writes on is *Beyond a Reasonable Doubt*, in which everywhere are the signs of the mortification of classical cinema. Gunning's arguments have their basis in Lang's more overtly allegorical German silent films and in which the language of German tragic drama is much more obvious.

80. See the description in McGilligan of Lang's walking away from *Scarlet Street* (1945) before the editing had been completed to begin preproduction on *Cloak and Dagger* (1946), leaving the film in the hands of the producer, Walter Wanger. On viewing this cut, Lang reportedly accused Wanger of "stabbing him in the back." *Fritz Lang*, pp. 323–324.

81. Gunning, p. 11.

82. In a 1958 essay on Lang, Truffaut writes of *While the City Sleeps*, "The most overwhelming thing in this movie is the way Lang looks at his characters with unrelieved hardness; they are all damned. Nothing could be less soft or sentimental, really more cruel, than a love scene Lang directs." "Fritz Lang in America," in *The Films in My Life*, trans. Leonard Mayhew (New York: Simon and Schuster, 1978), p. 66. Likewise Rivette has written that *Beyond a Reasonable Doubt* is "obviously the antithesis of the idea of 'an entertaining evening.' " "The Hand," in *Cahiers du Cinéma: The 1950s*, p. 141.

83. Martin Scorsese, "Learning from Lang," in *Fritz Lang 2000*, Anthology Film Archives, ed. Robert Haller, 2000, p. 31. Scorsese's attitude toward the later American films directly follows the *Cahiers* approach, "In his last American films, there's nothing left but the design—the brutality and physical excitement is gone from *While the City Sleeps* and *Beyond a Reasonable Doubt*, and there's only the trap: it's as if you're observing a lab experiment. I think Lang had finally had it with America. . . ." Scorsese, p. 31.

84. Kalat argues, "This minimalism is in part a consequence of Lang's feeling out of place in postwar Berlin: unable to recognize the landscape, he had no ability to translate it cinematically. However, the restricted terrain also serves to focus the film's energies." P. 118.

85. Deleuze isolates a central category in modern cinema which he calls the "crystal image." In the crystal image, "narration ceases to be truthful, that is, to claim to be true, and becomes fundamentally falsifying." Protagonists in this new image are no longer in control of the sensory-motor situations of the films and the forger becomes the character who now seems to preside over this cinema. His falsifying status is one that "assumes an unlimited figure which permeates the whole film." This permeation creates an environment in which "investigators, witnesses and innocent or guilty heroes will participate in the same power of the false." This is a world in which uncovering the truth becomes increasingly difficult and in which the detective figures likewise begin to reflect the de-centering of the process of investigation, "degrees of which they will embody, at each stage of the narration. . . . There is no unique forger, and, if the forger reveals something, it is the existence behind him of another forger." *Cinema 2*, pp. 131–134.

86. Before working for Lang, Addams had also worked for E. A. DuPont in *Return to Treasure Island* (1954) and Chaplin in *A King in New York* (1957), making her something of a darling of aging silent directors. Addams and Van Eyck had appeared together in another Brauner production made the year before *The Thousand Eyes*, Ralph Habib's *The Black Chapel*.

87. Compare this to what Visconti does with Alida Valli and Farley Granger in their scenes together in *Senso* (1954). Whereas Valli speaks Italian with other Italian actors, all of her love scenes with the American Granger are in English. (Granger is dubbed in the Italian prints but both he and Valli speak in their own voices in the English-language version.) This still carries a major mark of inauthenticity about it because Granger is playing an Austrian officer and there is no reason why he should be speaking English to an Italian countess. But playing their scenes together in the same language at least allows the actors to directly connect with one another on the set, something that apparently did not take place with *The Thousand Eyes*. *Hiroshima, mon amour*, by contrast with both of these films, actively foregrounds its own international coproduction status by having the language difference of its two lovers (one French, one Japanese) become part of the subject matter of the film.

88. Gunning, p. 473.

89. Michel Mourlet writes of Lang's last films prior to *The Thousand Eyes*, "The bodies are seized by a paralysis which restricts their movements within an almost fixed frame. The faces are closed, impassive not only in reticence but because the world is already dead, petrified, each individual being imprisoned without recourse, therefore devoid of anguish, beyond solitude, dispatched purely because of the bond of antagonism, indifference or contempt." Michel Mourlet, "Fritz Lang's Trajectory," in *Fritz Lang: The Image and the Look*, p. 16. Originally published in *Cahiers du Cinéma*, no. 99, September 1959.

90. Deleuze writes of this general shift, "The configuration of power was also inverted and, instead of converging on a single, mysterious leader, inspirer of dreams, commander of actions, power was diluted in an information network where 'decision-maker' managed control, processing and stock across intersections of insomniacs and seers (as in, for example, the world-conspiracy we saw in Rivette, or Godard's *Alphaville*, the listening and surveillance systems of [Sidney]

Lumet, but above all, the evolution of Lang's three Mabuse's, the third Mabuse, the Mabuse of the return to Germany, after the war." *Cinema 2*, p. 265.

91. One of Vernon's most notable screen performances prior to *The Thousand Eyes* was as the "sensitive" Nazi officer in Jean-Pierre Melville's *La Silence de la mer* (1947), a character who is the very antithesis of what he is asked to play for either Lang or Godard.

92. Deleuze refers to two of the great figures of modern cinema, the body and the brain. The body in modern cinema is defined by its state of sheer exhaustion, of never seeming to exist fully in the present. On the other hand, there is the cinema of the brain, which is not necessarily opposed to the new cinema of the body but exists in relation to it. "Tiredness and waiting, even despair are the attitudes of the body." *Cinema 2*, p. 189.

93. The author of the play on which *Grand Hotel* was based, Vicki Baum, also wrote a play during World War II that became the basis for another Hollywood film, *Hotel Berlin* (1945) with Peter Lorre. The film is set in the declining years of the Third Reich with the hotel (once again) serving as a microcosm of Germany at the time.

94. As Gunning writes of *The Thousand Eyes*, "A locale takes on the pivotal role that the figure of Mabuse or Haghi played in the earlier films, character giving way to architecture." P. 464.

95. Such a desire for surveillance through the act of filming and recording is consistent with the ways in which the Nazi regime viewed such apparatuses as extensions of ideological domination and control. As Rentschler points out, the National Socialist Party's attempts to monitor human activity were pervasive and ongoing. "To this day, Nazi cinema in many minds resembles Mabuse's 1,000 eyes or 1984's panoptic state apparatus." P. 374.

96. In a letter Adorno wrote to Lang from Germany in 1950 he notes, "the Germans are suffering from the most indescribable feelings of guilt (and not only the Nazis by any means). But they are repressing these feelings, probably because they could not breathe otherwise, and so they deaden them and try to overcompensate, a task made very easy for them, of course, by their present political role . . . they are merely a function of a great field of tension, and have ceased to be a political subject." In *Fritz Lang: His Life and Work*, p. 404.

97. Siegfried Kracauer, *The Mass Ornament: Weimar Essays*, trans., ed. and intro. Thomas Y. Levin (Cambridge, Mass.: Harvard University Press, 1995), p. 175.

98. Kracauer, *Mass Ornament*, pp. 182–83.

99. In Kracauer, *Mass Ornament*, p. 184.

100. Gunning writes of the function of hotels in Lang as "a place of meetings, erotic encounters, role-playing and mutual observation." P. 474.

101. Perhaps the most potent and condensed image in all of modern cinema in this regard is that of the closed elevator doors in the Overlook Hotel in Stanley Kubrick's *The Shining* (1980), in which torrents of blood flow out from the sides of the doors, flooding the hallways and covering the lens of the camera: a symbolic blood, not only the blood of the previous caretaker and his murdered family but the blood that rises up from underneath the hotel, the blood of the

Native Americans who fought and died to prevent the construction of the hotel itself (built, we are told early in the film, on one of their burial grounds), a blood that contains the history of American racism, imperialism and expansion.

102. As Gunning points out, "The Nazi past pervades *The Thousand Eyes of Dr. Mabuse* without needing to be rendered visible." P. 473.

103. Very quickly this act of repression became the subject of farce in another Billy Wilder film with a postwar German setting, *One, Two, Three* (1961), made the year after *The Thousand Eyes* and as dominated by images of this new architecture as *A Foreign Affair* was by images of immediate postwar ruin. But perhaps the most interesting and neglected of the postwar German films that deal with this issue in relation to architecture is one directed by yet another former German émigré, Robert Siodmak, *Mein Schulfreund* (1960). Here we see the passage from rubble to renewal over approximately fifteen years played out strongly through architecture and decor, with modern architectural design (including a hotel) clearly serving as sites of ideological repression and cover-up.

104. See Brian Ladd's *The Ghosts of Berlin* (Chicago: University of Chicago Press, 1997), p. 175. Ladd refers to a 1994 explosion in East Berlin in which construction workers accidentally detonated one of these bombs, killing three people, injuring seventeen, and blowing a large hole in the wall of an apartment house. Ladd writes, "Berliners did not need such a cruel reminder that memories of the war lurk in the depths of their city."

105. Truffaut writes, "Of all the German filmmakers who fled Nazism in 1932, [Lang is] the one who has never recovered. . . . Lang did not doubt that man is born wicked, and the terrible sadness of his last films reminds us of Alain Resnais' *Nuit et Brouillard*." In "Fritz Lang in America," p. 67.

106. See Eisner in *The Haunted Screen*, especially chapters 7 (" 'Decorative' Expressionism"), 8 ("The World of Shadows and Mirrors"), and 9 ("Studio Architecture and Landscape").

107. Kerry Brougher, "Hall of Mirrors," in *Art and Film Since 1945*, p. 24. For Deleuze, the mirror also function as a fundamental device within the crystal image in which an exchange between the virtual image within the mirror and the actual image of the characters or events caught within it takes place. Here mirrors often assume baroque proportions, multiplying themselves within the space of the film as the distinction between the real and imaginary, between the actual and the virtual becomes confused. The funhouse sequence from *Lady from Shanghai* is likewise crucial for Deleuze, "a perfect crystal-image." *Cinema 2*, p. 70.

108. "In those days," Welles has said of the 1930s, "*Caligari* was the cinéaste's dream picture, you know. It hasn't stood up, thank goodness [!], but it used to be considered a great classic." In Orson Welles and Peter Bogdanovich, *This Is Orson Welles*, ed. Jonathan Rosenbaum (New York: Da Capo Press, 1998), p. 42.

Chapter 2. Fascination and Rape: *Marnie*

1. Slavoj Žižek, "Introduction: Alfred Hitchcock, or, The Form and Its Historical Mediations," in *Everything You Always Wanted to Know About Lacan (But Were Afraid to Ask Hitchcock)*, ed. Slavoj Žižek (London: Verso Press, 1992), p. 5.

In a more recent essay, Emil Stern refers to *Marnie* as "messy and almost seemingly on the verge of explosion, and almost as unpopular now as it was on its initial release in 1963[*sic*]." In "Hitchcock's *Marnie*: Dreams, Surrealism, and the Sublime," *Hitchcock Annual*, 1999–2000, p. 30. In the same issue of the magazine is Ken Mogg's essay on the film, the title of which says it all in terms of *Marnie's* ongoing problematic status: "Defending *Marnie*—and Hitchcock."

2. Truffaut, *Hitchcock*, p. 327.

3. Raymond Durgnat argues that the three films "form a group, moving from bleakness to a positive faith in a humiliated moral decency." *The Strange Case of Alfred Hitchcock or, the Plain Man's Hitchcock* (Cambridge, Mass.: MIT Press, 1974), p. 368.

4. See Tom Ryall, *Alfred Hitchcock and the British Cinema* (London: Athlone, 1996). Originally published in 1986 by Croom Held, London. During the British period, Ryall notes, Hitchcock "seemed to be straddling the two branches of the film culture [in Britain], the commercial and the artistic, the world of entertainment and the world of 'film art.'" Pp. 88–89.

5. Robert Kapsis, p. 78.

6. Andrew Sarris, "Movie Journal," *Village Voice*, August 11, 1960, p. 8.

7. Critical response to *Psycho* was initially mixed but in the aftermath of the enormous financial success of the film, several critics reversed or modified their initial reviews. See Kapsis, p. 63. Hitchcock received an Oscar nomination for best director for *Psycho* the following spring. Such an immediate turnabout did not take place with *The Birds* and *Marnie*.

8. Fieschi states, " I think too that we have all noticed [*Muriel's*] links with Hitchcock in general . . . and to *Vertigo* in particular. . . . So we have a thriller but a thriller where the enigma is the intention of the film itself and not its resolution. (It's worth noting that *The Birds* is also Hitchcock's first film where the tension isn't aimed at solving a mystery, but at elaborating and developing it.) The analogy doesn't stop there. It also relates to the actual way the mystery is treated: the first part of *The Birds*, which is banal, everyday and simple in its use of *signs*, is a preparation for the appearance of the fantastic element. The first part is therefore not fantastic itself but rather, looked at retrospectively, it's oneric." Jean-Louis Comolli et al., "The Misfortunes of *Muriel*," in *Cahiers du Cinéma, The 1960s*, ed. Jim Hillier (Cambridge, Mass.: Harvard University Press, 1986), p. 73.

9. Kapsis, pp. 64—68. These letters were responding to the film in both its initial theatrical release and its first television showing in 1968. Kapsis also quotes from a *Time* magazine review of *The Birds* stating, "Fans hooked on Hitchcock may be dismayed to discover that, after 38 years and more than 40 films, dealing mainly in straightforward shockery [*sic*], the Master has traded in his uncomplicated tenets of terror for a new outlook that is vaguely *nouvelle vague*." P. 93.

10. Kapsis, p. 80. Kapsis also notes that the film's production files "indicate how important the film's psychoanalytic framework was to Hitchcock's campaign to improve his artistic reputation among the serious critics." P. 82.

11. The *New York Times* felt that with *Marnie* "Hitchcock is taking himself too seriously—perhaps the result of listening to too many esoteric admirers"

(cited in Kapsis, p. 94), however more typical of the American response was Judith Crist's *New York Herald Tribune* complaint that the film is "pathetically old-fashioned and dismally naive." Cited in Kapsis, p. 123.

12. In *Village Voice*. Sarris complained of the distracting nature of "fake sets" and "appallingly dated" process work. Cited in Kapsis, p. 123. Robert Boyle told Kapsis that neither he nor cinematographer Robert Burks were happy with the matte work and rear projection on the film and suggested to Hitchcock that they reshoot the footage. Hitchcock's response, "I don't see anything wrong with it, Bob. I think it looks fine." From this, Kapsis deduces that critics who have defended these devices in *Marnie* were wrong. Pp. 129–130. In later years, Hitchcock began to side with the film's detractors on this matter. He confessed to Peter Bogdanovich that the matte shot of the ship looming over Mrs. Edgar's street "wasn't well done in *Marnie*." Peter Bogdanovich, *Who the Devil Made It: Conversations with Legendary Filmmakers* (New York: Ballantine Books, 1997), p. 539.

13. Compare Ken Mogg's eloquent defense of the film's use of rear projection and matte work in "Defending *Marnie*" from *Hitchcock Annual* 1999–2000 with Jacques Aumont's passing reference to the "unbelievable backdrop" of the looming ship at the end of the Baltimore street on which Marnie's mother lives. "Paradoxical and Innocent," in *Hitchcock and Art: Fatal Coincidences*, ed. Domique Païni and Guy Cogeval (Montreal: Montreal Museum of Fine Arts, 2000), p. 79.

14. According to Hedren, Hitchcock continued to keep her under personal contract for two years after *Marnie*, but then refused to loan her out to anyone or to use her in any future projects of his own, presumably as punishment to her, in spite of what Hedren maintains were numerous offers. Her only other major screen appearance in the 1960s after *Marnie* is a supporting role in another disastrously received work by an aging master, Chaplin's final film, *A Countess from Hong Kong*. See Tony Lee Moral, *Hitchcock and the Making of Marnie* (Lanham, Md.: The Scarecrow Press, Inc., 2002), p. 129.

15. Truffaut, *Hitchcock*, p. 327.

16. Aumont has drawn attention to Hitchcock's melancholy oscillation between an idealization and a victimization of women in his films, seeing in this position a strong nineteenth-century sensibility: "The man is hurt not so much because he has been deceived, but because the woman is not equal to the task." The woman must then be banished from Paradise whereas the man who is responsible for the banishment is often a feminized man. "Paradoxical and Innocent," pp. 91–92.

17. In their discussion of *Marnie*, Truffaut refers to this theme as one that has always strongly appealed to Hitchcock and Truffaut tells Hitchcock, "I hope that someday you can work it out to your satisfaction." *Hitchcock*, p. 306. Donald Spoto writes, "The film was becoming the story of a director's desire for an inaccessible actress who, therefore, became even more an object of fantasy." Donald Spoto, *The Dark Side of Genius* (New York: Little, Brown, 1983), p. 500.

18. When Bogdanovich asked Hitchcock how the situation with Hedren had gone on *Marnie*, Hitchcock's cryptic reply was, "Svengali has a few more gray hairs." *Who the Devil Made It*, p. 483. Truffaut refers to Hitchcock's behavior during the production of the film as being that of a "frustrated Pygmalion." *Hitchcock*, p. 346.

19. In writing on the later works of Lang and Hitchcock, Jean-Pierre Oudart writes that the image comes to signify "the absence of the subject or the presence of the master, whose fantasy suspends the discourse, breaks its transitivity and introduces an intolerable *play* into the fiction. It was actually in terms of suspense and play that these directors initially posed their transgression. However, in their latest films . . . and within the framework of a system where this was inconceivable, the image itself does indeed end up, for Lang, representing what the object had at first signified (the phallus), by its very emptiness and lack . . . ; and for Hitchcock, even more strangely, it is charged with directly producing the figuration of the fantasy." "Work, Reading, Pleasure," p. 133.

20. Jacques Aumont, Jean-Louis Comolli, Jean Narboni, and Sylvie Pierre, "Time Overflowing," interview with Rivette from *Rivette: Texts and Interviews*, p. 12.

21. Cited by Fieschi, "Jacques Rivette," in Roud, p. 875. Review originally appeared in *Cahiers du cinéma*, no. 132, June 1962, pp. 35–37.

22. Fieschi, p. 875.

23. Umberto Eco, "Casablanca: Cult Movies and Intertextual Collage," in *Travels in Hyperreality*, trans. William Weaver (New York: Harcourt Brace Jovanovich, 1986), p. 209.

24. A particularly flamboyant example of quotation in relation to *Marnie*: The performance artist John Epperson, in his drag performance as Lypsinka, has used excerpts from the soundtrack of *Marnie* in several of his stage acts, lip-syncing to the voices of Hedren and of Louise Latham as Mrs. Edgar. One of the acts periodically makes use of Herrmann's "madness" theme to connote Lypsinka's own camp, theatricalized onstage breakdowns while another act draws upon *Psycho's* shrieking violins as a form of transition.

25. Eco, p. 198.

26. Pascal Bonitzer, "*Notorious*," p. 153.

27. Bonitzer, "Hitchcockian Suspense," pp. 17–18.

28. Bonitzer, "Hitchcockian Suspense," p. 19.

29. "Everything is proceeding normally, according to routines that are ordinary, even humdrum and unthinking, until someone notices that an element in the whole, because of its inexplicable behavior, is a stain. The entire sequence of events unfolds from that point." Bonitzer, "Hitchcockian Suspense," p. 20.

30. In Robert Daudelin's 1965 review of *Marnie* he writes, "In *Marnie*, you have *L'arrivée d'un train en gere* and *Hiroshima mon amour*; *Greed* and *Rio Bravo*." From "*Marnie*: Early Testament?" in *Hitchcock and Art*, ed. Païni and Cogeval, p. 191.

31. This concern with the human subject not acknowledging the camera is not, however, entirely typical of the Lumière films, many of which seem actively to encourage their subjects to engage in a direct acknowledgement of the camera's presence.

32. In an early production conference for the film, Hitchcock originally described a crowded train station through which Marnie would walk for this opening sequence. But he also expressed a desire to "cheat like they do in the Italian films and have nobody around if we can." Sidney Gottlieb, ed., *Hitchcock on Hitchcock: Selected Writings and Interviews*, (Berkeley: University of California

Press, 1995), p. 319. Production conference originally published as "Hitchcock at Work," *Take One* 5, no. 2, May 1976. According to Moral, the Italian connection was obvious enough for the film critic of the *New York Post*, Archer Winsten, to compare *Marnie*'s train station and "the abstract train depot in [Fellini's] *8½*." P. 125.

33. Stern refers to the "deadness of atmosphere that pervades the film and gives it a ghoulish aspect—if the film's narrative concerns love . . . its form suggests death. . . ." P. 35.

34. Hitchcock told Truffaut that what primarily bothered him about *Marnie* were the supporting characters: "I had the feeling that I didn't know these people, the family in the background," while also complaining about the casting problems with Connery. *Hitchcock*, p. 304. Jay Presson Allen (on the making-of *Marnie* DVD) also speaks with amusement over the "fake British" nature of Hitchcock's casting and directing choices for the American upper-class Rutland family, particularly the father. When Allen objected to the inauthenticity of the characters and the costuming and decor of the social world Hitchcock was depicting, Hitchcock reportedly told her that Americans would not believe the reality of how their own upper classes lived and behaved. What is also interesting according to Allen's testimony is that she claims she and Hitchcock cast Connery with a full awareness that he was not ideal for the role in terms of verisimilitude.

35. In an early production conference for the film, Hitchcock's description of his original plan for this opening conforms to his earlier conception of movement as one from far away to close up on the object. He describes Marnie walking through a train station, buying a ticket, and then going to the platform (only shown from behind): "And we end up with a close shot on a rather bulky handbag under her arm." Gottlieb, p. 318.

36. As John Russell Taylor writes, Hitchcock "never cared too much, right back to the silent days in England, about giving more than a formal nod towards what he considers technical inessentials. If you get the idea that a character is riding a horse, that is all you need; to be completely literal about it is excessive." *Hitch: The Life and Times of Alfred Hitchcock* (New York: Pantheon, 1978), pp. 273–273.

37. Truffaut, p. 304.

38. David Freeman, *The Last Days of Alfred Hitchcock* (Woodstock, N.Y.: Overlook, 1984), p. 49.

39. Mary Ann Doane (working out of Thierry Kuntzel) writes, "The opening and closing of a door (the ruling rhetorical figure of a film like *Spellbound* (which deals directly with psychoanalysis) is quite frequently a metaphorical representation of the opening and closing of the mind, repression and disclosure. This forcing of the discourse is symptomatic of difficulties in the classical film's representation of interiority." *The Desire to Desire: The Woman's Film of the 1940s* (Bloomington: Indiana University Press, 1987), p. 138.

40. Elsaesser argues, "The somewhat facile generalization that in Hitchcock evil does not lurk *behind* a door but is there, in broad daylight, and comes out of a blue sky, might be rephrased by saying that montage, in Hitchcock (as in Eisenstein) is the very sign of a categorical refusal to give the cinematic image any kind of transcendental value." "The Dandy in Hitchcock," in *Hitchcock:*

Centenary Essays, ed. Richard Allen and Sam Ishii-Gonzalès (London: BFI Publishing, 1999), p. 9.

41. Deleuze, *Negotiations*, p. 55.

42. "What matters is not who did the action . . . but neither is it the action itself: it is the set of relations in which the action and the one who did it are caught." Deleuze, *Cinema 1*, p. 200.

43. Deleuze, *Cinema 1*, p. 200. Deleuze is strongly working out of a French tradition of looking at Hitchcock, from André Bazin's review of *Rear Window*, to much of the Claude Chabrol and Eric Rohmer Hitchcock book, and, especially, Jean Douchet's essay on *Psycho*, which also concerns itself with Hitchcock's propensity to structure his films in relation to three elements although in Douchet's case the three elements are related to Hitchcock's desire to "unmask reality and show it to us in *triple* form." See Douchet, "Hitch and His Audience," trans. Norman King, in *Cahiers du Cinéma, The 1960s*, p. 151. Originally published in *Cahiers du Cinéma*, no. 113, November 1960.

44. "The film is no longer a relation between the director and the film but the relation between the director, the film and the public whose reactions 'complete' the film, put together the sets of relations." Deleuze, *Cinema 1*, p. 202.

45. See my essay on the role of the face and the close-up in Hitchcock, "The Object and the Face: *Notorious*, Bergman and the Close-Up," in *Hitchcock: Past and Future*, ed. Richard Allen and Sam Ishii-Gonzalès (London: Routledge, 2004).

46. As Krohn writes, "The new problem posed by *Marnie* was not how to film someone with a guilty secret, which Hitchcock had been doing since *The Manxman*, but how to photograph someone driven by unconscious desires." P. 264. Krohn's argument (in relation to one moment near the end of the film when Hitchcock surprisingly does not show us Marnie's face as she says goodbye to her mother) could apply to much of the film. Krohn writes that this shot of Marnie's face is absent "because the director who had spent his life filming his actors so that we can read the thoughts on their faces had understood that [there] are thoughts which cannot be photographed." P. 266. The production designer on the film, Robert Boyle, has explained the difficulty Hitchcock faced on *Marnie*: "Hitchcock was trying to get at something you couldn't see. He was trying to tell a story of things that are not at all overt. . . . He was trying desperately to really dig into the psyche of this woman. Kapsis, p. 129.

47. This conception of the face bears some relationship to Deleuze's argument that the protagonist of postwar cinema (initiated by neorealism) is caught in a situation in which he "outstrips his motor capacities on all sides, and makes him see and hear what is no longer subject to the rules of a response or an action. He records rather than reacts." *Cinema 2*, p. 3.

48. Jean-Luc Godard, *Godard on Godard*, trans. and ed. Tom Milne (London: Secker and Warburg, 1973), p. 38. Durgnat argues that most of Hitchcock's films are fundamentally comedies "of a new kind—comedies in a sense somewhere between the older sense of not being tragedies, and the newer sense of not quite being dramas." P. 57.

49. Deleuze writes, "the whole of English thought has shown that the theory of relations is the key element of logic and can be both the deepest and

most amusing element." Deleuze, *Cinema 1*, p. 202. We should also note that the fascination with contrast in Hitchcock most likely has a strong basis in late nineteenth- and early-twentieth-century perceptions of London (Hitchcock's native city) as an urban space strongly marked by contrast and in such a way that it affected much of art and literature of the period. See Malcolm Bradbury's useful survey, "London: 1890–1920," in *A Guide to European Literature*, pp. 173–190.

50. Hayden White, *Metahistory: The Historical Imagination in Nineteenth-Century Europe* (Baltimore: Johns Hopkins University Press, 1973), p. 233. In 1952 Bazin noted this ironic assertion of Hitchcock's own power as author, arguing that Hitchcock's films offer a "certain between-the-lines reading of the scenario by those who can see beyond the most obvious effects." Bazin, "Must We Believe in Hitchcock?" in *The Cinema of Cruelty*, trans. Sabine d'Estrée, ed. and intro. Francois Truffaut (New York: Seaver, 1982), p. 122. Originally published in *L'Observateur*, January 17, 1952.

51. Charles Barr, "Introduction: Amnesia and Schizophrenia," in *All Our Yesterdays: 90 Years of British Cinema* (London: BFI Publishing, 1986), p. 24. Christine Gledhill has written of the differences between British and U.S. conceptions of melodrama that are relevant for understanding Hitchcock. She argues that in American cinema, melodrama becomes part of a system of narration and characterization, which took as its ideal a fictional environment in which conflicting forces (metaphoric and referential, psychological and social) are reconciled and brought into line with the demands of psychological realism. But in British cinema, these conflicting forces are displayed rather than reconciled and become the site of a "dynamic disjunction." The unreconciled split between the psychological and the social, for example, creates narratives built around "looking, spying, overseeing" as a response to this split. In *Classical Hollywood Narrative*, "Between Melodrama and Realism: Anthony Asquith's *Underground* and King Vidor's *The Crowd*," pp. 160–166.

52. As Bellour notes in his essay on *Psycho*, in Hitchcock's earlier films an investigating couple attempts to uncover the fundamental mystery at the center of the narrative. Although this investigation may finally be completed by an outsider or third party, we are still within a classical narrative situation of a "uniform dynamic leading from the riddle to its solution." In *Psycho*, on the other hand, dividing the investigation among five characters, none of whom is in full possession of the truth but only gain access to separate aspects of it, leads to a film in which a "veritable split occurs between the materiality and the awareness of experience." Bellour, "Psychosis, Neurosis, Perversion," in *The Analysis of Film*, ed. Constance Penley, trans. Nancy Huston (Bloomington: Indiana University Press, 2000), pp. 240–241. Book originally published as *L'analyse du film*, Paris: Editions Albatross, 1979. Essay originally published in *Ça cinéma*, no. 17, 1979. Published in *Camera Obscura*, no. 3–4, 1979.

53. Durgnat, p. 367.

54. See Bellour, "Psychosis, Neurosis, Perversion," p. 239.

55. A major sequence that would have at least clarified Lil's relationship to Marnie and Mark was shot but later deleted, originally because Hitchcock's wife, Alma Reville thought the scene unnecessary. Hitchcock and Jay Presson Allen

eventually agreed with her. Baker later said, "There seemed to be a missing dot to the sentence of my character." Moral, p. 133.

56. Hitchcock told Truffaut that he was "bothered by the long period between the time she got her job at Rutland's and the time she committed the robbery. Between the two, all we had was Mark on the make for the girl. That just wasn't enough." P. 307. In her favorable review of the film, Dilys Powell compares the racetrack sequence with the sequence of the policeman trailing Marion in *Psycho* in that they are both "a kind of irritant in the smooth flow of action and enigma." Powell argues that the racetrack sequence allows the audience to become more receptive "to the tale of obsession which is to follow." Dilys Powell, *The Golden Screen: Fifty Years of Film*, ed. George Perry (London: Pavilion, 1989), p. 205.

57. Truffaut, *Hitchcock*, p. 315.

58. Truffaut tells Hitchcock: "I believe you're right to hang on to that rising curve. For you, it works very successfully." *Hitchcock*, p. 315.

59. See Daudelin, pp. 193–194.

60. Truffaut says, "As it is, there's nothing redundant in the story; in fact, on many points, one would like to know more." *Hitchcock*, p. 304.

61. Doane, *The Desire to Desire*, pp. 39–43.

62. Doane, p. 39.

63. Doane, p. 41.

64. Corinn Columpar has also discussed how *Marnie* diverges from the traditional medical discourse film. Although some of our arguments overlap, we also raise separate issues in terms of this divergence. See "*Marnie*: A Site/Sight for the Convergence of Gazes," *Hitchcock Annual* 1999–00, pp. 51–73.

65. Brooks, *The Melodramatic Imagination*, p. 19.

66. Within the persecuted wife melodrama, the heroine's point of view may be problematized provided that a male investigative figure is placed within the narrative to uncover the mystery surrounding her. This is how Adare functions in *Under Capricorn*, and this may also be found in other films of this type such as Cukor's *Gaslight* (1944) and Jacques Tourneur's *Experiment Perilous* (1944).

67. All of these categories (except for the one dealing with issues of class differences) as well as the term *persecuted wife melodrama* may be found in Michael Walker, "*Secret Beyond the Door* (1947)," *Movie 34/35* (Winter 1990): 18.

68. Bonitzer, "*Notorious*," p. 152.

69. Žižek, *Looking Awry: An Introduction to Jacques Lacan through Popular Culture* (Cambridge Mass.: MIT Press, 1991), pp. 102–103.

70. Durgnat, for example, in his chapter on *Marnie* refers to "the glamorously doomy air" of *Rebecca* now seeming "somewhat archaic, in this age of amnesic cool and fun morality." P. 352.

71. Adrian Martin, "Lady, Beware: Paths through the Female Gothic," *Senses of Cinema* (January/February 2001). Martin also notes, in ways that have relevance to *Marnie*, that the female gothic "is, at its core, a genre based on instability, ambiguity and ambivalence, in relation to the very status of reality as much as to questions of identity politics." Electronic journal: <www.sensesof cinema.com/contents/01/12/gothic.html>.

73. Dialogue was written in which Mark talks about his mother to Marnie but this was ultimately regarded as expendable and removed from the final cut. See Moral, p. 48.

73. Žižek, *Looking Awry*, p. 104.

74. When Bogdanovich asked Hitchcock for his own understanding of the ending, the director's own reading of it is contradictory and ambiguous. When Bogdanovich asked Hitchcock if he thought Marnie was cured at the end, Hitchcock responded, "Not at all—no, no—and he [Mark] still had a problem. But I believe that it was hopeful. In time, he'd wear her down." *Who the Devil Made It*, p. 538.

75. "Interview with Rainer Werner Fassbinder," conducted by Wilfried Wiegand, in *Fassbinder*, trans. Ruth McCormick (New York: Tandam Press, 1981), p. 90.

76. Fassbinder also repeats the idea of the neurotic heroine obsessively walking a straight line in *Martha*, although in the Fassbinder the walk is done in a much more insistent manner. Martha's extreme and heavy 1940s-style high heels and tight dress suits cause her to take steps that are at once fast, tiny, and loud as she seems to clump across hardwood floors.

77. Pier Paolo Pasolini takes the latter approach in his famous and controversial essay, "The Cinema of Poetry" in which he argues that in *Red Desert* Antonioni makes use of the "'indirect subjective'" approach: "[Antonioni] has finally succeeded in representing the world seen through his own eyes because he has substituted, wholly, the world-view of a sick woman for his own vision, which is delirious with estheticism." In *Movies and Methods*, ed. Bill Nichols (Berkeley: University of California Press, 1976), p. 553. English translation originally appeared in *Cahiers du Cinéma in English*, no. 6.

78. Wood argues that the ending of *Marnie* "is arguably the nearest thing to a convincing and *earned* happy ending in any Hitchcock film." *Hitchcock's Films Revisited*, p. 405. Durgnat approaches the resolution in a similar vein, p. 361.

79. Michel Delahaye and Rivette, "Towards a Semiotics of Cinema," in *Cahiers du Cinéma: The 1960s*, p. 284.

80. Jean-Louis Comolli et al., "The Misfortunes of *Muriel*," p. 78.

81. Roland Barthes, "Dear Antonioni," in *L'avventura*, p. 64.

82. Barthes, p. 65.

83. Writing in 1965 Wood argues, "To wish that Hitchcock's films were like those of Bergman or Antonioni is like wishing that Shakespeare had been like Corneille." P. 58 However, in his study of Antonioni (cowritten with Ian Cameron) Wood's chapter on *Red Desert* draws a number of parallels between the two directors as well as between *Marnie* and *Red Desert*. *Antonioni* (New York: Praeger, 1965), pp. 120–123. In his study of Resnais, John Francis Kreidl writes, "In 1978 [the year of the book's publication], we should be free of the 'art house syndrome' and be able to enjoy *Muriel* more as the Hitchcockian suspense film it is." *Alain Resnais* (Boston: Twayne Publishers, 1978), p. 111.

84. Bellour, "To Enunciate (on *Marnie*)," trans. Bertrand Augst and Hilary Radner in 1977; rev. Constance Penley in 1990, in *The Analysis of Film*, p. 224. Originally published in *Camera Obscura*, vol. 1, no. 2, Fall 1977, as "Hitchcock the Enunciator."

85. Bellour, "To Enunciate (on *Marnie*)," p. 223.

86. Bellour, "To Enunciate (on *Marnie*)," p. 233. In spite of some early feminist support for Bellour's essay on *Marnie*, more recent approaches have quite seriously challenged many of its assumptions, both in terms of interpretation of the images themselves and of the positioning of the female spectator in relation to these images. See, for example, Lucretia Knapp's lesbian reading of the film in "The Queer Voice in *Marnie*," *Cinema Journal* 32, no. 4 (1993): 6–23.

87. That strategies of this nature are strongly modernist is something to which Peter Brooks has drawn attention. Writing of "that impossible enterprise of arresting and fixing the object of inspection," Brooks argues that as "realism develops into its 'modernist' phase, the frustrations of knowing produce a questioning of the epistemophilic project itself. The observer/knower is put into question, and the very principle of knowing—or of possessing—another body comes to appear hopeless." *Body Work*, p. 106.

88. Adrian Martin has drawn links between the opening of *Marnie* and the fragmented montage opening of *Muriel*, described in chapter 1 herein. Martin made this comparison for an Editor's Day column on the MacGuffin Web site in January 2002. <http://www.labyrinth.net.au/~muffin>.

89. Bellour, "To Enunciate (on *Marnie*)," p. 221.

90. Truffaut, *Hitchcock*, p. 301.

91. According to Spoto, in the early stage of production on *Marnie* Hitchcock was declaring that Hedren was his "ultimate actress, the one he had waited years to direct, and that she was giving the finest performance in any of his films." P. 501.

92. Two years after making *Marnie*, Hitchcock made a comment to the screenwriter Howard Fast: "My God, Howard! I've just seen Antonioni's *Blow-Up*. These Italians are a century ahead of me in terms of technique! What have I been doing all this time?" Spoto, p. 525. Hitchcock and Fast collaborated on the script for the aborted *Kaleidoscope*, the film Hitchcock intended to be his most formally audacious film up to that point. The executives at Universal rejected the project although *Frenzy* (*Kaleidoscope*'s original working title) contains certain elements of this earlier project.

93. Bonitzer, "The Disappearance," in *L'Avventura*, ed. Seymour Chatman and Guido Fink. Trans. Chris Breyer, Gavriel Moses, and Seymour Chatman (New Brunswick, N.J.: Rutgers University Press, 1989), p. 216. Originally published in *Michelangelo Antonioni: Identificazione di un autore*, ed. Giorgio Tinazzi, Parma, Societa Produzioni Editoriali, 1985. In 1982 Antonioni referred to the limitation of standard thrillers, "even Hitchcock's," as being insufficiently "real." He claims, "They have an amazing format, great suspense, but they aren't realistic. Life is also made up of pauses, of impurities; in both content and its representation there is a sort of dirtiness . . . that should be respected." In *The Architecture of Vision: Writings and Interviews on Cinema*, ed. Carlo di Carlo and Giorgio Tinazzi (New York: Marsilio Publishers, American Edition, 1996). Interview originally published in *Cahiers du Cinéma*, no. 342, December 1982.

94. See Krohn, p. 230.

95. See, for example, Mary Ann Doane's *Femmes Fatales: Feminism, Film Theory, Psychoanalysis*, in particular, "Veiling Over Desire: Close-ups of the Woman,"

"The Abstraction of a Lady: *La Signora di tutti*," and "Woman's Stake: Filming the Female Body" (New York: Routledge, 1991).

96. See Spoto, pp. 496–497.

97. Hedren says that when Hitchcock told her Connery had been cast as Mark she was upset. Hedren knew that creating audience sympathy for the character was already going to be difficult, so to also have the woman refuse the advances of Connery would make Marnie an especially implausible character in the eyes of many spectators. Jay Presson Allen claims she did not see the problems Hunter did in having Mark commit this violent act on his honeymoon. For Allen, the problem was easily overcome by Connery's star charisma. On the making-of *Marnie* DVD.

98. In both *Gone with the Wind* (1939) and *The Foxes of Harrow* (1947), the wives are sexually assaulted by their husbands, and in the latter film (as in *Marnie*) on their wedding night. In both cases, the films clearly imply that the wife, in a sense, provokes her husband into raping her. The wives overreact to their husband's virility and their refusal to have sex is something the films do not view sympathetically. In *Gone with the Wind*, not only is Scarlett's rape viewed positively, but also when she wakes up the next morning, she is shown to be happy and relaxed. Again, *Marnie* is partly within this tradition while also complicating its implications. Significantly, in all three films the closed or locked bedroom door at once signifies the wife's refusal to have sex with her husband, whereas the breaking down of the door itself marks the husband's violation of both the space of the bedroom and the body of the woman.

99. Gledhill, "Between Melodrama and Realism," p. 165. We should also recall here that Mark calls Marnie a "cold, practiced little Method actress of a liar."

100. Interestingly, Rupert Crosse, one of the stars of Cassavetes's *Shadows*, makes a brief appearance at the end of the sequence of Marnie robbing the Rutland safe.

101. Moral, p. 36.

102. Moral, p. 45.

103. Wood, *Hitchcock's Films Revisited*, p. 393. Wood also offered this interpretation to Allen herself during a question-and-answer session at the Hitchcock Centennial Conference in New York City in 1999. Allen agreed with Wood. See Richard Allen, "An Interview with Jay Presson Allen," *Hitchcock Annual* 2000–01, p. 20.

104. Durgnat has described this sequence of Mark taking Marnie back to her mother's home to relive the moment of her initial trauma as "an abduction, an emotional rape, just as much as his earlier, seduction-rape of his bride." P. 363.

105. Spoto, p. 500.

106. For Allen, this monologue was utterly central to the meaning of the film. But to her the importance of Mark's description of the fattid bugs was "that in any aspect of beauty there may be extremely ugly elements, but the overall thing is beautiful." Moral, p. 48. Murray Pomerance has offered a fuller reading of this sequence than I have here in which he aptly notes that the reference to the fattid bugs also ties in very strongly to the issue of camouflage and "the way in which a

particular creature might have need of camouflage in a warm climate. . . ." Murray Pomerance, *An Eye for Hitchcock* (New Brunswick, N.J.: Rutgers University Press, 2004), p. 164. Note here the importance of this reference in relation to numerous naturalist motifs that occur throughout the course of the film. A complete addressing of this topic in relation to *Marnie* (and to Hitchcock in general) must be done elsewhere. For now, I would simply note how the naturalist attraction for what Deleuze defines as "originary worlds" driven toward a death impulse, the behavior of the characters determined by impulse and instinct and in which the fetish becomes the central form for representing this fragmented world (see *Cinema 1*, pp. 128–130) is one which *Marnie* is both attracted to but pulls back from.

107. Deleuze, *Cinema 2*, pp. 12–13.

Chapter 3. Staging the Death of the Director: *Two Weeks in Another Town*

1. John Houseman, *Final Dress* (New York: Simon and Schuster, 1983), p. 210.

2. Houseman, p. 215.

3. Higham and Greenberg, p. 182.

4. Houseman, p. 213.

5. Houseman, p. 210.

6. One important exception to the overwhelming number of negative reviews of the film in the mainstream media is a typically insightful review by Dilys Powell from the London *Sunday Times*. See Powell, p. 187.

7. Paul Mayersberg, "The Testament of Vincente Minnelli," *Movie* 3 (October 1962): 10–14.

8. Peter Bogdanovich, "*Two Weeks in Another Town*," *Film Culture* 26 (Winter 1962): 54.

9. Quoted in Ben Hecht, *A Child of the Century* (New York: Ballantine, 1970), p. 467.

10. See, for example, George Morris's reference to *Two Weeks* as "one of the great testament films," a claim evocative of Mayersberg on the film fifteen years earlier. In *The Films of Vincente Minnelli* (New York: Thousand Eyes, 1978), p. 36.

11. Stephen Harvey, *Directed by Vincente Minnelli* (New York: Museum of Modern Art/Harper and Row Publishers, 1989), p. 278.

12. See Hillier, ed. *Cahiers du Cinéma: The 1950s*, pp. 175–176.

13. Hillier, ed., *Cahiers du Cinéma: The 1960s*, p. 177.

14. Hillier, ed., *Cahiers du Cinéma: The 1960s*, p. 6.

15. In a 1987 interview with Daney and Narboni, Douchet stated that only he and Domarchi of the *Cahiers* critics loved Minnelli's work. Jean Douchet, *L'art d'aimer* (Paris: Petite bibliothèque des Cahiers du cinéma, 2003), p. 11.

16. In Harvey, p. 270.

17. In Harvey, p. 276.

18. For Bordwell and Staiger, however, these appropriations never move beyond the level of pastiche. Writing of the New Hollywood directors who emerged

in the late 1960s and early 1970s, they argue that "only minor instrumental changes" are at work between this historical development of the Hollywood paradigm and classical Hollywood cinema as it solidified within the studio system after 1918: "Classical film style and codified genres swallow up art-film borrowings, taming the (already limited) disruptiveness of the art cinema." Borwell et al., p. 375.

19. Naremore, p. 17. Naremore also writes, "Minnelli was . . . both a creator of a personal style and a clever manipulator of the storehouse of art; in this sense he was a true modernist, prefiguring the death of romantic expression and the birth of endless quotation." P. 24.

20. Elsaesser, "Vincente Minnelli," p. 19.

21. Naremore, p. 47.

22. Cited by Hillier, *Cahiers du Cinéma: The 1960s*, pp. 2–3. As recently as 1998, Rivette accused Minnelli of being a director who, in his obsession with mise-en-scène, ignores his actors who find themselves "working in a void." From "The Captive Lover—An Interview with Jacques Rivette," by Frederic Bonnaud, trans. Kent Jones, *Senses of Cinema* 16 (September/October 2001), electronic journal: <http://www.sensesofcinema.com/contents/01/16/rivette.html>. Originally published in *Les Inrockuptibles*, March 25, 1998. See my response to Rivette's statement in "Medium-Shot Gestures: Vincente Minnelli and *Some Came Running*," *16:9* 3, electronic journal, <http://www.16-9.dk/2003/-061side11_minnelli.htm>.

23. Elsaesser describes Minnelli as "an artist who knows one big thing, and never tires to explore its implications." "Vincente Minnelli," p. 13. In a 1996 television interview, Deleuze refers to Minnelli (and Joseph Losey) as filmmakers who are "overwhelmed" by an idea, in the case of Minnelli the idea being What Does It Mean to Be Caught Up in Someone's Else's Dream?

24. Walter Benjamin, *Charles Baudelaire: A Lyric Poet in the Era of High Capitalism*, trans. Harry Zohn (London: Verso, 1983), p. 167. Outside of American cinema, Jean Renoir's films arguably treat the subject of the private space of the individual in relation to decor the most extensively although often in a very different manner from Minnelli.

25. Benjamin, p. 168.

26. Elsaesser refers to Minnelli's "existential theme of a character trying to construct the world in the image of the inner self, only to discover that this world has become uninhabitable because it is both frighteningly suffocating and intolerably lonely. . . ." Thomas Elsaesser, "Tales of Sound and Fury," in Gledhill, p. 54.

27. Benjamin, p. 169. Douchet refers to Tacy's need to collect rocks and illogically and destructively stash them in her trailer as "the will literally to appropriate the world." Cited by French [Krohn], p. 38.

28. Elsaesser, "Vincente Minnelli," p. 21.

29. Naremore, p. 34.

30. Within his extended analysis of *Home from the Hill*, Edward Gallafent has drawn attention to the ways that doors function in the film. Like *Marnie*, *Home from the Hill* has a female protagonist, Hannah, who refuses to have sexual relations with the male protagonist, her husband Wade, while living in the same

house with him. But in Minnelli's film, Hannah's rejection of her husband "is figured here in the insistent concentration on open doors, part of a sustained thread of imagery in the film." Hannah does not, like Marnie, take refuge behind the closed and locked bedroom door but instead seems to take pleasure in "leaving her sexuality standing, as it were, in the open." "The Adventures of Rafe Hunnicutt: The Bourgeois Family in *Home from the Hill* (1960)," *Movie* 34/35 (Winter, 1990): 67.

31. Bachelard, p. 222.

32. David Gerstner, "Queer Modernism: The Cinematic Aesthetics of Vincente Minnelli," *Modernity* 2 (2000). Electronic journal: <http://www.eiu.edu/~modernity/gerst—html>. Gerstner draws particular attention to the struggle at MGM between Minnelli's visual sensibility and that of the head of the art department, Cedric Gibbons. Gibbons was devoted to this streamlined modernist approach, but Minnelli ultimately won his battles with Gibbons.

33. Andrew Sarris, *The American Cinema: Directors and Direction 1929–1968* (New York: Dutton, 1968), p. 102.

34. Godard, p. 231.

35. André S. Labarthe, "Mort d'un mot," *Cahiers du Cinéma* 195 (November 1967): 66.

36. As Dana Polan argues in relation to *The Band Wagon*, what the film (and by extension Minnelli's work in general) celebrates "is the conversion of culture and nature alike by Hollywood spectacle, a reality of unreality, a form which claims to be beyond the merely cultural or the merely natural." "It could be Oedipus Rex: Denial and Difference in *The Bandwagon* [*sic*] or, the American Musical as American Gothic," *Cine-tracts* 4 (2/3) (Summer/Fall 1981): 23.

37. Gérard Guégan's statement that if you "build a world which is in all respects like the real world and then distort it in the filming" to the point where you suppress the first of these elements then "you have *The Sandpiper*" is typical. In "A Discussion about American Cinema and the politique des auteurs," from *Cahiers du Cinéma; The 1960s*, p. 201.

38. Michèle Manceaux, "A Movie Is a Movie: Interview with Jean-Luc Godard on *Une Femme est une femme*," in *Focus on Godard*, ed. Brown, trans. Royal S. Brown (Englewood Cliffs, N.J.: Prentice-Hall, 1973), p. 29. Originally appeared in *l'Express*, January 12, 1961 and July 27, 1961. Godard also said of the musical during this period "the genre itself is dead. It would be pointless even for the Americans to remake *Singin' in the Rain*. You have to do something different. . . ." *Godard on Godard*, p. 182.

39. Bachelard, pp. 6–7.

40. In Shaw's novel, Andrus and several other American and Italian characters are haunted by their memories of their experience of World War II and this often profoundly affects their physical and psychological inertia. This historical context is eliminated in the film version, which ascribes all manner of behavior to individual psychology. A similar jettisoning of the possibilities of this type of neurosis having a social and material basis in World War II (rather than simply being tied to the family and psychology) was also removed from the adaptation of *Some Came Running*.

41. Polan has argued that the 1940s is a decade that "offers Hollywood its last great chance to be a narrative art of a classic sort." *Power and Paranoia: History, Narrative, and the American Cinema, 1940–1950* (New York: Columbia University Press, 1986), p. 18. During this decade, classical narrative begins to show signs of breaking down "while spectacle and a nonnarrativized flow of performances serve as markers of a newly emergent aesthetic possibility." P. 35. One example of this new aesthetic possibility can be found in Minnelli's musicals, which do not simply reproduce the artifice of a cinema produced under the studio system but "instill an ambiguity into the very representation of the natural." In Minnelli's musicals we find an intensification of artifice to the point where the spectacle is not simply an artificial one but one that opens up onto and refers to the possibility of additional realms of artifice beyond the immediate represented one. P. 258.

42. Deleuze writes, "And it is precisely after the war—at the very moment when the American Dream is collapsing, and when the action-image is entering a definitive crisis, as we will see—that the dream finds its most fertile form, and action its most violent, most detonating schema. This is the final agony of the action cinema, even if films of this type go on being made for a long time yet." *Cinema 1*, pp. 157–158.

43. Elsaesser, "Tales of Sound and Fury," pp. 64–65.

44. As Deleuze writes, "From the outset, the rules of the Actor's Studio applied not only to the actor's acting out but also to the conception and unfolding of the film, its framings, its cutting, its montage." *Cinema 1*, p. 155.

45. Elsaesser, "Vincente Minnelli," p. 10.

46. Elsaesser, "Vincente Minnelli," p. 13.

47. Elsaesser, "Vincente Minnelli," p. 9.

48. Elsaesser, "Vincente Minnelli," p. 14.

49. Deleuze has written that in Minnelli (and unlike the more classical conception of dance and movement found in the musicals of Astaire/Rogers or Donen), "dance is no longer simply movement of the world, but passage from one world to another, entry into another world, breaking in and exploring. . . . Musical comedy has never come as close to a mystery of memory, of dream and of time, as a point of indescernibility of the real and the imaginary, as in Minnelli." Deleuze, *Cinema 2*, p. 64. This absorbent conception of the image may also explain the ease with which Minnelli was able to move between musicals and melodramas, something a comparable figure within the musical such as Stanley Donen was never able to do. Many of Deleuze's observations about Minnelli have their origin in Douchet's writings for *Cahiers* and *Objectif* in the 1960s as well as subsequent work on Minnelli by Jacques Fieschi and Tristan Renaud (all of which Deleuze cites).

50. See Andrew Sarris's reference to the "curiously depressing" tone of *An American in Paris* and *Gigi* and to Minnelli's "unusual, somber outlook for musical comedy." In *The American Cinema*, p. 101. Likewise, Robin Wood writes of the Minnelli musicals containing "tension, excess, dislocation" and how this produces "continuous uneasiness." In Wood's entry on *Meet Me in St. Louis* in *The International Dictionary of Films and Filmmakers*, ed. Christopher Lyon (New York: Macmillan, 1984), p. 291.

51. In his autobiography, Minnelli describes his relationship with the studio and his status as an artist in this way: "I was the resident specialist in sophisticated musicals, in adapting visual influences from the higher world of art, in using a realistic framework for fantasy. . . . But did anyone call it the Minnelli touch? Come now. We all realized we were cogs in the business machine and, as such, we weren't allowed the luxury of such affectations." Vincente Minnelli, with Hector Arce, *I Remember It Well* (Garden City, N.Y.: Doubleday, 1974), p. 245. However, a few pages earlier he describes his work on *An American in Paris* thusly: "Some erudite types point to *An American in Paris* as the perfect example of the studio-as-auteur theory. I disagree. . . . Though I don't minimize anyone's contributions, one man was responsible for bringing it all together. That man was me." pp. 228–229.

52. Naremore has traced this sensibility in Minnelli's work to one that has its origins in nineteenth-century European and U.S. culture in which the close relationship between aestheticism and commodification, which began during the early part of that century, is recognized by the artist. This recognition provokes attitudes from the artist that are at once ironic and melancholic in that the artist recognizes that what he produces will inevitably be tainted by commerce and mass production. Naremore, p. 8.

53. Farber, p. 154.

54. Aumont, "The Fall of the Gods," p. 218. Robert Rosen has called *The Bad and the Beautiful* "self-reflexive [*sic*] without revealing anything of itself. Instead, it self-confidently celebrates and reaffirms the pleasures and sufficiency of the culturally dominant film language and its mode of production." In "Notes on Film and Painting," in *Art and Film since 1945*, p. 256.

55. Naremore sees Von Ellstein as a parody of Lang whereas the other major director character in the film he sees as a parody of Hitchcock, p. 118.

56. Pairing him with Claire Trevor as his wife also evokes their earlier costarring roles in John Huston's *Key Largo* (1948) in which Robinson not only portrays a gangster but his relationship with Trevor is based on an endless, sadistic round of confrontations and humiliations toward her in a manner anticipating what happens between the two of them in *Two Weeks*.

57. The presence of Eric von Stroheim Jr. in the supporting cast (who looks like a taller, gaunter version of his father) serves as a physical reminder of Teutonic genius directors who suffer at the hands of Hollywood.

58. See Catherine Russell on *The State of Things* in relation to the question of the death of the director, pp. 67–104.

59. Deleuze, *Cinema 2*, p. 77.

60. Aumont, "The Fall of the Gods," p. 218.

61. Rosenbaum, *Rivette: Texts and Interviews*, p. 27. Also relevant to the problem of representing film production is Comolli's argument that the cinema has difficulty in filming all types of work, not just filmmaking. For Comolli, the cinema is driven toward "the idealization of matter and of the body" and to "the exaltation of forms." In this world, "the worker becomes an athlete, a dancer, an acrobat. . . . Representing work means de-realizing it, through the estheticization of gesture and of posture, through the body's ludic mechanization and virtualization."

In "Mechanical Bodies, Ever More Heavenly," trans. Annette Michelson, *October* 83 (Winter 1998): 21.

62. Comolli, "Mechanical Bodies," p. 21.

63. Naremore has written of *The Bad and the Beautiful* that "no other film or novel captures so well the sense of the movie colony as a small, patriarchal family... possessed of suburban values...." P. 127.

64. Michel Chion, *The Voice in Cinema*, ed. and trans. Claudia Gorbman (New York: Columbia University Press, 1999), p. 156.

65. This is, in fact, what happened on Minnelli's previous film, *Four Horsemen of the Apocalypse*, in which Ingrid Thulin's voice was later dubbed in (against Minnelli's wishes) by Angela Lansbury. See Higham and Greenberg, *The Celluloid Muse*, p. 181. That film also contains extremely inexpressive looping of much of Yvette Mimieux's dialogue.

66. Minnelli has claimed that the new head of the studio cut the orgy sequence because it offended him and did not want MGM to be associated with a film that would include such a sequence. Minnelli, p. 347. But Houseman maintained that the sequence was cut "not for obscenity but for obscurity and tedium." P. 213.

67. *Four Horsemen of the Apocalypse* includes a brief citation of a shot from the Odessa Steps sequence from Eisenstein's *Battleship Potemkin* (1925).

68. See Deleuze, *Cinema 1*, p. 148. Bogdanovich argues for the superiority of Minnelli's orgy over Fellini's: "This bizarre group gets together in Minnelli's gaudy, flashy, cynical and debauched Roman world—a picture of perversion and glittering decay that in a few precise and strikingly effective strokes makes Fellini's *La Dolce Vita* look pedestrian, arty and hopelessly social-conscious." P. 53.

69. *Tea and Sympathy* (1956) is one exception to this in that Laura functions as both lover and mother figure for Tom. However, Tom continues to live out a relationship with his emotionally distant father in a way that is typical of many of Minnelli's other protagonists.

70. Mayersberg compares the relationship between Davie and Kruger to the relationship between Brick and his father Big Daddy in Tennessee Williams's *Cat on a Hot Tin Roof*, p. 12.

71. Naremore, pp. 147–148.

73. Gerstner, p. 20.

73. Harvey, p. 277. Harvey attributes the misogyny entirely to Schnee's script, detecting what he believes to be Minnelli's lack of comfort with it on this matter.

74. Mayerbserg, p. 12. Mayersberg also notes that the portrait of Veronica that Jack places on his hotel mantel has "the quality of a pseudo-Renaissance Madonna." P. 11. A portrait of a Madonna and child ironically hangs on the wall of the hospital behind Clara as she tells Kruger to "go back to the nuthouse where you belong."

75. Godard, p. 200. We might also note here that when Clara slams down the issue of *Now* magazine on Kruger's desk, the cover image is not something "now" but a painting of the Trojan horse, suggesting a tie to the origins of the Faustian archetype, Simon Magus, who had scandalized early Christianity by claiming that a prostitute, Helen, was a reincarnation of Helen of Troy.

76. Houseman, p. 211.

77. See Pauline Kael's review of the film in which she writes of "orgies designed to out-do *La dolce vita*, and Cyd Charisse done-up like the heroine of *Marienbad*." *Kiss Kiss Bang Bang* (New York: Bantam Books, 1968), p. 458.

78. Cited by James Monaco in *Alain Resnais*, p. 73. Monaco quotes Resnais, "Thanks to *Cahiers du Cinéma* we learned that American directors were just human beings and that maybe Vincente Minnelli knew more about art than any French director who was so proud of his culture." P. 9.

79. Georges Bataille, *The Accursed Share*, vols. II and III, trans. Robert Hurley (New York: Zone Books, 1993), p. 53. Douchet discusses the relationship between the human and the animal in *Two Weeks* in *L'Art d'aimer*, pp. 123–124.

80. Bataille, p. 56.

81. Dennis Giles, "Show-making," from Altman, p. 97.

82. The car crash in Godard's film, in fact, collapses both the car ride in *Two Weeks* and the plane crash in *The Bad and the Beautiful*. In the latter film, as in Godard's, a crash kills the screenwriter protagonist's wife who is engaged in an adulterous affair; in Minnelli's film with a movie star, in Godard's with a producer. This resolution differs somewhat in the details from the resolution to Moravia's novel. In the novel, the screenwriter's wife dies as a result of a spinal injury sustained in a narrowly avoided car accident with the producer (who is neither injured nor killed) at the wheel. As in Godard's film, this accident takes place off-screen (as it were) and is described in retrospective detail by the writer.

83. See chapter 3, "The Text of Muteness," from Brooks, *The Melodramatic Imagination*, pp. 56–80.

84. Naremore, pp. 131–134.

85. Harvey, p. 278.

86. Naremore, p. 117.

87. Elsasser, "Vincente Minnelli," p. 27.

88. Harold Bloom, *The Western Canon: The Books and School of the Ages* (New York: Harcourt Brace, 1994), p. 233.

Conclusion: Or The Death of Cinema Is No Solution

1. See David L. Overbey, "Fritz Lang's Career Girl," *Sight and Sound* 44 (Autumn 1975): 240–243.

2. Wim Wenders, "Death Is No Solution: The German Film Director Fritz Lang," in *West German Filmmakers on Film*, ed. Eric Rentschler, trans. Sheila Johnston, p. 104.

3. Godard's opinion of De Palma, at least in 1981, was ambivalent. Although admiring De Palma because "he really works with the image, he starts with the image," De Palma also "goes too far when he puts his talent into such a lousy script." De Palma's reworking of *Psycho*, *Dressed to Kill* (1980) particularly irritated Godard because De Palma showed too much "disdain for the story." In Jean-Luc Godard and Pauline Kael, "The Economics of Film Criticism: A Debate," in *Jean-Luc Godard Interviews*, ed. David Sterritt (Jackson: University Press of Mississippi, 1998), p. 112.

4. Cited in Kapsis, p. 198.

5. Pauline Kael, *When the Lights Go Down* (New York: Holt, Rinehart and Winston, 1980), p. 421.

6. "Every cut," Scorsese said, "every frame was a reference to Vincente Minnelli, a reference to George Cukor, and many of the directors of the period." Mary Pat Kelly, *Martin Scorsese: A Journey* (New York: Thunder's Mouth Press, 1991), p. 103.

7. According to Scorsese, "Jean-Luc Godard came over for lunch one day and he was talking about how much he liked *New York, New York*. He said it was basically about the impossibility of two creative people in a relationship—the jealousies, the envy, the temperament." Kelly, pp. 111–112.

8. One of the very few favorable notices the film received when it opened was from George Morris in *Film Comment*. For Morris, *"A Matter of Time* emphatically vindicates auteur criticism, in that a real love and awareness of Minnelli's oeuvre is essential to its enjoyment." Although aware of the technical flaws of the film, Morris also argues that "few contemporary films can summon up a tenth of its personal expression and intensity." George Morris, "One Kind of Dream," *Film Comment* 12, no. 6 (November–December 1976): 21.

9. Harris also originated the role of Daisy Gamble in the stage musical *On a Clear Day You Can See Forever* in 1965 of which Minnelli did the film version in 1970 with Barbra Streisand in the lead.

10. Krohn, p. 274.

11. Krohn, "A Hitchcock Mystery," from the MacGuffin Web site: <http://www. Labyrinth.net.au/~muffin/krohn_c.html>. Originally appeared in *MacGuffin* #27, December 2000. This essay contains additional information on the production process of *Family Plot*.

12. Patrick McGilligan, *Alfred Hitchcock: A Life in Darkness and Light* (New York: Regan Books, 2003), p. 732.

13. See Harvey, p. 293.

14. *Anatahan* is a film whose stylistic paradox is principally based on the fact that Sternberg flew to Japan to make a film about the island of Anatahan and then shot the entire film in the studio.

15. Deleuze, *Cinema 2*, p. 63.

Index

249